The Dynamics

OF SOVIET SOCIETY

The Dynamics

OF

SOVIET SOCIETY

W. W. ROSTOW, in collaboration with
ALFRED LEVIN, and with the assistance of others at
the Center for International Studies,
Massachusetts Institute of Technology

W · W · NORTON & COMPANY · INC · New York

PRINTED IN THE UNITED STATES OF AMERICA
FOR THE PUBLISHERS BY THE VAIL-BALLOU PRESS

914.7
R 839d

CONTENTS

Part Two   COHESIVE FORCES, INSTABILITIES, AND TENSIONS IN CONTEMPORARY SOVIET SOCIETY

Contents

PREFATORY NOTE

THIS book is one result of a series of investigations carried out at the Center for International Studies of the Massachusetts Institute of Technology. The Center is dedicated to an attempt to bring to bear the resources of the academic community on problems of action confronting the United States in its relations with the rest of the world. Perhaps the most important of those problems is how we are to conduct ourselves with respect to Soviet Russia.

In considering whether to launch the studies of which this book is the first product we asked ourselves what use the government "operator" or the voter behind him might make of the work of the academic fraternity. The field of Soviet scholarship has proved exceedingly fruitful over recent years. Despite the iron curtain, a large body of information and insights has been accumulating in scholarly monographs and journal articles. What kind of distillation of this growing fund of knowledge would be of most help to the harried official who must plot daily moves in the chess game and to the worried citizen who must decide whether to support or oppose the general national strategy?

One answer we got when we asked this question was, "Facts, give us facts. Every added scrap of information helps." This suggested the preparation of an encyclopedia conveniently indexed and cross-referenced. But the suspicion grew as we worked that no amount of "facts" would really help those whom we thought of as our customers. The questions which were keeping men awake nights in Washington were exactly those which trouble us all: What will the Kremlin do next? Why did they take this step or that step? What makes these people tick, anyhow? And what kinds of changes in the Soviet system may conceivably come about which could abate the cold war? No simple compilation of facts would be much help to people struggling with these imponderables. We concluded that just because facts on the Soviet Union were hard to come by, the illusory impression had grown that if only you could get more information the whole exasperating puzzle would be somehow solved. That this was an illusion was suggested by our difficulties in understanding other societies that are completely open to our questions.

We finally concluded that what was most urgently needed was not new information but a way of making sense out of what was already known. Could a set of ideas be provided, an interpretive framework, which would give the nonexpert the feeling that he understood to some degree what was going on, and what might go on in the Soviet Bloc?

The experts, whether academic or governmental, did not of course need this. Each has developed his own conceptual picture of why the Soviets are as they are. Nobody can devote his life to the study of a society without developing a set of hypotheses as to the prime motivating forces within it. The question was whether there had developed sufficient consensus among close students of Russian society so that it might be possible to present, for the nonexpert, a picture with which, in the main, most of them would agree.

The Center asked Mr. Rostow to attempt such a synthesis with the assistance of a number of specialists to help him with particular aspects of the problem. Starting as a nonspecialist, he read voraciously, and consulted endlessly with everyone he could find who had knowledge, scholarly or direct, of contemporary Russia. He finally emerged with the conviction that there was a common pattern sufficiently clear to justify his trying to draw it for the benefit of others.

The responsibility for an interpretive job of this kind must ultimately fall upon a single mind. This is essentially Mr. Rostow's book. There will be many who will say they would have used different language or placed their emphasis differently. There will no doubt be some who will go so far as to say that the whole interpretation is wrong from beginning to end. But the Center has been gratified that, in spite of every scholar's compulsive necessity to be original and to disagree with his colleagues, so many of them have accepted this analysis as a useful approximation.

One of the most valuable characteristics of this analysis is that it attempts to portray the Soviet system not as something static and unchanging but in a recognizable process of historical evolution. This emphasis upon change and the forces that bring it about may mislead some readers as to the objectives of the book. The temptation to seek in its pages a daily explanation of the news in the morning paper will be strong. In one sense it is appropriate that the thesis of the book should be tested against current events. The forces analyzed by Mr. Rostow are powerful ones which will not alter their direction abruptly. If the analysis is valid, new developments should be at least partly explainable in terms of those forces.

It was for this reason that Chapter 15 was added. The other chapters of the book were completed prior to Stalin's death. The author felt that this event was likely to be of such critical importance in Soviet history that some discussion of its implications should be added.

Since Chapter 15 was completed there have been a number of other notable incidents which invite comment. We have witnessed the disorders in Eastern Germany beginning on June 17, the dramatic downfall of Lavrenti Beria, the purging of numbers of his henchmen and supporters, especially in Georgia, the Soviet agreement to meet with the Western powers on German unity and other problems, and the major speech of Premier Malenkov (which lies before me in the morning paper as I write this) announcing Soviet possession of the hydrogen bomb and—perhaps even more significant—suggesting a serious intention to shift resources to a heavier emphasis on consumer goods. Undoubtedly by the time this book appears in print there will have been many other events calling for interpretation.

But this is not primarily a commentary on the current scene, and it would be foolish to try to weave into this prefatory note an explanation of the very latest news. In any case a number of alternative interpretations of what has happened in the last six months are still plausible, all of them consistent with what we know of earlier history. We still cannot say with any confidence what is meant, for example, by the continued emphasis in Soviet statements on the principle of collective leadership. We still cannot establish with certainty the role which has been played of late by the military. We still do not know how far-reaching are the internal decisions to pursue, both externally and internally, a "softer" policy, or what factional disagreements if any lie behind these. To this reader at least, however, the analysis in this volume persuasively eliminates certain notions as to what the Soviets are about and casts much light on the plausibility of the remaining alternatives.

We do not present this or any of our other studies as representing the views of the Center for International Studies, much less those of the Massachusetts Institute of Technology. It is one purpose of the Center to encourage presentation by individuals of thoughtful, responsible and stimulating ideas bearing on the issues America faces today. We feel they will do this more effectively if the force of their ideas is not diluted through "clearance" with their colleagues or sponsors. But we do present this volume in the conviction that Mr. Rostow's analysis deserves serious attention by all who would understand more fully the nature of contemporary Soviet society.

MAX F. MILLIKAN, Director
Center for International Studies
Massachusetts Institute of Technology

Cambridge, Massachusetts
August 10, 1953

FOREWORD

THIS extended essay is the outgrowth of an experiment conducted by the Center for International Studies (Cenis) at M.I.T. It was regarded as useful to attempt to pull together, in the compass of one short volume, what modern Russian studies could contribute in answer to two fundamental questions: (1) What determines the policy of the Soviet state, at home and abroad? (2) What are the prospects for change in Soviet society? It was further regarded as useful to draft someone from outside the field of Russian studies to conduct this experiment. I was asked to take this job, and accepted. The reader deserves to know, therefore, how this intrusion by an outsider into a highly specialized field was conducted.

I am by profession an economic historian, most of whose work has been on problems of the nineteenth century. I have been privileged to take a small part in postwar diplomacy at the Department of State in 1945–46 and at the UN Economic Commission for Europe (Geneva) in 1947–49. I learned a little of Soviet diplomacy and Soviet diplomats at these posts. By no stretch of the imagination, however, could I qualify as more than a moderately informed layman in this complex and even treacherous field. I took it to be my responsibility to learn enough about the Soviet Union to form independent judgments. This I have done. I read extensively and was most generously educated by my colleagues. Further, we have had the benefit of criticism and advice from many responsible authorities in and out of academic life. A considerable proportion of whatever value this essay may have derives from the unstinting support of the Russian Research Center at Harvard and from the wise advice of its director, Clyde Kluckhohn.

This essay attempts to put within a coherent framework of thought, embracing the whole structure of Soviet society, the creative scholarship of many men. As the text will reveal to Russian scholars, and the footnote references and bibliography try to make clear, Part One is built on the foundations laid by the whole international community of students of modern Russia: among others, on the work of Bauer, Bergson, Berman, Beck and Godin, Carr,

xiii

Chamberlain, Deutscher, Fainsod, Gerschenkron, Gurian, Hoover, Inkeles, Jasny, Karpovich, London, Maynard, Moore, Mosely, Nicolaevsky, Robinson, H. Schwartz, S. Schwarz, Struve, Sumner, Timasheff, and Wolfe. Parts Two and Three venture into areas less well charted. Although, as is wholly proper, the interests, perspective, and emphasis of Russian scholars differ widely, the observer of the field cannot but be impressed by the devotion and quality of their work, which, as a body, conforms to the highest standards of scientific scholarship in our society.

The basic analytic structure, the balance given to various elements in the story, and the sequence of presentation have been discussed with my collaborators extensively; but full responsibility for this document must be taken by myself alone. I have profited much from the observations of Mr. Levin and others. But they bear no responsibility for such eccentricities of emphasis and structure as this analysis may present. Mr. Levin, for example, would treat differently from Chapter 7 the relation between the Soviet regime and the Russian autocratic past; and he has reservations on my interpretation of the present role of the Communist Party in the Soviet system. Had he borne the responsibility for this analysis, or, in fact, had any other social scientist borne that responsibility, it would have emerged different in organization, in emphasis, and, to some extent, in its conclusions. And this is not to say it would have been less correct or useful. Social scientists are not yet far advanced in the techniques for analyzing the various parts of a moving society in relation to one another. It is, moreover, difficult to achieve objectivity on problems at once so close to us in time and so charged with meaning in terms of our fundamental values. With an awareness of my own limitations in this task I have, nevertheless, chosen to present as clearly as possible the view which has emerged in my mind rather than to organize this book as a series of discrete and disparate essays, or to find compromises by forms of words. This method mainly reflects the view that team research is most likely to be fruitful if, in the end, after the fullest possible exchanges of view, intellectual responsibility is assumed by one man.

Mr. Levin was responsible for writing first drafts of the following portions of the text: Chapter 2, Section 1; Chapter 3, Sections 2–6; and Chapter 7. Chapter 3, "The Bureaucratization of the Instruments of Power," is to be regarded, even in its final form, as primarily his work.

Mr. R. V. Daniels wrote first drafts which served as the basis for

Chapter 13, Sections 2 and 4; Chapter 14, Sections 1, 4, and 5. Mr. A. Lowenfeld wrote first drafts which served as the basis for Chapters 8 and 9. Chapter 11 is based, in part, on the work of Mr. R. W. Hatch, whose advice and judgment are reflected at many other points, as well. Chapter 13, Section 2, is based on the researches of Mr. Isaac Patch and Mr. Alexander Korol; and Chapter 14, Section 6, on an investigation of Mr. Harry Naylor. Other portions of the text were initially as well as finally drafted by myself.

I also had the benefit of reading first drafts written by Mr. Daniels covering Chapter 1, Sections 3–4; Chapter 2, Sections 2–4; Chapter 5, Sections 1–5; and Chapter 6, Sections 1–7. When these emerged in final form Mr. Daniels expressed disagreement with the analytic framework within which his drafts had been placed and, at certain points, with my revisions. Since he himself intends to write on the subject matter of these portions of the text, they were wholly rewritten by me from the sources. Nevertheless, I should like to pay tribute to Mr. Daniels' contribution to the project as an organizer of basic materials, as a critic, and as the author of the following pieces of research which I have read: "The Kronstadt Revolt of 1921," *American Slavic and Eastern European Review*, December 1951; and "The Left Opposition in the Russian Communist Party to 1924" (unpublished doctoral thesis, Widener Library, Harvard University, 1950). I am sure Mr. Daniels' colleagues on this project join with me in expressing the hope that his interesting and original views will soon be generally available.

I should like to express my appreciation to Mr. Paul Aron for his kind permission to use unpublished materials presented to the seminar of the Russian Research Center at Harvard, and here used as background for Chapter 6, Section 7.

Mr. Ernest Hollis kindly made available to us preliminary chapters of his study of the Soviet secret police. We all have benefited indirectly from the preliminary research of Mr. Levin, sponsored by the Research Foundation of the Oklahoma Agricultural and Mechanical College, conducted before he joined Cenis.

I am greatly in the debt of a group of experts, in addition to my colleagues on this project, who read and criticized this essay in an earlier draft. This group included men busy with tasks of government and academic experts, whose extraordinarily generous and constructive response to this intervention in a specialized field was heartening to us all. The scholars who gave of their time to criticize this book in draft, aside from Mr. Levin, Mr. Daniels, and others on the project, were: Raymond A. Bauer, John E. Burchard, Merle Fainsod, George C. Homans, Albert Kervyn, Clyde Kluckhohn, William L. Langer, Alfred Meyer, Barrington Moore, Jr., Elting E. Morison, and Bertram Wolfe. I wish to thank them all.

In the final revision of the text and its preparation for publication I have been ably assisted by Mr. Robert E. Macmaster of M.I.T., and by my learned colleague Alexander Korol. Mr. Francis Bator, Assistant to the Director of Cenis, has been, throughout this enterprise, a most valuable and constructive critic.

My acknowledgments would, indeed, be incomplete if I did not record the personal debt I owe to Julius A. Stratton, Vice President and Provost of M.I.T., and to Max F. Millikan, Director of Cenis. Their unfailing confidence in this project and substantive support of it were the foundations on which it has been built.

W. W. Rostow

Center for International Studies, M.I.T.,
Cambridge, Mass.
May 1953

The Dynamics
OF SOVIET SOCIETY

"Tyranny . . . has no regard to any public interest which does not also serve the tyrant's own advantage."

—Aristotle

INTRODUCTION

THIS essay aims to contribute in a limited way both to the study of Soviet society and to the clarification of certain issues basic to the making of U.S. policy toward the Soviet Union. As a study, it might be described as an exercise in analytic history, or, what comes to the same thing, an exercise in bringing together the various social sciences around a single dynamic problem, i.e., a problem of change over time. In this academic aspect, it seeks to establish one possible conceptual frame which would contain and relate systematically the areas of knowledge and data now available on Soviet society. Its purpose is to stimulate further thought on the interrelations among the various sectors into which Russian studies, in common with the social sciences in general, have come to be divided.

The unifying hypotheses adopted here can in no sense be regarded as final. The study of modern Russia is at an early stage of its evolution. More than that, historians and other social scientists have only begun to address themselves systematically to the problem of making a frame for the dynamic analysis of societies such that the whole area of knowledge can be made greater than the sum of its specialized parts. This essay is, frankly, a tentative and exploratory effort.

The present analysis is also meant to assist the makers of American policy. Any act of policy must be based on some implicit or explicit generalization, or net judgment, concerning the forces at work in the area to which it is addressed. Public action involves an effort to achieve some aim in the light of the capabilities available and in the light of an intelligence judgment based on better or worse information, and better or worse analysis of it. The conventions of specialization in the social sciences permit the academician to evade a net intelligence judgment in this sense; the responsible official is denied the luxury of such evasion. Whatever the state of knowledge and analysis available to him, the responsible official must act. His action, by definition, involves some net judgment concerning the interplay of forces at work in the camp of his ally, his negotiating partner, his potential or actual enemy.

3

This unavoidable link between evaluation and action has a special importance in U.S.–USSR relations. The United States stands in what economists might call a duopolistic (or oligopolistic) relation to the Soviet Union: the influences exerted by the United States and the Soviet Union on the world arena of power are so great that each faces an environment it has helped to create by its own past actions and by the reactions to them of the other power.

The American view of the motivations and intent of the present Soviet rulers, and of the future prospects of that society, is, therefore, an essential and unavoidable part of American policy-making. Similarly, the Soviet view of American intentions and the future course of American society is a basic determinant of Soviet policy. But, even more than that, the world environment which the United States confronts is partly determined by prior and current U.S. foreign policy, including the reaction of the Soviet Union to that policy. The world environment which the Soviet Union confronts is partly determined by prior and current Soviet policy, including the reaction of the United States to that policy. The interaction of these two centers of power is thus exceedingly intimate. One consequence of this interaction is that, in a quite formal sense, even perfect knowledge of the workings of Soviet society would not permit firm prediction of its future course, since its course will be partially determined by events in the external world, including the course of U.S. policy.

Out of its accumulating experience the United States Government has formed a range of simplified working hypotheses concerning the operative motivations of the Soviet rulers, and the probable course of change of Soviet society as it may impinge on the policy of the Russian state. Implicit or explicit in the work of the academic community concerned with modern Russia are views on these decisive matters. It has thus seemed possible that an analytic review of modern Russian studies focused, in the end, on the questions which responsible officials must try to answer might lead to formulations which would contribute to U.S. policy. Prima facie, the vast swings in American public opinion and policy toward Russia over the past thirty-five years, and in the appreciation of Soviet society, which underlay and partly determined those swings, appear to justify an effort of this kind. If, with all its imperfections, this essay can contribute in a small way to producing a more stable general understanding of the Soviet Union, its primary purpose will have been achieved.

This is evidently not a task to be undertaken once and for all. Russian studies are evolving rapidly. The present effort, undertaken a year or two from now, would have the advantage of many important pieces of organized knowledge not now available as well as a more certain feel for the shape and stability of the Soviet structure as it is revealed in the post-Stalin process of readjustment. It is certainly the first of our conclusions that an analytic effort of the kind attempted here be made a regular part of the work of the various Russian research organizations in this country, and that, at periodic intervals, one group or another take responsibility for this kind of formal analytic reappreciation of what we know and do not know concerning the operative motivations of the Soviet rulers and the alternative courses Soviet society as a whole may take in the future.

Any attempt at a unified analysis of a whole society must involve assumptions and hypotheses which cannot be fully tested in the present state of information. It is partially for that reason that no fully responsible academic analysis of Soviet society of the kind presented here now exists, although Barrington Moore's *Soviet Politics: The Dilemma of Power* covers, with somewhat different intent, a part of the same ground. If some such effort is to be made, empty boxes must be filled and hypotheses advanced which relate the boxes to one another. These hypotheses inevitably touch on interrelations among sectors of a moving society about which formal knowledge is now extremely limited. This analysis is, as it was meant to be, an experimental performance.

The problem confronted in this essay consists in depicting how the various parts of Soviet society have moved in relation to one another. The life of a society in movement consists of action at analytically separable levels, which may be roughly defined as economic, social, political, and cultural. These levels continuously interact, but each also has a certain degree of independent continuity. Both the interaction of the various levels of society and their continuity take their shape from the nature of human motivations and the related requirements of human beings in organized societies. In the analysis of relatively free societies, where the play of individual motivations helps directly to determine the dynamic sequence of events, no priority of (say) economic over other human motivations can be assumed. Economic action, for example, may result from any of a wide range of human motivations or may, in terms of the society, be instituted from the level of politics, the social system, or the culture, as well as from within the economy itself. The essence of this system of thought is the notion of continuing interaction among the various levels into which society may be usefully but arbitrarily divided, reflecting the complex interactions within the minds of individual men as they confront and solve or fail to solve the endless stream of problems thrown at them for decision by the physical environment and society within which they live.[1]

It is our view that even in a modern totalitarian society such interaction takes place, although in a somewhat different manner from that in relatively more atomistic structures. The trends in Soviet history which emerge from an ex post examination of events are taken to result not from conscious long-term planning, but rather from a succession of key decisions of the Soviet state made in the context of particular sets of circumstances created by the historical course of events. These strategic decisions appear to have been governed by a remarkably continuous set of priorities (or value judgments) in the minds of those who prevailed in the Soviet structure. The shapeliness of the story which emerges is, thus, not the consequence of full control and forethought by the men who have dominated the Soviet system, but rather of the continuity of priorities in their minds in confronting issues thrown at them for decision by the course of world history and the continuity of certain fixed or slowly changing forces operating within the society they have sought to control. It is this view of the dynamic process by which Soviet society has evolved which appears to justify the emphasis given to the factors which may have shaped the priorities in the mind and personality of Lenin; for these priorities emerged in greater simplicity but full continuity in Stalin. And, since the late 1930's, they have been crystallized into remarkably stable institutional procedures and attitudes. There is, as yet, no reason to believe that these priorities do not also dominate the minds of Malenkov and his colleagues who, as this Introduction is written, uneasily manipulate in coalition the controls unified, at least since 1929, in Stalin's hands.

The analysis opens with an effort to establish the source of what

---

[1] The fundamental approach to the analysis of a moving society used here closely relates to that used by the author in his work on economic problems. See especially *British Economy of the Nineteenth Century*, Oxford, 1948, Chapter 6, and *The Process of Economic Growth*, New York, 1952, Chapters 2 and 3.

is here called the priority of power. A converging series of influences made Lenin and the hard core of the Bolshevik Party he dominated choose that course which would increase their own direct short-run power, as opposed to any other possible goal open to them, at moments of decision. The means to power early became, in fact, an end in themselves—a result implicit in Lenin's conception and organization of the Bolshevik Party and fully evident in the policy of the Soviet regime by 1921. This fundamental transition appears to have substantial roots in the philosophic bases of Marxism, in Russian history, and in the personalities of the men who dominated the Bolshevik group initially and who subsequently proved best capable of surviving in power.

The concept of the priority of power, which is used throughout the following essay, is a shorthand phrase for a complex phenomenon. It appears important that this conception be distinguished from the notion that, psychologically, the rulers of the Soviet state are motivated, in a personal sense, simply by the desire for power. Indeed, there is an evident enjoyment of power present in the lives of Lenin, Stalin, and the others who made the Russian Revolution of November 1917; and they certainly belong with those many figures of history who found it easy to believe that, if power remained concentrated in their hands, larger beneficent purposes would be served. More than that, one of the dynamic, self-reinforcing processes to be discerned in this story is the progressive selection of men who had a respect for power, knew how to use it, and were prepared to take risks in order to achieve it. And there is an equally consistent process of elimination of those unwilling to resolve their conflicts between idealism and their own power position, or less able in the pursuit of the latter. The love of personal power is a legitimate element in the analysis; but we do not attempt to pierce behind it to the deeper psychological roots of the behavior of the chief Bolsheviks; and, more important, this element in the analysis is not taken to be the sole root for the priority of power that has consistently dominated the behavior of the Russian Communists. This essay is not simply a Newtonian elaboration on the theme of personal power maximization.

The priority of power is based, in the first instance, on a combination of Marx's view that there was a determinable form which future history would take and Lenin's conception of the Communist Party as a chosen instrument for the achievement of Marx's prognosis. The Party thus acquired in its own eyes both legitimacy of status and the moral right to force the "correct" historical path—against the will of the majority and against the will, even, of the industrial working men who were designed to be the primary beneficiaries of the whole revolutionary development. In prerevolutionary Russia this essentially conspiratorial conception attracted emotional support due to the frustration of economic, social, and political reform by the tsarist state which led many reformers to concentrate their energy on the task of overthrowing by violence that autocratic regime. The overthrow of a regime by force is, essentially, a problem in the strategy and tactics of power. Further, since the "correct" line is always arguable, in its Russian context this conception had the consequence of moving the Communist Party itself toward a dictatorial form of rule, in which, in the end, one man's judgment would determine the line; and, in the anarchic state of revolutionary and postrevolutionary Russia, the right to lay down the "correct" line was likely to rest with him who knew best how to conduct a struggle for power. The bases for the priority of power lie, then, in converging aspects of the history of Russia and Communism, as well as in the personal characteristics of Soviet leaders. It is inseparably bound up with one aspect of Communist ideology, and gathered its initial emotional force from that fact. The reader should constantly bear in mind that this essay is not based on a simple opposition of ideology and a lust for power. Both conceptions are much more complex than common usage would credit; and, in the Soviet case, they partially converged.

Communist ideology also included, however, a fairly explicit set of economic, social, and political goals, incorporated in the aspirations and programs of various revolutionary groups. Some of these specific goals converged with the effective pursuit of power—for example, the nationalization of industry. Some of them conflicted —for example, the placing of political authority directly in the hands of trade unions and the Soviets, those Bolshevik-dominated organizations of workers and soldiers on whom the November Revolution was built. The inner core of consistency in the story of the Russian Communists is the priority they were prepared to give to the maintenance and expansion of their own power over other lines of policy, including their willingness to go to any lengths judged to be required to organize and control the Russian peoples in an effort to secure their own continued ascendancy as a regime. In the end, the society they have organized represents a projection out onto an entire state and its peoples of the form and concepts of organization created largely by Lenin for the operation of the Communist Party itself.

Despite the impressive continuity of the priority of power the manner in which it has been exercised has, of course, changed. Lenin, in the immediate postrevolutionary days, may be seen groping among the conflicting leads offered to him by the complex and contradictory heritage of Russian Marxism. There are, in his performance as a political leader, certain unresolved contradictions which, for some historians, justify for Lenin a higher moral status than for Stalin; for example, the relative freedom in which he left Soviet intellectual and cultural life, his unwillingness to use the death penalty against fellow Communists, the bonhomie with which he led the Communist Party (except when seriously challenged), and the relative freedom within the Communist Party for open controversy in his day. There are some real differences between the rule of Lenin and that of Stalin which are of historical interest. On balance, however, in the key decisions he made, the priority of power over other goals, including goals professed by Russian Communists, is evident in Lenin.

Stalin, in this context, appears less hampered than Lenin by the problem of overriding those elements in the Communist heritage which conflicted with the priority of power. His performance has a massive consistency, both in the extensive changes he brought about in the decade after 1928 and in the subsequent stability of the policies and institutions he elaborated. Increasingly, in the years before Stalin's death, one sensed that the Soviet regime was operating less from a conscious and fresh set of decisions, in which alternative possibilities were examined in the light of relatively fixed principles (including the priority of power among them), than from habits and procedures built into heavy inflexible bureaucratic structures. The historical roots of the priority of power and the living experiences which brought it to life seemed far distant from the Soviet Union, enshrined, at best, in such ritualistic documents as the *Short History of the Communist Party of the Soviet Union* and in the youthful memories of the middle-aged and elderly men who now rule Russia. Like almost all else in the Soviet Union, the priority of power as the dominant test for policy appears to have been bureaucratized.

The interaction of the pursuit of power, thus defined, with the problems and resistances it met resulted in decisions which had, in turn, their consequences; and these consequences created new situations (often in the form of increased resistance) which required further decision. It is essential to this argument that the secondary consequences of given decisions did not lie fully within the control of the Soviet regime and were not, in all cases, either fully predictable or compatible with its primary purposes. The successive application of the priority of power thus yielded an unfolding sequence of decisions which shaped modern Soviet society and, in particular, shaped the institutional form it has assumed since the late 1930's. To understand the present position of that society and the alternatives for it which the future may hold, it is, therefore, necessary to look back to the process by which it has arrived at its present position.

One might have expected that the study of the first professedly Marxist regime in history would constitute an exercise in the analysis of the relations between the economy on the one hand and the social, political, and cultural superstructure on the other. On the contrary, the philosophical implication of the priority of power has been that Hegel, having been allegedly turned on his head by Marx, is set right side up again by Lenin and Stalin. We are examining a peculiarly persistent and single-minded effort to use the maximum powers of a modern state to produce throughout the society it controls the economic, social, political, and cultural changes believed desirable for the maintenance and expansion of power by a small co-optive group. The *de facto* ideology of the Soviet Union would now more nearly identify the Great Leader and the State as the prime movers of history than the play of economic forces or even the interplay of economic, social, political, and cultural forces. The dilution of executive authority since Stalin's death is unlikely to alter this conception, unless much more drastic changes occur within the Soviet Union. But if our view of the history of society as a fully interacting process is correct, the actual course of the society is not to be determined or understood solely in terms of its political process, even when power is wielded absolutely with the full mechanisms available to a modern state. And, in fact, the evolution of Soviet society consists in large part of a sequence of interactions between the aims of Soviet rulers and the limitations imposed on them not only by Russia's geographical position and natural resources, but also by the stage of Russian history and economic development at which they came to power and by profound cultural forces in Russian society which are capable of only slow change.

Put more precisely, the forms which the efficient pursuit of power has taken have been more heavily determined by certain abiding or slow-changing aspects of the Russian scene than by the ideological or other presuppositions which the Soviet rulers brought to their self-designated mission. Those who seek to consolidate and enlarge their power wish their people to work hard and efficiently on the tasks they set. If men are to execute assigned tasks, their motivating interests must be taken into account, as well as the accretion within them of a long cultural heritage. In fact, men appear to be governed less in their actions by a conscious, rational calculus among alternatives than by habits, customs, and attitudes deeply ingrained in their heritage and personal experience, and tenaciously held. The existence of these forces embedded in cultures does not eliminate the need for men to exercise choice among alternatives; but it limits the range over which those choices are likely to be found acceptable. Lenin said of the Russian peasant: ". . . he is as he is, and will not become different in the near future . . . the transformation of the peasant's psychology and habits is something that requires generations." Although the motivations and cultural outlook of men are certainly subject to change over time, the ruler who wishes prompt as well as efficient performance must take men as he finds them. This, essentially, the Soviet regime has done. Despite varying efforts to shape more profoundly the human beings within Soviet society to its purposes, the regime has generally sought efficiency and conformity from the Russian peoples as it found them and as they have evolved in the past thirty-five years under influences longer lived and more complex than the policy of the Soviet state alone. The consequence of the regime's pragmatic decision, over the years, has helped give a distinct and persistent Russian character to the forms of Communist dictatorship; but it is an important conclusion of this analysis, elaborated in Chapter 7, that the Russian mannerisms of the Soviet regime do not imply an identification of the regime's interests with those of the Russian peoples or the Russian nation.

We are thus convinced that the story of Soviet Russia is not only a lesson in the awful potential of totalitarian rule in the context of modern societies; it is also a lesson in the limitations of even the maximum exercise of political power in the face of the nature of cultures and ultimately the resistance, often passive, of men.

Within this framework of assumptions, biases, and conclusions the analysis has been organized in the following manner:

Part One examines the evolution of Soviet rule. The first aspect of the process examined is the series of successive self-reinforcing steps by which the handling of executive power became concentrated in a virtual one-man dictatorship, and how the succession of a second thoroughgoing dictator came about. The consequence of the centralization of command over institutions, notably the Communist Party itself, the Soviets, and the trade unions, which originally themselves held elements of policy-making power is traced. The bureaucratic administration of power within the framework of its extreme centralization is then considered. A further stage of the argument examines the relationship of the economy to the dominant goals of Soviet policy, the adjustment of ideology consequent upon the fundamental priorities of the regime, and the adjustment in social and cultural policy stemming from the priority of power. This view of the changing course of the regime's organization and policies is followed by a summary consideration of the interaction of the goals of the regime and certain stable or slowly changing elements of Russian national life and culture. The historical portion of the analysis ends with a consideration of the relations of this internal evolution to the sequence of Soviet foreign policy since the Revolution and to post-1945 policy in the European satellites.

Having thus traced the course of the Soviet structure to its present point, the analysis turns to a consideration of the current impact of that changing system on certain individuals and groups within it and on its key institutions. This portion of the text (Part Two) takes the form of a cross-section evaluation of the cohesive forces, instabilities, and tensions in contemporary Soviet society. This evaluation is explicitly linked to the dynamic course of events traced in Part One as it has had its impact on different aspects of Soviet life and on particular groups within Soviet society.

Finally (Part Three), events from the Party Congress of October 1952 to May 15, 1953, are reviewed and certain conclusions are outlined briefly concerning the operational behavior of Soviet leaders and alternative possible evolutions of the society in coming years, as it confronts the awkward dilemma of the succession process. Conclusions are presented in this alternative, speculative form both because of evident limitations on our own knowledge and on our ability to predict the course of a moving society, and also because among the determinants of the outcome will be events external to the Soviet Union, including the course of U.S. policy.

It may be helpful at the close of this Introduction to note certain areas of doubt and ignorance which, to this observer of modern Russian studies, suggest possible priorities for future efforts of research and analysis. There is first, of course, the current position within the highest level of the Soviet regime. We need to know more of the manner in which "collective leadership" now operates. Has the authority of the secret police really been reduced? What of the political role of the armed forces? Has the bureaucracy asserted itself as a political force, in the face of weakened executive authority? Is Malenkov merely biding his time before making a play for the totality of Stalin's power? Second, and perhaps of even greater importance, is the need to gain knowledge and insight concerning the outlook within the current generation of higher bureaucrats, created largely by the dynamic workings of Soviet society. These men, forty-five and under, have had their mature experience since the crystallization of Stalin's rule in the 1930's. The Revolution of 1917 is a childhood memory at most, part of a propaganda-created folklore. These high officials are bureaucrats, trained to discipline and efficiency against a background of intense nationalism which was heightened by the experience of World War II, living under the orders, surveillance, and suspicion of a regime built by a different generation of men. They and their children who now enjoy hereditary, almost pre-1914 middle-class advantages, may well constitute the key to Russia's next historical stage.

Third, we would do well to learn more of the workings of the Soviet bureaucratic structure. Bureaucratic organization is a feature of all modern societies; and it is easy to fall implicitly into a view that all bureaucracies are the same, since they do, indeed, have common features. A careful comparison of bureaucratic processes under totalitarian and democratic societies, sorting out common factors and differences, would reveal much, both of modern Russia and of our own society.

Fourth, out of the growing mass of material on Soviet society we should try to establish some sense of the degree and nature of those democratic elements in political and social organization of which Russian society might be capable should it be freed from Soviet rule. American interests in the Russian future are, indeed, real; but they fall far short of the need to see established and maintained in that region particular social and political institutions. Nevertheless, it is important and will remain so for the United States to have some feeling for the underlying aspirations and capabilities of the Russian peoples with respect to the organization of their own society.

Finally, we would call attention to the fundamental issues of social science analysis which lie at the heart of this essay but which transcend the field of Russian studies. What is the process by which the rulers and the ruled interact in a totalitarian state? What are the limits of modern totalitarian rule? How best can one organize an analysis of a moving society, so that the relationships among its various parts may be sorted out with reasonable precision, despite the almost infinite complexity of the interactions which occur? What are the elements in Soviet (and other) societies which we cover by the word "ideology," and how do they play their part along with the other forces which move men to act? How, in the light of the complexities of modern social science, shall we treat the ancient tendency of men to strive for their own political power, without losing sight of this factor or ignoring the complexity of human motivation? These are some of the underlying questions this work has confronted and, in a tentative way, has sought to answer. I am acutely aware of the interim character of the answers offered, whose purpose, in substantial part, is to stimulate others to do better.

Part One

THE EVOLUTION
OF SOVIET RULE

Chapter One

THE PRE-1917 FOUNDATIONS FOR SOVIET RULE

1. A STATEMENT OF BASIC CONSIDERATIONS

IT IS the present hypothesis that the modern Soviet state is to be understood primarily as the consequence of a peculiarly single-minded effort by an extraordinarily centralized regime to pursue two related but not identical goals: the maintenance of its own absolute internal power over Russian society, and the maximization over time of its power vis-à-vis the external world. These twin objectives have interacted on each other. Moreover, they have to some extent supported each other, but not on all occasions; when conflict has arisen between them, the first has had priority thus far in the history of the Soviet regime.

These interlocking characteristics of the regime emerged step by step out of a historical process rather than from a conscious plan. The origins of the process can be traced back to certain elements in the history and thought and personality of the chief revolutionary leaders, notably Lenin, and reflected in the political party he organized. These men were predisposed to make certain policy choices when confronted with the alternatives open to them before, during, and after the Russian Revolution of 1917. They did not consciously plan the Soviet regime which emerged. Their predispositions, when confronted by events and forces outside their control, led to a series of short-run decisions which, over time, shaped the course of the Soviet regime. In particular, this accumulation of decisions led systematically: (1) toward the evolution of a system of centralized and absolute political power dominated by one man; (2) toward a bureaucratized, hierarchical structure of institutions and a related system of income distribution designed to maximize efficiency; (3) toward a systematic statist and nationalist alternation in Marxist ideology, and, within the framework of the modified ideology, toward a conservative, traditionalist pattern for social, intellectual, and cultural life; (4) toward that organization of the Russian economy which would maximize the rate of industrial growth and military strength, leaving for consumption that minimum compatible with the maintenance of life and efficiency within the working force. The emergence of this pattern for society—a pattern fully formed in the course of the 1930's—has set in motion forces, not fully within the power of Soviet executive control, which are, in turn, changing the pattern of Soviet life and institutions and which promise to alter that society still further in the future.

Since the value judgments which have been central to the shaping of Soviet life were effectively, if not finally, crystallized in the outlook of Lenin and some of his colleagues, it is important to examine the foundations of their thought, and, especially, to clarify the manner in which they differed from political figures of the Western world in this century.

The Russian revolutionaries who formed the Bolshevik Party evidently did not fully share the value judgments which underlie the political, social, and economic techniques of Western societies. These might be summarized as follows:

1. Individual human beings represent a unique balancing of motivations and aspirations which, despite the conscious and unconscious external means that help shape them, are to be accorded a moral and even religious respect; the underlying aim of society is to permit these individual complexes of motivations and aspirations to have their maximum expression compatible with the well-being of other individuals and the security of society.

2. Governments thus exist to assist individuals to achieve their own fulfillment; to protect individual human beings from the harm they might do one another; and to protect organized societies against the aggression of other societies.

3. Governments can take their shape legitimately only from some effective expression of the combined will and judgments of individuals, on the basis of one man one vote.

4. Some men aspire to power over their fellow-men and derive satisfaction from the exercise of power aside from the purposes to which power is put. This fundamental human quality in itself makes dangerous to the well-being of society the concentration of political power in the hands of individuals and groups even where these

groups may constitute a majority. Habeas corpus is the symbol and, perhaps, the foundation of the most substantial restraint—in the form of due process of law—men have created to cope with this danger.

From Plato on, political scientists have recognized that men may not understand their own best interest, and, in particular, that they may be short-sighted and swayed by urgent emotions in their definition of that interest. As between the individual's limitation in defining wisely his own long-run interest and his inability wisely to exercise power over others, without check, democratic societies have broadly chosen to risk the former rather than the latter danger in the organization of society, and to diminish the former danger by popular education, the inculcation of habits of individual responsibility, and by devices of government which temper the less thoughtful political reactions of men. From Plato to Stalin, however, there have been those who have chosen, intellectually or in practice, to risk the latter danger.

From this definition the democratic element within a society emerges as a matter of degree and of aspiration. Aware of the abiding weaknesses of man as a social animal, the democrat leans, nevertheless, to the doctrine of Trust the People rather than Father Knows Best. The pure democratic conception is, however, compromised to some extent in all organized societies by the need to protect individuals from each other, by the need to protect the society as a whole from others, and by the checks installed to protect the workings of the society from man's frequent inability wisely to define his own long-run interest. Even when societies strive for the democratic compromise, the balance between liberty and order which any society can achieve and still operate effectively, and the particular form that balance will take, are certain to vary. They will vary not only from society to society, but also within one society in response to that society's cultural heritage, the state of education of its citizens, and the nature of the problems it confronts as a community. It is evident that some present societies, like their historical counterparts, have not had and do not now have the capability of combining effective communal action with a high degree of what is here called the democratic element. Both history and the contemporary scene offer instances of governments in which the balance of power is heavily in the hands of the state rather than in the hands of the individual citizens who comprise it.

Within the infinite array of possible balances, a totalitarian regime constitutes an extreme case. It can be defined as a state in which the potentialities for control over society by governmental authority are exploited to the limit of available modern techniques —where no significant effort is made to achieve the compromise between the sanctity of the individual and the exigencies of efficient communal life; where the moral weakness of men in the administration of concentrated power is ignored; where the aspiration toward a higher degree of democratic quality is not recognized as a good; and where, conversely, the extreme authority of concentrated power is projected as an intrinsic virtue.

Whether the democratic value judgments are regarded as good or bad, it is basic to an understanding of the Soviet system that they were only partially shared by Marx, and by Lenin and those others who made the Soviet Revolution and who, step by step and perhaps partially against their own expectations, formed thereafter a totalitarian regime in Russia. This transition is believed to have its roots in certain elements within Marxist thought; in the conspiratorial Russian revolutionary tradition which focused obsessively on the destruction of tsarist autocracy; in the problems and experience of prerevolutionary conspiracy; and in the human qualities of the revolutionary leaders. Its final extreme character has been permitted by the exploitation of control potentialities inherent in the techniques of modern society.

2. SOME OBSERVATIONS ON MARX AND LENIN

In view of the extraordinary energy and attention subsequently given by the Soviet state to the mechanics of handling power, it is ironic that Marx's political ideas were so incompletely developed and profoundly confused. They consisted of an ill-digested amalgam of three major elements which in practice have led to conflicting courses of action. The three elements are these:

1. The notion of a scientifically predetermined course for history in which political power and leadership belonged legitimately only to those who understood the scientific key, i.e., the true Marxists.

2. The notion that the achievement of certain democratic values, in the humanistic eighteenth- and nineteenth-century sense, would automatically accompany the transition from capitalism to socialism.

3. The notion that all societies would pass, by means of class struggles, from feudal to bourgeois-capitalist to socialist stages, in

each stage of which political power would be exercised on behalf of a dominating class; and that the process would end with the mystically enunciated withering away of the state upon the emergence of a classless society.

Soviet Russia has seen the gradual triumph of the first of these elements and the virtual, but not complete, elimination of the other two. As discussed below, the resolution of the human dilemma set up by a deterministic conception of history resulted in an identification of historical correctness with the ability to seize, hold, and expand power.

The first of these three elements in Marx was early harnessed, in the Bolshevik movement, to the eternal human craving for power and to familiar techniques for seizing and holding power. This mélange of quasi-philosophical rationale with ancient human motivations and methods dominated the careers of both Lenin and Stalin. Bolshevism only slowly divested itself (and then incompletely) of the second of these elements; that is, a heritage of humanistic democratic values. The third element which, if pursued, would have forced the Bolsheviks to conduct a revolution in 1917 on behalf of bourgeois capitalism was clearly jettisoned by Lenin before his return to Petersburg from Switzerland in April 1917. The mutilation of Marxism caused by the "premature" achievement of the "dictatorship of the proletariat" has been more or less successfully concealed in subsequent Soviet elaborations of Marxism, which have managed to rationalize the current existence of a powerful state while continuing to hold up the ultimate objective of its disappearance. To this rationale, an identification of the interests of the Russian Communist state with the ultimate goals of Communist ideology has been central.

Marx's doctrines were formulated at a time in the nineteenth century when men were excited by apparent analogies between the course of societies and the process of change in the natural world, as elaborated by a sequence of scientists who defined evolution in terms of certain fixed laws of adaptation. These laws, in Marx, assumed the form of a hypothesis which made the social, political, and cultural texture of societies dependent on material and economic forces.

Applied to societies, the evolutionary hypotheses resulted in theories of historical change. Men differed, of course, in their interpretation of the pattern history had followed and was likely to follow. The analogy with the evolution of the physical world had the following important effect: it appeared to define a future which would be correct in terms of natural laws and apparently independent of the individual judgments of men or of the short-run processes of politics.

It is the notion of a scientifically objective and, therefore, "correct" course for history which, in part, led to the frame of mind of the Marxist revolutionaries. They believed that Marx had formulated the theory which would determine and therefore permit prediction of the course of history; and they were led thereby to the view that those political actions were correct which moved societies along this historically predetermined path. The Marxists never accepted, or they abandoned, the lessons of some two thousand years of Western thought which regarded the handling of state power in relation to the individual as a distinct problem in all forms of society. Marxism, in one of its aspects, simply assumed away the problem. It held that the state was solely the instrument for class oppression by the historically dominant class and that the correctness of political action lay not in its substance or method of application but in its relation to the effective exercise of class power at different historical stages. It was on these quasi-scientific foundations that Lenin built his conception of the Party as the disciplined instrument of Marxist history, responsible only to its own correct analysis and for the application of correct laws of historical change.

The Party—the True Marxists—became a type of Hegelian hero. The acceptance of the notion of a correct and predeterminable path for history gave special status in the process of politics to those who understood that path. The Party appeared to receive sanction, by the acceptance of this doctrine, to take whatever steps might appear to them necessary, in the light of their Marxist analysis, to move the political process in the predetermined direction. The acceptance of this element in the Marxist dogma relieved the Soviet revolutionaries from the responsibility of considering systematically the manner in which the individual aspirations of men related to the political process, or the manner in which the political process must be shielded from the frailties of human ambition and ignorance in the handling of power.

In its own eyes the Bolshevik Party thus had the right and duty to force the correct path for history. Since a group finds it difficult to agree on what is correct at any given complex moment in history, the exigencies of political practice converted this doctrine into a system in which correctness was defined by that man who succeeded in surviving and dominating the political situation; and his consequent decisions were executed by the disciplined faithful.

This whole pattern of thought has been explicit in the Communist tradition since at least 1902 when Lenin published his famous *What Is To Be Done?* Lenin there combats the notions of his opponents within the revolutionary movement who wished to see a deterministic Marxism harnessed to some form of democratic or popular political process. He uses two main lines of argument:

1. Without the leadership of the proletariat by professional Marxist revolutionaries, the working class might seek, not revolution but ameliorative advances under a trades' union banner; and

2. Only a dictatorship of the proletariat, as opposed to the parliamentary play of political forces, would move history along the correct path.

On the basis of these fundamental judgments he called for a tightly disciplined organization of the revolutionary party.

There was another and more practical basis for Lenin's belief that a disciplined dictatorial group must dominate political action if such action was to be "correct." He and his colleagues were engaged in revolutionary agitation. They worked largely underground in Russia or from exile by illegal means. They faced real dangers and the practical problem of subversive action. Lenin's elder brother, Alexander, had been hanged as the result of an abortive students' conspiracy. Lenin's justification for a tightly disciplined, centrally directed political party was thus made not only in terms of one strand in Marxist political theory, but also in terms of efficient revolutionary practice. There was logic in the marriage of Marxism (with its ambiguities about the political process, but its special sanctions for the true Marxists) with the urgent tasks of energetic revolutionaries. This logic led to a conception of the handling of political power by a central small unit, operating without any formal check on the legitimacy or correctness of its judgments except that provided by discussion within the kind of politically irresponsible group which tends to fall under the domination of a single leader. Lenin fully accepted Engels' dictum: "Conspiratorial methods . . . require a dictatorship if they are to be successful."

The tactical aspects of Lenin's doctrine, with its emphasis on the need for flexibility in the face of any given situation, have a particular importance; for they reveal the vast simplification of his problem achieved by Lenin, and also suggest the manner in which the pursuit of power could become, in fact, an end in itself. Once Lenin, as a professional revolutionary, had defined his goal in terms of the seizure of power, he could build up in terms of the possibilities for action at any given moment a line of policy, regardless of substantive Marxist aims. Since, by definition, a professional revolutionary was operating without responsibility and outside of any accepted frame of government, it was wholly natural that, with respect to the handling of power, there should evolve an empirical, practical frame of mind which did not devote much time or effort to a consideration of the appropriate limits within which power should be used. Lenin was engaged in war against the tsarist state—and in warfare men tend to accept the view that the end justifies the means.

It was equally natural that revolutionary opposition should attract and stimulate adventurous utopian minds, many of which developed in Russia both outside and within the Bolshevik movement. But the discipline of seeking and then of exercising political control weeded out ruthlessly those who were not prepared to cut through the ambiguities of Marx and face the short-run manipulation of power as a serious professional task. Those who tended to take ideology rather than the techniques of power seriously on an abstract level were inclined also to underrate the latter in practical situations, to their ultimate extreme cost.

Although the full meaning of Lenin's simplification did not become clear until much later, and he was almost certainly not conscious of all its practical implications in 1917, it is evident in retrospect that the most important contribution of Marxism to his actual operations in the seizure of power was extraneous to fundamental Marxist thought, i.e., Marx's view that destiny lay with the industrial proletariat.

The peasants' desire for land was a powerful force in the Russian as in earlier European revolutions, and the strength of Bolshevik appeal among the soldiers lay partly in that fact. But it was in the cities that power was seized. At a time of crisis a peculiar strength attaches to those who control urban centers; an organized segment of the urban proletariat can be immensely helpful in seizing power, quite apart from its proportionate representation in the society as a whole.

3. THE RUSSIAN BASES FOR LENINISM

Lenin's peculiarly practical adaptation of one philosophical strand of Marxist thought had its roots not only in pre-1914 Russian conspiratorial practice but also in the contours of Russian political thought and experience over the previous century. Leaving aside its Marxist element, Lenin's thinking reflects three qualities which can be traced in a good many of his Russian predecessors:

1. The notion that there were unique problems and possibilities in Russia's position which required and made possible an evolution different from that of Western Europe.

2. A feeling that a gap existed between the mass of the Russian people and the intellectuals, which the intellectuals had, somehow, to fill.

3. The conception that a phase of violence, even destructive violence, might be required in order to put Russia on the right political and social path—a conception founded in the hard fact of the recurrent triumph of brute force in the long sweep of Russia's history.

It should be strongly emphasized that there were other vital strands in the evolution of Russian political thought before 1917. Russia generated its own version of the Western democratic tradition. Up to 1914, and even to 1917, these more familiar elements were the predominant forces making for change in Russian politics. Although such speculation is not very fruitful, there is a good case to be made for the view that Russia would have moved into a phase of fairly familiar Western democracy, had not World War I and its attendant disasters intervened. It is to be remembered that, in their only relatively free election, that of November 25, 1918, the Russian citizens gave at least 58 per cent of their votes to a party representing a moderate socialism, to be executed by parliamentary means. This was the predominant direction of Russian development in the century before 1914, and it was the trend which the Bolsheviks frustrated and repressed. Nevertheless, Lenin's view of appropriate political practice had some national roots.

In his perceptive little volume, *The Origin of Russian Communism*, Nicholas Berdyaev says: [1] "The Russian cultured class was suspended over an abyss, crushed by two fundamental forces, autocratic monarchy above and an unenlightened mass of peasantry beneath. Russian thought, without basis and rebellious, in the nineteenth century was inwardly free and audacious; it was not chained to a grim past and to tradition, but outwardly it was cramped and

[1] (London, 1948), p. 25.

even persecuted." Indeed, Russian political thought and speculation of the nineteenth century presents a wide spectrum, ranging from a philosophical anarchism with profound spiritual bases, through conventional Western conceptions of democracy to extreme autocratic and even totalitarian ideas. Despite this range, the persistent influence on intellectuals of the dual frustration isolated by Berdyaev can be discerned: frustration imposed by a backward tsarist autocracy and by the massive fact of a population consisting of a downtrodden peasantry, to the extent of some 80 per cent. These frustrations largely account for the three Russian elements, noted above, which found their way into Lenin's formulation of the mission, strategy, and tactics of the Communist Party.

The sense of Russia's unique problem and possibilities can be traced in many figures of the nineteenth century, of whom one of the earliest and most distinguished was Alexander Herzen (1812–1870), a cultivated and urbane nobleman who was also the first important Russian socialist. After many years of immersion in the Western political tradition, he reacted strongly against the "petty bourgeois spirit" which he felt had infiltrated even European socialism. Exiled from his native land, he came to feel that the oppressed Russian peasant had in him potentialities for a grander social and political evolution than the West had seen. The great social revolution which he envisaged would have begun in Russia and then swept over the West. Out of this holocaust would have arisen a purified and better world. Michael Bakunin (1814–1876), Herzen's contemporary and fellow-nobleman, further elaborated this view. He held it to be possible for Russia to escape what he regarded as the horrors of capitalism, and, in this respect, he ranks as one of the more important forerunners of Lenin. In general, not only Russian political thought but Russian literature as well, from Pushkin forward, reflects a sense of the special destiny of Russia. On the whole, it is fair to relate Lenin's decision in 1917 to forego a "bourgeois stage" and to move directly for "the dictatorship of the proletariat" to this strand in the national pattern of mind.

The struggle of Russian intellectuals to relate themselves to the mass of the Russian people, and their vacillation between romantic efforts at identification and an almost cynical harnessing of the people's energies to purposes the people did not share, is also a long story. The effort of the intellectuals to get close to their fellow-beings, and especially the peasantry, found major expression in the *narodnichestvo*, the populist movement which engaged in one way or another not only such political figures as Herzen and Bakunin, but also Dostoyevsky and Tolstoy. The emotional basis for this effort was exceedingly complex, reflecting, among other factors, the sense of isolation of the Russian intellectual community and its guilty conscience at the gap between its own civilized life and the brutal poverty in which the mass of Russians lived. Sir John Maynard, in his *Russia in Flux*, aptly entitles one of his chapters, "The Intelligentsia and the Worship of the Plain Folk."

By the 1880's, however, the romantic phase of Russian populism had largely played itself out. The most active *narodniks* in Russia were members of a terrorist wing which included Lenin's unfortunate brother Alexander; and their sporadic, amateur violence had also revealed itself as insufficient to the revolutionary goals they cherished. In this setting, various versions of Marxism, with its unemotional, allegedly scientific basis, were gaining in influence. Among many intellectuals (whom it is easy to overestimate, looking backward from the fact of the November Revolution) there was disappointment with the efficacy of the gradualist efforts at Russian reform, and a tendency to look harder at the facts of political power and ways to achieve it. Lenin, born in 1870, came to maturity at a period of reaction against this back-to-the-people movement, strengthened in his case by his brother's execution. Lenin's doctrine of Communist Party leadership, if necessary against the will of the proletariat, obviously bears the mark of the fairly widespread disillusion with the populist approach in particular and the concept of peaceful political evolution in general.

The third of these Russian elements in Leninism—the persistence of a faith in violence as an instrument for the seizure of power— obviously owes a great deal to the inflexibility of tsarist autocracy over the pre-1914 century. There were, indeed, important changes and concessions in the operation of Russian autocracy in these years. But reform came slowly, and against the background of a chronic, often brutal, reassertion of autocratic rights and privileges. From the failure of the Decembrist Revolt in 1825, with its conception that a military coup might achieve quick drastic social reform through dictatorship, down through Herzen, Bakunin, the Nihilists of the 1860's, the terrorist wing of the populist movement, to revolutionary Marxism itself, this theme—that violence would be required—runs through much Russian political thought.

4. CONCLUSIONS ABOUT LENINISM

The conception of the Communist Party defined and applied by Lenin owes something, then, to Russian history as well as to the Hegelian strand in Marx and to the hard experience of conspiratorial practice. Under Lenin the Communist Party emerged with its power centered in a small disciplined organization, prepared to subject the means it used to no rigid framework of rules, facing with equanimity the prospect of imposing on the Russian majority or even on its own narrow group of adherents an overriding judgment from the top concerning the historically correct line of action.

It was essential to the process which occurred during and after the Russian revolution, however, that these doctrines were not the only ones which played a part in the thinking of Lenin and the Bolshevik Party. Marxist prerevolutionary thought contained within it an important element of general democratic conceptions derived from the progressive thinking of the previous two centuries, e.g., the right of free assembly, the notion of free and secret elections, the inviolability of the person and of the home, the freedom of conscience, of speech, of the press, the right to strike—all interwoven in the minds of both the leaders of the revolutionary movement and their followers with the hard core of practical rules for action. The process of removing this "ideological baggage of parliamentary democracy" [2] represents an important part of the evolution of the Soviet state after it achieved power.

A second piece of the Marxist inheritance that had to be abandoned was, as noted above, the Marxist conception that societies must pass from a feudal through a bourgeois- to a proletarian-dominated phase. It was probably not until shortly before Lenin returned in 1917 to a Russia already in revolt that he permitted himself, at last, whole-heartedly to contemplate the possibility of a direct seizure of power by the Bolshevik Party without a preliminary phase of more conventional bourgeois parliamentary government.

It is thus the conclusion of this stage of the argument that even before 1917 the inheritance of an important element in Marx's political theory converged with the bitter and practical experience of conspiracy, and with aspects of nineteenth-century Russian political thought. These converging influences gave to Lenin and his colleagues a fundamental bias in the following form: when a choice

[2] A phrase from Barrington Moore Jr., *Soviet Politics—The Dilemma of Power* (Cambridge, Mass., 1950), p. 36.

had to be made between a course of action which would enhance
the power of their own political group as opposed to its being in
conformity with Marxist doctrine, the substantive goals of revolution, the broad ideological aims and traditions of the progressive
movement, or the majority will of the peoples concerned, the choice
would lie on the side of short-run political realism and practice.
It is in this precise sense that Aristotle's subtle definition of tyranny,
which appears at the beginning of this book, directly applies to the
evolution of the Soviet state. In some instances the ideological
inheritance of the revolution converged with the pursuit of power;
in many instances there was conflict—consistently resolved and enforced in the interests of short-run power. The evolution of the
Soviet regime since 1917 is, in its essence, the dynamic consequence
of this persistent, gradually strengthening, and ultimately institutionalized bias in the context of Russia and the world scene. Its story
is a profoundly reinforcing commentary on the doctrine that, in the
handling of political power, there is no meaningful separation to
be made between ends and means. This is no empty cliché. Its substance derives not only from the demonstrable transition of a political movement initially dedicated to ideological goals of substance
into a regime organized around the goal of its own power; if the
views presented in Parts Two and Three of this essay are just, it is
further supported by the fact that the fundamental forces likely
to make for change and instability in this regime derive, in turn,
from the means it has chosen to pursue the goal of power.

Chapter Two

THE HIGHER POLITICS
OF SOVIET RULE

1. THE RUSSIAN REVOLUTION AND THE BOLSHEVIKS

THE RUSSIAN Revolution of March 1917 was a national upheaval, generated out of Russian history, to which the Bolsheviks were at the most secondary contributors. It thrust Lenin and the small Bolshevik Party into a wholly new setting. Up to that time they had been concerned with the building of a conspiracy against the tsarist state, with the organization and discipline of their own party, and with a considerable controversy with competing revolutionary groups. The major historical forces which brought about the disintegration of the tsarist state in March 1917 put them for the first time into a position of opportunity, and even responsibility, with respect to the exercise of the power of the state.

By March 1917 Russian military difficulties in the field, combined with hunger and inflation at home, placed tremendous strain on the tsarist government. That government itself was split into two factions, neither of which was capable of coping with the situation. The coterie of the Empress and her spiritual adviser and favorite, Rasputin, dominated by an inflexible desire to preserve the autocracy against further encroachment, was unwilling to make the political and administrative concessions necessary to deal with the domestic situation and the problem of military supply. The administrative machinery was disorganized as incapable ministers followed in rapid succession. The death of Rasputin placed the responsibility for the state of the nation squarely on the throne and upon the Tsar as Commander-in-Chief. Tsar Nicholas II had to assume direct responsibility for huge manpower drafts, for military defeats, for harsh discipline, and for hunger in the Russian cities. Important groups in

30

the court, army, and administration were aroused by the weakness of the Tsar's performance, and by a belief that the Tsarina was exercising an influence both stultifying to the efficiency of the state and overly reactionary. These groups began to think in terms of a further liberalization of the state and a further limitation of the power of the monarchy. They would have pushed on with the gains that had been made in 1905 and the following years. By March 1917 the regime was isolated from virtually all elements of Russian society, and the stage was set for the formation of an alternative government.

As in earlier European revolutions, the urban areas took on, under these circumstances, an importance beyond their numerical proportion in the population. The first effective action against the regime assumed the form of crowd demonstrations in Petrograd on March 8, 1917, against the local food shortage. These developed rapidly into riots lasting about a week. The crowds, which consisted chiefly of industrial workers and various middle-class elements, although restrained, were fired on by troops garrisoned in Petrograd and by a police force commanded by men frightened and insecure. Within a few days, on March 10–11, the troops, mainly peasant conscripts of the Petrograd garrison, were themselves transformed into a revolutionary force. Affected by the popular mood, reacting against orders to fire on the crowds, concerned about a possible movement to the front, they mutinied against their officers. The crowds, now reinforced by the military, mobbed uniformed police. Strategic public buildings and fortified points were taken from weak defending forces. In the face of a lack of unity of purpose in the high levels of the tsarist state, neither army nor police nor administration stood up against the wave of popular feeling. The regime had lost control over the capital city, and other major centers followed Petrograd's lead.

This, then, was a revolution begun with popular dissatisfaction against which the regime was incapable of mobilizing adequate military and political counter-strength. A key stage in the process was the decision of the military high command to join with liberal and conservative leaders of the Duma—Russia's parliament, established in 1905—to defy the order proroguing the Duma. Thus the Duma remained in session and organized the Provisional Government, the purpose of which was envisaged as the restoration of order and the establishment of a new permanent regime which would better meet the desires of various elements in opposition to tsarist rule, and which might more efficiently conduct the war against the Central Powers.

Political success at this juncture depended on the ability of the government to gain and hold the loyalty of troops, workers, and peasantry by action or by promise that their basic demands and aspirations would be satisfied. In this context, the position of the Provisional Government was most difficult. It inherited the obligations of the disestablished monarchy and faced the same military and economic circumstances which had brought on the upheaval. Its personnel, moreover, were representative of only a small segment of Russian society. Its authority was promptly challenged on two major questions: the continuation of the war, and the establishment of economic stability. A Soviet (Council) of Workers' and Soldiers' Deputies, under the leadership of Social-Democratic and Social Revolutionary intellectuals, and modeled on an institution that had played a prominent role in the revolution of 1905, soon became the focus of this challenge. The Soviet demonstrated its ability to control the effective (mainly urban) forces of revolution by undermining discipline in the army and instigating, or articulating, popular demands against the reestablishment of the monarchy and against the continuation of the war. Seeking at first only to curb the alleged conservative tendencies of the government, the Soviet to some extent identified itself with the latter by accepting cabinet posts. Kerensky, soon to be the leader of the Provisional Government, was the most prominent example. Despite such links to the government, however, the Soviet maintained its freedom for independent action.

A key stage in the Provisional Government's disintegration was its loss of military support at both high and low levels. It proved incapable either of establishing military discipline or of controlling uprisings stimulated by leftist propaganda and leadership. It thus alienated the military command as well as conservative and liberal elements. Although an armed challenge from the Right under General Kornilov in September 1917 disintegrated in the face of official and Soviet opposition, the Government's position became increasingly difficult. The failure of an offensive in the field in July 1917 had lowered its prestige; and the Kornilov affair revealed (to both the Bolsheviks and the Government) the Government's reliance on forces under Soviet rather than its own control. More generally the Government had lost popular confidence through its inability or unwillingness to cope with peasant and labor unrest, land redistribution, widespread desertion, and economic chaos. Having lost support from the more conservative elements, in October 1917 it faced an extreme challenge from the Bolshevik Party.

Until Lenin returned from Switzerland in the famous sealed train on April 16, 1917, there had been cautious collaboration between the Bolsheviks and the Provisional Government. From the moment of his return it was Lenin's policy to move from the fluid position he confronted to a seizure of the power of the state by the Party. There was a false start on July 17, when an abortive popular uprising was associated by the Government with the Bolsheviks and Lenin fled to Finland to escape arrest. Aided, however, by the growing unpopularity of the Provisional Government and by shrewd "Land-Bread-Peace" propaganda, the Bolsheviks were able to gain sufficient support from the workers, soldiers, and sailors to control and organize the key Petrograd Soviet and utilize this body and its Military Revolutionary Committee to seize power in Petrograd on November 7. Similarly, power was seized in Moscow. The essential elements in this process were the willingness of the troops in these towns to work with the revolutionary parties in the seizure of power, and the ineffectiveness of either the Government or the conservative opposition to hold the army together or otherwise to mobilize effective military or political counterforce.

The actual seizure of power in 1917 required that Lenin and the Bolshevik Party overcome two elements and clarify a major obscurity in the Marxist doctrine. They had to overcome Western democratic ideas concerning the political process which clung tenaciously to much Marxist thinking and which have not been totally eliminated from official Soviet propaganda to the present day. Specifically, they chose to prevent the continued meeting of the Constituent Assembly after it had been duly elected and convened with a strong anti-Bolshevik majority in January 1918. In its place they affirmed the exclusive power of the Soviets, where the inside guiding influence of the Bolshevik Party was great. The conception of political democracy was strong in the Russia of 1917, and strong even in the Communist Party. Communists, it is true, were generally disdainful of parliamentary democracy as a bourgeois device. But in a part of their minds they looked to the Soviets (and the trade unions) as purer forms of political democracy. Thus, the support of the Soviets as opposed to the Constituent Assembly had ideological roots among the Communists. It also had, of course, a meaning in terms of Lenin's power, which was strong in the Soviets, but weak in the elected Assembly. The dismal fate of the Soviets, as serious political bodies, revealed soon the dominance of the latter element in Soviet policy.

The Bolsheviks also had to overcome the Marxist notion that societies could move to a stage of socialism only after a historic passage of bourgeois capitalism—a leap in which Lenin's leadership from April 1917 was decisive. Finally, they had to fill the gap left by Marx in his theory covering the actual handling and administration of power. This they did, step by step, by extending, from the practice of conspiracy to the practice of government, the notion of a highly disciplined elite corps whose leadership was justified in terms of their knowledge of Marxist theory and the correctness of the decisions they would make in terms of the course of history.

2. FROM THE NOVEMBER REVOLUTION TO NEP

The extension of the disciplined practices of a conspiratorial party to the operations of a state took shape in a succession of practical decisions which had to be made by the Bolshevik rulers in the period, roughly, from 1917 to 1921. The suppression of the Constituent Assembly and the majority will it reflected did not end the problem of the part which the democratic process would play in Soviet political life. The "dictatorship of the proletariat" proved to be a mightily ambiguous conception; and further conflicts in Marxist thought and tradition had to be resolved, one way or another, in the face of living problems and decisions which the regime confronted. The form of their resolution in these few years left decisive marks on the Soviet state: and knowledge of this period is, therefore, essential to an understanding of the process whereby the Soviet regime has evolved to its present position.

In his biography of Stalin, Isaac Deutscher discusses the period from November 1917 to March 1921 in terms of a general pattern for revolutions.[1] "Each great revolution," he writes, "begins with a phenomenal outburst of popular energy, impatience, anger, and hope. Each ends in the weariness, exhaustion, and disillusionment of the revolutionary people." Deutscher describes how, progressively, the revolutionary leaders are trapped between the promises and aspirations which sparked the revolution and the limitations imposed on their achievements by a harsh reality. Step by step the leadership becomes divorced both from the men who initially supported it and from the aspirations they initially shared. As the gap

[1] *Stalin, a Political Biography* (New York, 1949), pp. 173–76.

between aspiration and reality, between the people's goals and the acts of the revolutionary government, reveals itself, the leaders face a grave dilemma: Should they hold power in the face of a developing opposition; or should they abdicate to others, less burdened with the weight of broken promises? Something like this sequence can be seen in the French Revolution and, even more remotely, in the American Revolution from 1775 to 1787. What is distinctive in the Russian revolutionary sequence, in contrast to others, is that, in the face of changing problems and possibilities and at a high point of popular disillusion, one group of revolutionaries which had seized power at a radical stage clung to it successfully, defying the full force of the revolutionary undertow with whatever measures of repression were judged necessary for this purpose.

The meaning of this sequence in Russia, over the years 1917–21, can be seen by examining the problems faced by the new regime; the methods chosen by the leadership to solve them; the popular and Party reaction which resulted; and the resolution of his dilemma achieved by Lenin in 1921.

While the Bolshevik victory of November 1917 was achieved with ease in Petrograd and Moscow, the new regime by no means controlled the whole of Russia. The Ukraine was mainly in German hands. Anti-Bolshevik groups formed up in many parts of the country—the Caucasus, the Baltic, the Arctic north, and Siberia. The first test faced by the regime was that of civil war.

The second major problem of the regime was the need for ending the war with Germany. The promise of peace had been one of the most powerful of the Bolshevik slogans in November 1917. And Lenin insisted that this promise be made good as a minimum condition for dealing with the internal problems of the regime. Peace involved, however, both national humiliation and a violation of the hope of many Communists that the Revolution be promptly spread westward, notably to Germany. Moreover, the terms of the Treaty of Brest-Litovsk in March 1918 left the Germans in occupation of the Ukraine and other provinces and contributed to the general food shortage in the cities during the year 1918.

The third problem of the regime was to achieve some minimum level of production. Industrial output was seriously disrupted by the breakdown of the tsarist regime, the revolutionary events of 1917 and the experimental Bolshevik policies which followed, as well as by the brute fact of civil war. The extremely low level of industrial production during the postrevolutionary years was linked to what was, perhaps, the most basic of all the difficulties faced; namely, the low level of agricultural production and, especially, the difficulty of getting an adequate supply of food to the cities. Having been granted by the revolutionary process a drastic redivision of the land, the newly independent peasant failed to place on the market adequate supplies of food, in large part because countervailing supplies of industrial products were not available.

The Provisional Government had doubled the price of grain as one of the measures intended to increase the supply. But the solution of the main agrarian problem—that of land ownership and land redistribution—was left for the future Constitutional Assembly. Meanwhile peasants everywhere, especially in Central Russia, had proceeded to appropriate the land of large estates by local action of individual communities. The peasant holdings of arable land eventually increased by some 31 per cent, but the marketed share of crops declined catastrophically. Formerly, the large estates furnished most of the marketed grain; the operation of these estates was totally disrupted by the local peasant action. Furthermore, under the chaotic political and economic conditions, the peasant rapidly lost the incentive to raise more grain than was needed for his own consumption.

After the November coup, the Bolshevik government took no immediate measures of substance on the land question; nor was it politically and administratively able to stem the precipitous decline of agricultural output during the War Communism period. The peasant mainly acquired his land in a common-law process out in the countryside, while the disorderly business of the Revolution proceeded in the cities.

A decree formally nationalizing land (February 19, 1918) and a series of other decrees, including the decree (February 14, 1919) intended to preserve the former large estates for operation as State Farms, did little to alleviate the shortage of grain. By 1921 the area of land under cultivation shrank to about two-thirds of what it was in 1916. The yield per acre also declined. The drought of 1920 and 1921 thus produced a famine of unprecedented proportions.

In addition to these difficulties, the anti-Bolsheviks were supported at various points by Allied Governments, adding somewhat to the military difficulties of the new regime but also furnishing it with a powerful national rallying point.

These urgent military, diplomatic, and economic difficulties were met by an emergency program imposed from the top by dictatorial means. The Red Army was created to cope with civil war and intervention. A secret police was created to protect the regime by terror if necessary. Nationalist and ideological considerations were overridden by Lenin, and the Treaty of Brest-Litovsk was signed. Industry was almost totally nationalized under the system of War Communism. Factories were put on a semi-military basis, and state-organized barter supplanted, for the time, free market exchange. Requisition, by force if necessary, was applied with indifferent success to mobilize the food necessary to avoid starvation in the cities.

The administration of such an effort required, of course, the existence of a substantial bureaucracy, as well as centralized, dictatorial rule. A large part of the tsarist state machinery and its personnel were retained. Workers in the factories soon found themselves under a discipline at least as harsh as that they had experienced when the factories were privately owned. Discipline and formal ranks were also soon restored in the army, which continued to contain many tsarist officers.

Thus, dictatorship on behalf of the proletariat took on, almost immediately, a meaning which differed sharply from what most men had thought was meant by "dictatorship of the proletariat." In both its form and its substance the emerging centralized bureaucratic dictatorship violated the revolutionary aspirations of its own minority group of supporters. It had been one thing to accept centralized dictatorship as a revolutionary party, conspiring for power. It was quite another matter to see these conspiratorial techniques elevated to state policy, after victory had, apparently, been achieved. More than that, the continued use of the state bureaucracy as an instrument for exercising centralized power offended some of the most deeply held views of the revolutionary movement. Lenin himself had shared the romantic view that the postrevolutionary state and its economy would be administered by men elected by their fellow-workers, and that no permanent class of supervisory officials would be permitted to form. The continuity of bureaucratic practice and discipline was a distinct shock to many adherents of the revolution.

Finally, the decision of the regime to make prompt peace with Germany, foregoing the possibility of detonating a German revolution, was a major setback to many of those Communists who took their Marxism seriously. The whole notion of the seizure of power in November 1917 had been opposed as premature by many within the Bolshevik ranks. Some of these ideological dissidents were prepared, however, to envisage a Communist revolution so long as it was simply the catalyst which touched off Communist revolutions throughout Europe. The notion that Russia could go it alone, implicit in the Brest-Litovsk decision, deeply disturbed many of those close to Lenin.

The Communist bureaucratic dictatorship which took shape in the postrevolutionary days differed drastically, then, from the vision which had inspired many of those who had contributed to the Communist cause. Outside of the Communist Party, the fact of dictatorship by a minority party, the hunger of the cities, and the resentment of the terror with which the civil war was conducted produced widespread disaffection. Thus, the rulers of the Communist Party alienated some of their most idealistic supporters by the bureaucratic and dictatorial character of the regime, and they defied what was almost certainly a majority sentiment, already largely impotent in the making of policy, for some of the substance of political democracy.

Aside from the ruthless use of military and police power developed by the regime two factors, above any others, held the country together through these grim days. First, the intervention of foreign governments in the Russian civil war stirred in many a national loyalty to the regime which overrode their grave doubts about its course. Second, the anti-Bolshevik opposition lacked a political program which was an attractive alternative to that of the regime; notably, it failed to assure the peasants that the overthrow of the regime would not lead to a return of their newly gained land to the old landlords.

Nevertheless, opposition to the regime, both inside and outside the Communist Party, mounted considerably as the civil war came to an end in 1920. Within the Party the so-called Left Opposition focused its attack on the centralized and bureaucratic character of the regime and made impressive inroads on Lenin's leadership at the Tenth Party Congress in March 1921. In the midst of that Congress, a more dramatic symbol of dissatisfaction took shape in the Kronstadt Revolt. This revolt involved virtually all the elements of the opposition to Lenin's rule, ranging from Communists to anti-Bolsheviks, although the leadership and predominant spirit of the uprising derived from within the Communist ranks. Some of these elements demanded the overthrow of the regime in the name of the November Revolution itself: "Soviets without the Communists" was one of their slogans. Others had steadily opposed the

November Revolution on principle. And for still another element, the revolt reflected the chronic acute hunger of the city of Leningrad. Special military units of unquestioned loyalty to Lenin, and some of the delegates at the Party Congress itself, were rushed to Leningrad to put down the Kronstadt Revolt with force.

Speaking of Kronstadt, Lenin said, "This was the flash which lit up reality better than anything else." [2] He met that reality by using military strength to assert his rule while attempting to correct a part of the situation which had created the Kronstadt opposition. In recognition of the reality of popular dissatisfaction with the policy of War Communism, Lenin said: ". . . we had advanced too far. . . . We had not secured an efficient base. . . . The masses had sensed what we ourselves could not as yet consciously formulate . . . namely, that the direct transition to purely socialist forms, purely socialist distribution, was beyond our strength, and that, unless we proved able to retreat and to confine ourselves to easier tasks, we would be threatened with disaster." [3] Lenin refused, however, to bow to those who criticized his bureaucratic dictatorship of both the Communist Party and the country. On the contrary, he evoked with new force and meaning the overriding criteria of loyalty to the Party by its members and of unique authority for the Communist Party within Russia.

Confronted with the Kronstadt Revolt, members of the Left Opposition within the higher ranks of the Communist Party on the whole supported Lenin despite their deep reservations. These men were trapped in a dual contradiction from which they never were able to extricate themselves, down to the time of their ultimate liquidation in the Great Purge of 1936–38. They were loyal to the Communist Party and, although some had opposed Lenin's direct seizure of power in November 1917, they were loyal also to the concept of the November Revolution. But they advocated internal policies which would, almost certainly, have destroyed the possibility of continued Communist rule in Russia. The nondictatorial, nonbureaucratic techniques of organization they supported would have resulted in a drastic dilution of the regime's ability to control events. If not coupled with a return to capitalist and democratic forms of organization their domestic policies would almost certainly have also produced chaos. Their external policy, of looking to prompt world (or at least European) revolution, was equally at odds with the

[2] *The Essentials of Lenin*, II, 693, quoted in Deutscher, *op. cit.*, p. 220.
[3] *Ibid.*, pp. 813–14, quoted in Deutscher, *op. cit.*, p. 221.

realities of Communist power within Russia, and with Russian power vis-à-vis the external world.

Lenin's policy as it crystallized in 1921—dictatorial power at any price, including the abandonment of much of the revolutionary program at home and abroad—violated important aspects of their beliefs. In the end, however, their misgivings were overridden by their loyalty to the concept of a disciplined, unified Communist Party. They could not free themselves from a primitive faith in the concept of the Party as the chosen instrument of the Marxist historical sequence in the twentieth century. To do so would have brought into question not only Lenin's policies but also the meaning of their pre-1917 lives as conspirators and the meaning of the November Revolution itself. Although they found the logical consequences of this Hegelian element in their Marxism repellent at times, they had deeply accepted and lived for years within its major premise: that there was a scientifically and morally correct course for history which men, acting through the national state, had a right to impose, if they could, on others, without check.

Specifically, they remained loyal to the November Revolution. Their dilemma as early as 1920–21 forecast that of many others throughout the world in the next decades who, as the unsatisfactory consequences of Soviet rule emerged, clung to a rationale which would leave still intact the legitimacy of the November Revolution itself. In his account of the Great Purge Weissberg describes the Left Opposition dilemma at a later stage with acuteness, on the basis of his prison experience: [4]

After the experiences of the Great Purge most of us felt, consciously or unconsciously, that up to the death of Lenin the policy of the revolution had been more or less correct. The isolation of the revolution in a peasant country without wide-scale industrialization and without a strong and homogeneous industrial proletariat had then led to the Bonapartist dictatorship of Stalin. We completely approved of Lenin's theories and we just as completely opposed Stalin's practices.

In fact, of course, Lenin's theories were a confused amalgam which led in practice to an overriding priority for power. The road back to a coherent position was exceedingly painful for those emotionally attached to the November Revolution. There were few like Weissberg's fellow prisoner Sborovsky: [5]

[4] Alexander Weissberg, *The Accused* (New York, 1951), pp. 376–77.
[5] *Ibid.*, p. 377.

Sborovsky was the first Communist I met who went further. . . . "When Lenin seized power [Sborovsky says], he had a comparatively short period of dictatorship in mind, and he thought it would end with the civil war. Well, it didn't happen that way. The dictatorship went on and on and grew more and more totalitarian. And it wasn't a dictatorship of the working class, or even of the Party, but of a single man. But that development started in the very first days of the revolution. The Constituent Assembly should never have been overthrown."

While the strategic and philosophical position of Lenin's opposition within the Communist Party contained this basic flaw, its tactical position was weakened as well by internal developments in Communist Party—and thus governmental—organization which were of the greatest importance for the future. Throughout the civil war national power was vested by the Central Committee of the Communist Party in the Politburo, consisting of five men: Lenin, Trotsky, Stalin, Kamenev, and Bukharin. This policy-making body was linked to the day-to-day operations of the Communist Party by the Organization Bureau (Orgburo), which was in charge of Party personnel. Stalin was the only link between the Politburo and the Orgburo. The bureaucracy, with its mass of old tsarist and new inexperienced officials, was controlled by a Workers' and Peasants' Inspectorate. Stalin was Commissar of the Inspectorate from 1919. Finally, as Commissar of Nationalities, he was in a unique position to build up connections of personal loyalty with key Communist figures in the non-Russian areas. Although Stalin was the least well known and least ideologically distinguished member of the Politburo, he came early into control of the essential pieces of machinery of the bureaucratic dictatorship. And when, in 1922, he became Secretary General of the Central Committee, charged with preparing the agenda and policy papers for the Politburo and transmitting its policy decisions downward, his influence was formidable indeed. Thus, in putting forward its policies within the Communist structure, the Left Opposition was confronted at every turn by the fact that the machinery of party and government had been gathered into the hands of a man who was not a Left Oppositionist.

And so, in 1921, Lenin launched the New Economic Policy. The state of affairs under NEP violated in two basic respects the wishes of the Left Opposition. In terms of the structure of the Party and government Lenin's dictatorship was strongly confirmed, and the centralized machinery of control and direction was progressively strengthened. In terms of the substance of public policy, the goals of the Revolution were postponed. The peasantry were appeased by the substitution of a tax in kind for grain requisitioning. Wide areas of industrial and commercial life were freed of state control and a substantial capitalist sector developed in the Soviet economy. Commercial treaties, normalizing trade arrangements with foreign countries, were sought as a matter of high priority; these economic objectives of Soviet foreign policy conflicted to some extent with the interests of the Comintern. Limited amounts of capital imports were tolerated, and technical assistance was sought and obtained on a substantial scale. Thus Lenin set about building the "efficient base" which he had found lacking in 1921—a base which Stalin was to exploit from 1929 forward.

3. FROM NEP TO DECEMBER 1929

The essence of the political story of Russia from 1922 to 1929 is the gradual development behind the scenes of Stalin as an absolute and personal dictator, a status publicly confirmed on the occasion of his fiftieth birthday. The principal stages in that sequence are well known, since, until the end of the 1920's, the politics of the Communist Party in Russia were given a considerable degree of publicity.

Lenin suffered his first attack of cerebral hemorrhage in May 1922 and in March 1923, his final stroke, which incapacitated him until his death in January 1924. In 1922 Stalin, previously head of the Orgburo, became Secretary-General of the Communist Party. From his base in the Party Stalin gained increasing control over the whole political apparatus, including ultimately the Politburo itself; his position carried with it control over the secret police, as well. Although the politics within the Politburo before Lenin's death are somewhat obscure, it would appear that in 1922 Stalin and the bulk of Party organization stood for centralized control and discipline of the Party, conciliation of the peasantry, and a low priority for the Comintern's international activities. With Stalin were Zinoviev, Kamenev, and Bukharin. On the other side were Trotsky, Rakovsky, Piatakov, Preobrazhensky, Radek, and others who stood for a higher degree of party democracy, rapid industrialization, a curbing of the peasantry, and a reliance on world revolutionary forces to support the completion of socialism in Russia in the near future. The split between those who favored the pursuit of the Communist program as opposed to the short-run consolidation of power had its roots in attitudes and, even, alignments within the revolutionary movement which went back into the pre-1914 decade. The whole of the ideological struggle of this period was inextricably involved with power maneuvering within the Party structure.

In his sporadic pronouncements of 1922–23 Lenin, who had made the line of Kronstadt-NEP, moved, toward the last days of his life, nearer the position of the so-called Leftists on the question of the internal organization of the Party. It is evident from Lenin's "Testament," his final recommendations to the Russian Communist Party, that he feared the emergence of a personal dictatorship of Stalin based on his position as Secretary-General; but the alternative form of political organization for the Communist Party that he had in mind is not wholly clear. It is absolutely clear that at no time did Lenin envisage anything but a dictatorship of the Communist Party as the means of governing Russia. On the other hand he was unprepared to turn his powers over to a single successor. What he appeared to hope for was that the most important men in the Politburo might operate collectively and that, within the Central Committee of the Communist Party at least, a degree of free expression of opinion would be preserved. The Central Committee might thus manage to help keep the collective Politburo and the Party secretarial apparatus moving along a compromise line which maintained unity. Roughly, within the Party Lenin seemed to hope for a balance between the deliberative and the executive elements, with the latter avoiding domination by one man.

He was, perhaps, led to envisage this possibility out of his own previous experience with the management of the Communist Party. By his qualities of personal leadership and the personal connections that had developed between himself and the other key figures out of a common revolutionary experience, Lenin had, somehow, kept the Communist leadership together and effective as the chief instrument of executive power in the state without either totally repressing the expression of opposition views or losing personal control over the making of policy. This personal tour de force may well have encouraged him to believe there was some method for institutionalizing a tolerable balance of power relationship within the executive organs of the Communist Party and the Soviet state— some method short of one-man rule by force. Lenin clearly saw that Stalin's personality as well as his party powers were likely to prove incompatible with such a solution.

There had existed, it is true, the ideal of a majority vote system for making decisions within the Party Congress, the Central Com-

mittee, and the Politburo itself, carried over from the prerevolutionary Party organization. Communist Party procedure had some of
the trappings of democratic practice, and for a time, even some
carefully limited substance. Lenin preferred to persuade rather than
dictate policy within the various organs of the Russian Communist
Party. He did not regularly use the full measure of the power which
inhered in his personal prestige. However, when, late in 1920 and
early in 1921, his control of the Party was challenged, he used the
naked force of the party machine and, at Kronstadt, simple military
strength. Lenin was, after all, the prerevolutionary leader of a
Communist faction which prided itself on its operational tough-
ness.

Stalin quickly realized that here was a political system without an
institutional foundation. Elections within the Communist Party
could be controlled by those who dominated the Party machinery
at the top. There was no appeal outside the Party. At every level
the Communist Party, despite its elective apparatus, was or could
be converted by the high-level machinery of its organization into a
co-optive body. He who controlled the machinery of organization
controlled, in the end, the voting. And although it took Stalin
some time to work out satisfactorily the full implications of his
perception, the result was implicit in his effective domination over
the Communist Party organization at a time when that organization, in turn, dominated the instruments of power in the Soviet
state. A bench-mark in this process was the mass recruitment into
the Party of hitherto nonpolitical workers, early in 1924, which assured those in control of the Party apparatus of control from the
bottom up.

Lenin's apparent belief that a self-appointed party dictatorship,
the exercise of whose power in the nation was governed by no clear
or fixed rules, could maintain inner unity and discipline on the one
hand and, on the other, a real diffusion of authority or even democratic procedures, can only be described as naive in the face of the
centuries of political thought and experience available to him. It
reflects once again the fundamental gaps in Marxist thought about
the political process and the relations of man to power. Lenin was
certainly not the first, and perhaps not the last, autocratic ruler of
Russia to face, in the end, the unsatisfactory long-run consequences
of his personal tour de force. Democratic centralism was, from the
beginning, an impossible conception for the long pull unless the

organization of the Communist Party itself were put on a strong constitutional basis; and a party which was prepared to recognize no fixed rules in its relations to the power of the state was unlikely to generate a constitutional approach to its internal arrangements.

At the formal political level Stalin's operation over the period of 1922–29 was devoted to the elimination of major figures who initially shared power with him within the Politburo. Trotsky was in opposition from 1923, expelled from the Party in 1927, exiled from Moscow in 1928, and deported in 1929. In 1925 Zinoviev and Kamenev were maneuvered into opposition within the Communist Party and joined with Trotsky. The issue of their break was mainly the disposition of power, although overtones of the so-called Left-Right controversy were involved. In 1929–30 the major figures of the Right Wing in the Politburo, Bukharin, Rykov, and Tomsky, were eliminated.

The issues of policy, as opposed to power, were, at first, the handling of the peasantry and industrialization. The so-called Leftists opposed the continuance of the laissez-faire aspects of the NEP and deplored the political and social trends they had set in motion or permitted to continue throughout Soviet society. Second, there was the issue of the appropriate relation between Russian and International Communism. The failure of the German Revolution in 1923 and of the Chinese Revolution in 1927 strengthened the nationalist bias in the Russian Communist Party, as it took shape under Stalin's rising authority. To the Leftists, however, this trend represented a violation of Marxist doctrine.

The elimination of the Right Wing figures in 1929–30 confirmed an older *de facto* situation. The Five-Year Plan of industrialization was launched in 1928 and carried with it the policy of wholesale collectivization of agriculture. The apparent shift of Stalin from the Right to the Left Wing on the issues of internal policy is to be understood in terms somewhat different from the doctrinal language in which the issues were argued within the Russian Communist Party. Stalin is quoted by Trotsky as follows on the Western European Communist movements of the early 1920's: "There is no revolutionary movement in the west; there are no facts; there are only potentialities; and we cannot take into account potentialities." [6] Stalin's whole career had been concerned with facts rather than potentialities and his decisions on industrialization and collectiviza-

[6] L. Trotsky, *Stalin* (New York, 1941), p. 250.

tion are of this realistic character. Although considerable ambiguity still surrounds the whole process which led Stalin to the brutal decisions of 1929–30, the key facts appear to be these:

1. The success of NEP was strengthening the hand of the independent peasantry and even small businessmen, and was producing a political, social, and economic situation which threatened the power of the Communist state over the country.

2. Russia's industrial advance from the Revolution to 1928 had been slow, representing merely a recovery back to 1913 levels. Russia as an industrial and military power was still weak.

3. By 1928 Stalin fully controlled the instruments of power within the Soviet state: the Party organization, secret police, army, and state administration, all of which were much strengthened since the days of decision in 1921–22.

It should be noted that this was one of the major occasions when the priority of power converged with the ideological heritage of the regime. Industrialization and collectivization had been on the Communist agenda, and the subject of discussion and debate, from the days of the Revolution forward. Stalin undoubtedly shared, in part of his mind, the revolutionary aspirations and beliefs which commended these policies to the Russian Communists. The timing and the form which his decisions took, however, and the operative rationale which led him to reverse his earlier go-slow position on these policies, are probably incorporated in these three power factors.

The policies of 1928–30 add up, then, to a decision by a personal ruler who had fully consolidated his position, to increase his hold over his own domain and to enlarge the strength and power which his state might exercise in the world arena of power. A symbol of the personal character of the new effort was the celebration in 1929 of Stalin's fiftieth birthday—the beginning of a canonization which he henceforth imposed on the Russian scene.

Stalin's fundamental weapon in achieving dictatorial powers, and in his subsequent successful elimination of actual or supposed opposition, was his control of the Communist Party organization from Politburo to grass roots—a control which he developed from this base until it extended over the other instruments of power in the state. His position was achieved by an extension to the Russian state of the prerevolutionary principles of Bolshevik Party organization. Stalin's enemies were doomed by their acceptance of a doctrine of party organization which had carried over from the prerevolutionary period and which had been strengthened by the experiences of 1917–21. The Leninist conception of absolute unity in the execution of orders from above, no factional activity, no criticism of the basic party line, and rigorous enforcement of the organization's rules, both psychologically and in fact, facilitated Stalin's victory once he had seized the core of Party organization and reorganized its personnel on lines designed to sustain his personal authority.

The line from Lenin to Stalin is continuous. The men can be distinguished mainly by the fact that Lenin made the succession of decisions which led to a personal dictatorship after having struggled with and having been tempted by other choices more nearly in accord with the whole confused Marxist inheritance. Soviet society of 1922 was full of saving inconsistencies, by Western standards, and was markedly inefficient by later Soviet standards of totalitarian consistency. It is not clear at what moment Stalin clearly envisaged his own potentialities, but from the Revolution forward he not only exhibited a virtually exclusive interest in the organization of power but was also without inhibition in its pursuit. As an individual and as a politician Stalin was evidently prepared to ignore, distort, or to suppress those parts of the Marxist revolutionary inheritance which might impede his main aim. In the end, Lenin had done much the same. But Lenin had created the pattern of the Soviet state, step by step, out of a confused and contradictory heritage; and, in his last days, he may have been somewhat dissatisfied with the result. Stalin found the emergent pattern of the Soviet state congenial and, piecemeal, he worked out its implications in a manner which, after the event, exhibited a powerful logic. Like the third generation in other human and institutional sequences, Stalin's successors now face problems of a new and difficult kind.

4. THE DICTATORSHIP OF STALIN, 1929–53

Stalin's unchallenged dictatorship can be arbitrarily dated from his fiftieth birthday in 1929 to his death in 1953. Those twenty-four years witnessed, on the domestic scene, the transformation of Russian agriculture and industry, and abroad, the rise of Hitler, World War II, and the postwar enlargement of Russia's role on the world scene. The substance of Stalin's policy in these circumstances is dealt with elsewhere in this essay. The present section is designed briefly to indicate the evolution and vicissitudes of his organization of dictatorial power.

Stalin vacillated throughout the twenties on the appropriate rate

These substantial categories do not in themselves account for the enormous scale of the Great Purge. What appears to have happened is that Stalin indicated to his chief of the secret police the general categories he wished eliminated or decimated. In turn, it appears that the secret police were instructed to operate in some kind of bureaucratic order on the basis of "confessions" of guilt which would implicate individuals in alleged conspiracies to assassinate Stalin or otherwise overthrow Stalin's regime with foreign assistance. The method of gaining "confessions" (now quite thoroughly substantiated from a variety of independent sources) was to exert extreme and especially sustained psychological and physical pressure to induce some form of admission of guilt from the prisoners and, in addition, to induce them to list as many other persons as possible allegedly implicated in the alleged plots. Most prisoners, under the techniques of terror available to the secret police, agreed to a form of confession and named other persons. The secret police then proceeded to arrest those named; and a kind of wild geometric progression of arrests resulted, ramifying out far beyond any narrow group of categories. Thus, despite the public attention given to the major trials of this period, and although the Purge struck mainly at the higher echelons of Soviet official life, it developed a momentum and a scale that brought to the bulk of the Soviet population direct and memorable knowledge of the regime's capabilities for terror.

Like many great political events, the Purge may have been a consequence of different but converging forces, of which at least four almost certainly played a part.

1. The Bolshevik leaders deposed by 1929, as well as others, reacting against Stalin's policies of the early 1930's, certainly contemplated and perhaps even planned the overthrow of Stalin and his regime.

2. The continued existence of the Old Bolsheviks, even if they were wholly inactive, was an embarrassment to Stalin's canonization as personal ruler and sole inheritor of the Leninist mantle; their elimination by public trial, on grounds of counterrevolutionary activity, would both confirm Stalin's legitimacy and serve as a powerful intimidating example.

3. Perhaps most important, the process of bureaucratization had undoubtedly bred, by the 1930's, a generation of men in the army, the Party, industry, and elsewhere in the government who, whether in opposition or not, took their positions of quasi-authority for

granted and, in the age-old manner of bureaucrats, learned how to pursue a continuous line of policy somewhat independent of the executive arm of the state at its highest levels. Stalin may have felt that his bureaucracy, including even his own lieutenants in the Communist Party apparatus, was not sufficiently and directly responsive to his will.

4. Stalin may have felt that, with the rise of Hitler, war might come; and he wished to rearrange the structure of the state so that it was more positively under his direct control, with all possibilities of independent (let alone opposition) views eliminated from the instruments of power.

And so, in a unique, insane historical passage, virtually a generation of men was removed from key posts and destroyed or exiled, carrying with it millions of minor figures who fell within categories judged prima facie suspicious. The core of logic in the whole process, such as it is, derives directly from the Leninist conception of the disciplined and reliable party in absolute command, here projected out on to a full state structure and a whole society.

On at least two points the evidence on the purges now seems quite firm: first, whatever opposition may have existed to Stalin and whatever forms it might have taken in the middle thirties, such opposition was not the sole or even major basis for the purges; second, the formal charges made by the Soviet state against individuals involved bore no serious relation to their actions or to the facts.

The ability of the Soviet structure to survive this period hinged not only on Stalin's ruthless will but also on the fact that a new second generation of men was emerging toward the end of the 1930's. Unencumbered with romantic and ideological memories of the Revolution and of Lenin and trained in the Soviet system, these men were prepared to take over the posts in the bureaucracy (including the Party) vacated by the victims of the Purge. It is this new bureaucratic generation, directed by Stalin and the personal group of henchmen who surrounded him, which has operated the machinery of the Soviet state since 1939.

From the Great Purge until Stalin's death, the higher politics of the Soviet regime, and even its basic policies, remained remarkably constant. Almost alone among the countries of the world, the Soviet Union has maintained domestic policies which exhibit no overt signs of the profound changes wrought in the world by World

Chapter Three

THE BUREAUCRATIZATION OF
THE INSTRUMENTS OF POWER

1. INTRODUCTION

THE SELF-REINFORCING dynamic process whereby executive power in the Soviet state became concentrated in the hands of one man and his appointees had important consequences for the state's major institutions. In general, it may be said that Soviet institutions were progressively divested of executive policy-making power and converted into administrative arms of the executive, here defined narrowly as the Politburo, or more precisely still, as Stalin (at least after 1929). In particular, this process applies to the Communist Party itself, the system of Soviets, reaching from local to national level, and the trade unions. All of these institutions were envisaged, at the time of the Revolution and immediately thereafter, as fundamental policy-making bodies; all have been converted into bureaucratic agents (or "transmission belts") for the execution of policy determined within the Politburo—in the last analysis by Stalin.

Similarly, the executive power has taken extreme care to avoid an accretion of policy-making authority to the armed forces or secret police. These instruments of force were never envisaged, of course, as makers of high policy; nevertheless, from the beginning, the problem of maintaining executive authority over them was a major concern of the Politburo and its leaders. Significant elements in the evolution of the Soviet state have been the efforts to deny to the armed forces and secret police executive powers, and the fact that, as time has gone on, out of the dynamics of bureaucratic dictatorship, actual or potential elements of policy-making authority have grown up within them.

2. THE BUREAUCRATIZATION OF THE COMMUNIST PARTY

With respect to the Communist Party, the previous Chapter has already indicated the manner in which Stalin's authority developed in a manner such as to permit him control over the Party from the top down. At the higher levels of the Party the draining of power from the Executive Committee has already been described. With the purges of 1936–38, and the replacement of major Party officials, the fundamentally subservient role of the Party below the level of the Politburo—a fact since about 1924—was institutionally confirmed and reinforced.

As a result of these changes the Communist Party organization was gradually confined to limited, positive, functions of an essentially bureaucratic character. These may be summarized as:

1. Responsibility for surveying and guiding policy execution by other bureaucrats, reaching down to the local level of the Soviet state, in which task the Party functionary is meant to serve as model and leader and bears a partial, overlapping responsibility.

2. Reporting upward to the Politburo, giving to the leadership a sense of the success and failure of their policies in various areas and supplementary knowledge of the mood, aspirations, and frustrations of the Soviet peoples.

3. Propaganda, designed to expound and drive home to the people the official rationale for various lines of policy decided upon by the Politburo.

In short, the Communist Party by stages ceased to be an organ for the formulation of policy and become a propaganda organ charged also with responsibilities for the surveillance over and guidance of policy. In this role it shares its functions, in a complex overlapping arrangement, with the administrative lines of command of the Soviet state and with the secret police. Virtually all responsible officials throughout the Soviet administration and police, as well as officers in the armed forces, are members of the Communist Party and thus stand, as it were, in two formal chains of command. With the rise of discipline and efficiency, relative to ideological enthusiasm, as criteria for success in Soviet society, it seems likely, however, that the relative power of the Party tie of such key operational figures has somewhat diminished in its importance. And when the Party intervenes in the workings of the state machinery, it is as likely to intervene as a supplementary device to ensure efficiency in performance as to guarantee ideological conformity.

3. THE ATROPHY OF THE SOVIETS

Whereas the draining away of executive function from the Communist Party to Stalin and his Politburo has left the Party with substantial bureaucratic tasks to perform, the state structure of the Soviets has virtually atrophied. It will be recalled that it was the Soviets which formed, in Lenin's propaganda of 1917, the alleged democratic alternative to a parliamentary regime. The allocation of power to the Soviets was designed to give expression to the democratic political aspirations which figure so importantly in the popular support for revolution, and to fulfill one conception of the dictatorship of the proletariat. By the time of the November Revolution, however, the Bolshevik Party held a position of leadership within most of the Soviets. The Party moved fully into the Soviet organs at all levels and, in fact, came to replace them in all their vital functions. The transition took place, nevertheless, over some years, as a historical process, conquering step by step a variety of resistance as well as inertia.

After the November Revolution, the Party leadership assumed key posts in the government (the Council of People's Commissars, the Central Executive Committee and its Presidium); but the absorption of executive energies in civil war and the incomplete state of machinery of government delayed a clear delineation of functions as between Party and State. The association between them was close in the highest organs, where Party control was strong; but it was still relatively weak in the local Soviets, especially since the local Party organs were originally financed by local Soviet executive committees. The first effort at definition of functions was made at the Eighth Party Congress (1919), which declared that the Party must have a decisive influence and complete direction in all workers' organizations and especially in the Soviets. This was to be accomplished by daily, practical, self-sacrificing work by Party members in the Soviets and by placing the most dependable Communists in Soviet posts. At this stage, however, the Party was warned that it must carry out its decisions through the Soviets—that it must guide them but not supplant them. And later Congresses emphasized this distinction between the guiding role of the Party and the deliberative and executive functions of the Soviets.

To make the work of guidance more effective and to assure Party control over the Soviet apparatus as a whole, the introduction of Party personnel into Soviet organs at all levels was effected by 1921, following upon the virtual identification of Party and Soviet personnel at the highest levels. Up to the early thirties, however, the Party leadership took pains to emphasize the official separation of Party directives and the laws enacted by Soviet bodies, as well as the formal differentiation of Party and Soviet organization structures.

With Stalin's consolidation of the dictatorship and the initiation of intensive industrialization and collectivization, a more open fusion of Party and State developed. Not only did Party personnel occupy strategic Soviet posts, but the central organs of the Party began to issue directive resolutions to higher Soviet bodies which were followed by official Soviet legislation. At times the Party resolutions had the force of law. The Five-Year Plans, for example, went into effect before formal enactment by the Congress of the Soviets and the Central Executive Committee; and a Party decree of 1932 widely affecting the school curriculum and teacher self-government became law without formal legislation. Some acts of the Central Committee have repealed decisions of local governmental bodies. Since 1931, many laws have been published in the Official Gazette in the name of both the Central Committee and the Council of Ministers (People's Commissars). The identification of key personnel and functions, long since achieved in fact, was publicly symbolized in the assumption by Stalin of the post of Chairman of the Council of People's Commissars on May 7, 1941. The making of policy, the formulation of legislation and execution were, at last, obviously in the same hands.

The evolution of functions within the Soviets paralleled, then, the evolution of the Party. Lower bodies were subordinated to higher; information flowed upward and decrees downward; and the decision-making power of the central bodies—the Central Executive Committee and its successor, the Supreme Soviet—were transferred to their *praesidia* and to the Council of Ministers (People's Commissars). While the Supreme Soviet, like the Central Executive Committee, has met more frequently than the Party Congress, it too enjoys only brief sessions and has become too large for practical legislative and executive action. It functions as a policy-disseminating, information-tapping body. Legislative promulgation springs from the Presidium of the Supreme Soviet and from the Council of Ministers. These institutions are directly and almost completely controlled at every level by the Party, i.e., by Stalin and those few who handled power in his name, and now by Stalin's successors.

Control of the Soviet mechanism, as well as of other non-Party organisms, is effected mainly through the organized element within them. Party rules require that groups of at least three members in any state or public organization or any gathering must organize to carry through Party policy and secure Party control over them. These groups, or "fractions," establish their control by proposing candidates for all leading positions; they reach decisions on every issue before their organization or meeting at caucuses (and they alone can caucus); and they vote as a disciplined unit according to their agreed decisions which are, in turn, guided by the policies of higher Party bodies, and, especially, by the policy pronouncements of their immediately superior Party committee.

In addition to this pervasive procedure of Party control and leadership a special controlling institution has always existed in the Soviet structure under various names: Commissariat of Workers—Peasants Inspection (1920–34); Commission of Soviet Control (1934–40); and, from 1940, Commissariat (Ministry) of State Control. The essential functions of these institutions have varied little. They have worked in close association with the Commission of Party Control to check the performance and practices of governmental organs and the loyalty and efficiency of state employees. Like the Commission of Soviet Control, the members of the Commission of Party Control were nominated by the Party Congress; and as a ministry its leading officials, and probably all of its operative personnel, are Party members.

Further Party control is expressed through the management of elections to the Soviets. Only persons of unquestioned loyalty to the regime can legally become candidates. They are chosen by a joint pre-election area meeting of selected "non-Party Bolsheviks" and Party representatives; they must be registered by area election commissions in which Communists predominate; and they can be replaced even after their names appear on the ballots. And, since the thirties, only one nominee per office has been permitted. This has resulted in the achievement of the desired proportion of Party and non-Party people at various levels, generally allowing for a predominance of the latter at the lowest levels and their complete elimination in the Presidium of the Supreme Soviet and the Council of Ministers. The control of the entire structure from the Politburo is thus premeditated and complete in detail, given the information

available to the Politburo through the Secretariat, the full dominance of the Politburo over the Party, and its ability to control the
Party at all levels.

4. THE EMASCULATION OF THE TRADE UNIONS

The development of authority in the trade unions of the Soviet
Union followed much the same pattern as that of the Soviets. The
contrast between the original conception of the trade unions and
their ultimate subordination and bureaucratization is, perhaps, even
more striking, given that strand in Marxist ideology which not only
conceived of revolution as a historical act on behalf of the industrial
worker, but which also looked to his instinctive wisdom, as organized in trade unions, for the making of a large part of public policy.

Up to the end of the civil war the power and prestige of the Soviet
trade unions were considerable. Under the Provisional Government
the Bolsheviks pressed to enlarge the powers of the Factory Committees (composed of workers who had more or less spontaneously
taken over the factories in which they had been employed), as
opposed to the unions. In addition, perhaps under a momentum
not fully controlled by the Party, the Factory Committees began to
take over or share in the control of industry and thus to hasten the
disintegration of private control over the economy. This latter
process much accelerated after the November Revolution. The concentration of Bolshevik effort on the Factory Committees had
special point, for Mensheviks then controlled the trade-union organizations. But when the Bolsheviks won control of the unions, shortly
after the November Revolution, the Factory Committees were subordinated to the unions and the workers' sections of the Soviets were
removed from the sphere of trade-union activity.

The centralized and now effectively controlled trade union organization was immediately given the task of mobilizing labor and
production, as the Soviet regime fought for its existence in civil
and external war. Conscious of its position, the All-Russian Central
Council of Trade Unions guarded the prerogatives of the unions
and insisted on their independence from governmental control. It
instructed subordinate organizations to allow no interference by
the Soviets with trade union direction of industrial administration.
The All-Russian Council's position in the government itself was
strengthened as it held up to a third of the seats in the Central
Executive Committee. The Council was asked, in fact, to participate in so many other governmental bodies that it had to call on

subordinate trade-union organizations to supply personnel. Applying the principle of "workers' control," the trade unions participated in the management collegia (councils) of government plants, and private industry was in large measure controlled by the trade union "control-distributive" commissions. The unions were empowered to assess manpower requirements and mobilize workers. All workers were automatically enrolled as members; union dues were deducted at source; and rationing of food, clothing, and lodging depended, in part, on trade union membership. The unions formed special supply services for the Red Army and mobilized and armed half of their membership. As the government extended the socialization of industry, as a war measure, the unions' control functions expanded. Their right to dominate industrial administration was recognized. They were empowered to name the Commissar of Labor and his collegium and to propose legislation. The power of the unions was, however, short-lived. In the course of the civil war their authority was whittled away by the imperatives of bureaucratic organization at a time of military conflict in an increasingly dictatorial state. The policies of economic rehabilitation pursued by the regime after the civil war further weakened their position.

The establishment of the Supreme Council of National Economy to direct industry through the national trust, and the principle of single management, eliminated "workers' control," replacing it with a bureaucratic administration holding full power to control production. As a result, a reaction within the trade-union leadership developed which forced the Party to clarify the relationship of the trade unions to the Soviet government. The debates on the subject, which had cropped up ever since November 1917, came to a head at the Tenth Party Congress, March 1921, which met at a time of economic chaos and political rebellion (Kronstadt). The Eighth Party Congress, March 1919, had promised the unions complete administrative control over the national economy; but the marked tendency of the Supreme Council to disregard or act independently of the unions brought a direct challenge from some of the trade-union leadership (within the Communist Party) to the authority of the Soviet government in matters concerning labor. The Workers' Opposition at the Tenth Congress, under the leadership of A. Shlyapnikov, demanded that the regime honor its promises of the Eighth Congress and recommended complete trade-union authority through heavy representation in all economic controlling bodies and appointment of all management. This argument was elaborated within a theoretical framework which held that, until the socialist society had been established, the unions must be independent of the state in order to represent the special interests of labor.

The opposite viewpoint was expressed by Trotsky, who applied to the workers and their organs the sole criterion of ability to produce. He was prepared to see the unions absorbed completely into the state and subordinated to it. He opposed the demands of the Worker's Opposition for a guaranteed living standard, maintaining that the workers should elevate the general standard by raising individual productivity. The promise of the Eighth Congress, Trotsky asserted blandly, would be carried out in the form of the gradual absorption of the unions into the government. Trotsky's position was not accepted at this time. The resolution which was adopted by the Congress, and became the official position of the Party, was presented by Lenin and nine cosigners as a compromise. It maintained that Party promises would be fulfilled, but requested the unions, for the moment, to take a greater part in the organization of production by assigning their members to the administrative machinery. It required subordination of the unions to the government but not their absorption by it—so that they would be free to perform their proper functions as labor organizations, to keep the peasant majority under proletarian influence and to avoid becoming a mere bureaucratic agency. Hence, membership in the unions was to be voluntary and the unions were to accept Party leadership rather than having it imposed upon them. Lenin propounded his old idea of the trade unions as a "school of Communism" where the workers would acquire administrative experience; and he recommended that they help work out economic plans, propose candidates for administrative posts, inspect the economic administration, and assume responsibility for the distribution and productivity of labor, and for its wages and discipline. The unions thus found themselves with perhaps even less administrative power over the economy than was implicit in Trotsky's formulation, and in the ambiguous position of defending both state and labor interests.

After the introduction of the NEP the process of narrowing trade-union powers continued at the Eleventh Party Congress in March 1922. While strikes were not forbidden, the unions were asked not to call them against the proletarian state. Then, contrary to the decisions of the Tenth Congress, the unions were denied direct control over production. Individual management in private and public industry was firmly intrenched as the most efficient means of raising output, and the trade unions were warned that interference in the work of management was "harmful and inadmissible." The plant manager was given the decisive power to determine labor living standards, with the right to fix rates, to set rations, and to distribute work clothing in accordance with collective agreements with the unions. Finally, the unions were placed more firmly under Party control; for the Congress required that all chairmen and secretaries of the union central committees and members of leading regional bodies be Party members of long standing.

The subsequent Congress (Twelfth) reserved to management alone the right to appoint, transfer, and replace economic personnel —with no binding commitments to the trade unions. Moreover, it emphatically affirmed the "productionist" viewpoint, which sought to make the essential function of unions the assistance of management in raising productivity and lowering costs.

Henceforth the unions reflected primarily the interests of the state; and with the publicly enunciated ascendancy of Stalin in 1929 any serious element of trade-union autonomy was definitively ended. The unions were required to work out higher production norms; to accept compulsory arbitration—with management in a strong position; to tolerate state regulation of hours and state control over recruitment, the over-all wage bill, and contract-making.

The last real opposition to the process of total subordination of the unions came from the trade-union leadership under Tomsky. His "Right Opposition" program, calling generally for a continuance of the NEP, for curbs on bureaucratic centralism, and for less rapid industrialization, also demanded a stronger position for the unions. Up to this point Tomsky had not firmly opposed a trade-union policy focused primarily on the increase in output; but he came to appreciate the connection between the emasculation of the unions and Stalin's intent to press on with a rate of capital development which he felt to be intolerable. Further, he may have seen in the unions the basis for a last stand in his losing battle with Stalin for power in the Party and the regime. At the Eighth Trade Union Congress (December 1928) he called for more real democracy in the unions, more concern for the needs of the rank and file who were afraid to express themselves, and more real autonomy as against the Supreme Council and other state economic agencies. Spokesmen for the Party leadership insisted that the unions must support a sharp rise in worker productivity for the security of the regime; they secured the ouster of Tomsky and his replacement by the (then) loyal Stalinist, Rudzutak. From this point there was no longer any question of the subordination of the trade unions to the interest of Party and state, but the question of how close would be their identification with the state apparatus.

The development of the Stakhanovite movement, starting in 1935, symbolizes the outcome of this process of identification. De-rationing at about that time had opened the possibility of the individual's improving his living standard by increasing his earnings in a system of differentiated wage scales. The regime took full advantage of this circumstance to popularize the possibilities for increasing individual and group productivity and to raise progressively the required norms for individual production.

The campaign began with statements by Stalin and Ordzhonikidze (then Politburo member and Commissar of Heavy Industry), widely echoed in the Soviet press, concerning the need for improvement of technical standards and for reorganization of production processes and wage rates to increase production. On August 30, 1935, in the presence of a pit manager, a representative of the Party, and the editor of the local Party paper, Alexei Stakhanov cut a record 102 tons of coal in six hours, thus earning 225 rubles for the shift—more than a coal miner's average monthly wage. Stakhanov had rather thoroughly rationalized the coal cutting process by separating principal from auxiliary operations and by improved use of tools, although his *tour de force* involved, as well, the exploitation of his fellow-workers.

Stakhanov's results and methods were immediately subject to an intense publicity campaign. For a solid month the press concentrated on explaining, encouraging, and spreading Stakhanov's method, to the virtual exclusion of all other press material. Numerous conferences of trade unions and management were held for the same purposes, and Stakhanov's record was soon broken in his own field and his method widely applied. Productivity was raised not by increased physical exertion, as with the old shock-workers of earlier days, but by rationalization of the process through division of labor and by better utilization of working time and implements.

Within two months after Stakhanov's feat, "Stakhanovite" workers held an all-union conference, and in December 1936 the plenum of the Central Committee of the Party ordered the industrial commissariats to revise norms of technical equipment and of productive capacities on the basis of the best Stakhanov workers' experience. These efforts were to be discussed at conferences of management and of various categories of workers and trade unions. Designated categories of workers were required to take courses to meet compulsory technical minima which were to be revised in the light of new possibilities. Similar orders were issued for other branches of production, and norms were raised generally several times in the late 1930's, the increase ranging from 15 to 50 per cent. Many increases remained on paper, and the management was, in all probability, cautious about raising production to avoid the imposition of high planning figures. Yet the new standards were generally attained by the most skilled workers, yielding a marked expansion in industrial output. This activity was accompanied by a wider application of the piecework system of payment until three-fourths of all industrial workers were on a piecework basis by the end of the Second Five-Year Plan. Technical, engineering, trade, and transport personnel received bonuses for qualitatively and quantitatively exceeding planned output.

The system remains essentially the same in the postwar years, with perhaps greater emphasis on Stakhanovite teams. Rewards are still high for individual Stakhanovites, and the average of the best workers rather than the average performance of all workers is proposed to the directors as the basis for production quotas for all workers.

In addition to financial rewards, the regime has utilized every medium to make the Stakhanovite status socially desirable and to demonstrate the possibilities of individual advance in the Soviet system. High wages and wide publicity have transformed the Stakhanovites into a new elite among the workers, and they offer subject matter for endless Soviet success stories.

Since the inception of the Five-Year Plans, then, the prime function of the trade unions has been to press for maximum labor productivity in the interest of the state—through propaganda, campaigns of "socialist competition," and the control of certain social services which the trade unions administer. These include social insurance, vacation facilities, and cultural and recreational facilities. There also remain, formally at least, certain functions of representing the interest of the workers in plant administration. Collective agreements were gradually discontinued over the years 1933–35, although two were revived in 1947. Wage levels, set by the state, are specifically excluded from these later agreements; but they do embrace the application of wage norms and incentives, safety and working conditions, and the housing and welfare responsibilities of management. The unions serve as a mild and strictly limited check on the short-run administrative interests of the industrial managers, which might run counter to the state's long-run interest in maintaining that modicum of satisfaction among the workers required for their long-run efficiency.

5. POLITICAL CONTROL OVER THE ARMED FORCES

From the early days of its victory in revolution and its civil struggle to maintain power the Bolshevik leadership has been highly conscious of the importance of the armed forces to the internal and external security of the state. From its beginnings the regime sought to establish and maintain intimate control over the armed forces. In the first instance, it regarded with suspicion many in the high command and many of the officers taken over from the Imperial Army. Although discipline, party control, and checking from within have been the chief means for maintaining Party domination over the armed forces, these instruments have been reinforced on the positive side by the relatively high material and social status accorded the military, by constant public acclaim, and by intense, never-ending political indoctrination.

As in all agencies and organizations in the Soviet Union the Party has its committees and groups in every unit of the army; and these rest heavily on the Komsomol, the Communist Youth organization. The Ministries of the Army and Navy are now in all probability under the direction of Bulganin, a member of the Politburo; and a Military Department of the Central Committee of the Party carefully checks on armed forces activities. While the percentage of Party and Komsomol members is higher in the army than in other agencies, excepting the police, the usual pattern obtains of greater frequency in the higher echelons. Virtually all officers are Party members, and a high proportion of the enlisted men are members of the Komsomol.

Apart from the normal means of organizational control, the Party has resorted to a rigid system of "political control" at all levels, under the direction of the Political Administration of the Army. This body is simultaneously an agency of the Ministry of Armed Forces and a department of the Central Committee. It operates through political officers who are deputy commanders in every unit down to battalion level.

The history of political control in the Army is of some interest, reflecting as it does the pattern of the same forces in operation that have determined the evolution of other segments of Soviet organization; and it is of some importance, as it represents a problem alive down to the present. The institution of military commissars was created by the Fifth Congress of Soviets in July 1918, when civil war was getting under way. By the fall of that year the commissars were installed in the units of the Red Army. The War Commissariat described them as political agents of the Soviet government who were to assure that the army, which included many tsarist officers, did not become an institution apart from the Soviet system. More particularly their function was to prevent military establishments from becoming centers of conspiracy against the regime. The military commissars (M.C.'s) were empowered to participate in the direction of military operations. They were to see all letters and reports received by the unit commanders, and were to countersign all of their orders. They were responsible for the prompt execution of all orders and for the manner in which all personnel in the Red Army carried out their duties. They were appointed to all central and local institutions of the army to assure the economical use of funds and property, and were to act as a liaison between the army and local and central government agencies.

In an effort to arouse the peasantry to participate in the new military effort, the M.C.'s turned to political work of a broader kind. Recruited at first from heterogeneous elements, they were eventually drawn only from the Party, as the number of Party members increased. In December 1918, to supplement M.C. political work, Political Departments of Fronts, Armies, and Divisions were created to direct the political education of army personnel. These were subordinated by the Eighth Party Congress (March 1919) to the Political Department of the Military Revolutionary Council, under the chairmanship of a member of the Central Committee of the Party. The Eighth Congress designated the M.C.'s as the Party's representatives in the army and the bearers of its revolutionary spirit and discipline. They were to be appointed by the Political Departments at various levels, and these were to control all party life in the army. The same Congress also expanded the activities of the M.C.'s by placing supply and administrative problems under their control along with military officers, and by authorizing them to punish and bring to trial violators of the law. Moreover, the M.C.'s were to decide on the fitness of officers to command and were to direct special departments of the Cheka and military tribunals along with the Military Revolutionary Committee. Finding themselves in a position to exercise military as well as political authority, the more aggressive commissars began to neglect political work and engaged in more rewarding and interesting military operations. This development soon caused an unfavorable reaction among the professional military staff and their sympathizers in the Party organization.

By 1919 officers loyal to the Bolshevik regime won support from a group in the Party known as the "Army Opposition," who maintained that, as the Political Departments were sufficiently developed to direct all political work in the army, there was no need for the M.C.'s. The latter were held to be a barrier to the development of initiative on the part of the officer corps. Smilga proposed that military officers be allowed to issue orders in their own name, and called for the abolition of the M.C.'s in units where the loyalty of officers was beyond doubt. But Trotsky, People's Commissar for War, foreseeing stubborn opposition from the intrenched M.C.'s and their supporters, feared to disturb arrangements during the civil war and felt that in the interests of security the commissars had best be retained. The Tenth Congress of the Party, motivated by the same security interests, turned down the opposition demand to make the M.C.'s elective and place them under local Party control at the various levels.

But opposition to the aggressive M.C.'s persisted within the Party, and its leadership was torn between the need to maintain an efficient, loyal officer corps and the need to maintain a satisfactory check on its personnel. Some kind of compromise had to be devised. Pressure for elimination of the institution developed as many cases of violation of Party discipline and utilization of posts for personal ends were detected among the M.C.'s. In 1923 the Political Administration of the Republic (which had replaced the Political Department of the Revolutionary Military Council in May 1919), dominated by the Army Opposition, on its own initiative opened the subject of political work in the army for discussion in the army Party units.

The Thirteenth Party conference silenced all discussion, replaced Ovseenko by Bubnov as head of the Political Administration. On the other hand, in February 1924 election of company and regimental heads of political organizations in the army was permitted. Then, in June 1924, the Orgburo introduced the principle of unity in command, allowing some flexibility in the form and time of application to the various army branches and units.

Implementation of the policy of unity of command evolved slowly, as the Politburo sought to maintain the political organizations in the army as efficient propaganda machines and simultaneously utilize them as an effective check on officer antagonism to the regime. By 1926 the propaganda, morale-building, and liaison work of the M.C.'s had increased considerably, and for this work they were responsible only to their political superiors in the army. Political work was further centralized as the Political Administration was placed directly under the Central Committee of the Party. Moreover, wherever feasible, qualified commanders who were Party members (the great majority) were gradually given control of both military and political activity as true "single commanders."

But these measures, similar to the structural changes going on elsewhere in the Soviet system, apparently failed to improve relations between the officer corps and the M.C.'s. The latter were still responsible for securing the efficient fulfillment of all duties by the officers, and they had to investigate and make known the complaints of military personnel. Many of them were remarkably ignorant, and commanders found it difficult to reconcile themselves to the continued existence of an independent political organization in the army. Although the regime felt it necessary to retain such an organization during this period of Party struggle for power, in 1927 it was prepared to compromise sufficiently with the realities of military organization to abolish the requirement that purely military orders be countersigned by the M.C.'s. The latter were to countersign political documents only. Complete single command was thus instituted, and the M.C. became an assistant Commander for Political Affairs in charge of all political personnel and activities.

While officers appeared to have full control, they enjoyed wide independence only in making military decisions. Disputes with political personnel were referred to higher political organs in the army. The Political Administration was in charge of military justice, and the officers were thus under pressure to keep on good terms with the political deputies, since the latter sat on the attestation committees which investigated their service records for promotion and awards and helped prepare service reports. The sharp eyes of the M.C.'s—and, of course, the secret police—kept the regime well informed concerning its military officer corps.

Further measures taken during 1928 served to enhance the authority of the political deputies. Their duties were so defined as to require them to supply a summary of the political situation necessary for reaching operational decisions, and they were given broad authority to carry out political measures required in connection with combat activity. They were to be kept informed of the plans and operations of the commander; and the latter, prior to arriving at a decision, was to make the final summation of a situation in the presence of the deputy commander. The officer might execute his decision immediately, however, if the deputy failed to appear. The 1928 Service Regulations put the M.C. on an even footing with the military commander in supervising all training programs. Political personnel in the regiment were to have the same military training as military specialists, in an effort to make them a sort of duplicate chain of command. This rule remained, however, a dead letter. The general low educational level of the deputy commanders in fact did not permit them to share authority with the trained military specialists, and the deputies appear to have found it difficult enough to keep abreast of their political work.

During this period of Stalin's struggle for the dictatorship, while the M.C.'s control over military decisions was limited, their watch over the officer staff was judged fully as important as their educational-propaganda work. The army was successfully neutralized as a political force during this period. Similarly, during the collectivization campaign, the political organization managed to keep in line the peasant soldier who was getting disturbing news from home and was undoubtedly dissident.

The onset of the Great Purge brought a strengthening of the powers of the political personnel in the army. In September 1935 the professional ranks and duties of the M.C.'s had been more clearly defined. Political leaders or "Politruks" were established as the lowest rank and were commanded in ascending order by Senior Politruks, Battalion, Regimental, Divisional and Corps Commissars, topped by Commissars of the Army of the 2nd and 1st Ranks. As the purge made wide gaps in their ranks, junior Politruks were created who were to graduate as Politruks after a two-year period, thus opening a bureaucratic career for soldiers and noncommissioned officers with little formal military training. The decree of May 19, 1937, at a time when the Purge was gathering momentum, formally reintroduced the institution of Military Commissars already established in reality by the Table of Organization of 1935— that is, from regimental level up. The commissars were empowered once again to countersign all orders and were given functions of a security nature. The statute of August 15, 1937, required that they be appointed by the Commissar for Defense on the recommendation of the Political Administration. Together with the military officers they were to be responsible for all training, political and military, and for protecting their units against infiltration by enemies of the regime. The M.C. was also to be responsible for the execution of all laws concerning state secrecy. He was to direct all Party activity in the army. Together with the commander he was to prepare the service records of unit officers and to submit political characterizations of each member of the commanding personnel. Together with the commander he was to make appointments and recommendations for promotion.

While the training program for M.C.'s was developed somewhat, the generally low educational level that prevailed among them up to 1941 would seem to indicate that their cultural and educational activities were subordinated to their security and control functions. Despite their inadequacies they were allowed to interfere in the minutest military preparation. Had these rights been exercised under combat conditions the efficiency of military units would most certainly have been affected. During the Great Purge period, however, their services were regarded as vital. The number of M.C.'s doubled between 1934 and 1939, even while their own ranks were being decimated by the Purge.

In the war years policy shifted rapidly both for and against the Military Commissars. They took an active part in the Finnish campaign and, probably as a result of their incompetence and interference in military affairs, the officers succeeded in re-establishing single command in August 1940. The institution of M.C. was once again abolished. The rapid expansion of the active forces in the face of Hitler's attack brought the commissars back again in July 1941, by a decree of the Supreme Soviet. They were now drawn from the influx of Party members called to the colors and from the large number of newly recruited Party members. During the period of defensive operations they concentrated on expanding the Party organization in the army, maintaining discipline, and carrying on an intensive propaganda campaign designed to overcome apparently widespread apathy and defeatism as well as some cowardice. The heartening effect of the Moscow and Leningrad campaigns, and, probably, a great deal of fumbling resulting from amateurish interference in military operations, led the Party high command to feel that it could revert to the previous deputy commander system. In October 1942 single command was re-established and the M.C.'s.

again became Political Deputies. The evidence available does not allow for a detailed definition of the current functions of the reinstated deputy commanders for political affairs. If, however, their functions in any way resemble those of the late 1920's and early 1930's they not only carry on propaganda work but also keep a constant check on the officer staff and play an important role in determining promotions. Because of prolonged war experience many of them are probably better trained in military affairs than at earlier periods and the Politburo has probably made every effort to provide for a better military training program for the political personnel in order to co-ordinate political and military work as closely as possible.

Faced with problems of maintaining simultaneously the conflicting criteria of efficiency and political control, the regime appears to have imposed the dominance of the political commanders only at times of strongly felt political insecurity, while never relinquishing its intimate political surveillance and infiltration of the armed forces or abandoning its profound suspicion of their loyalty.

The Soviet leadership has also sought to dilute the feeling of unique power within the army by a variety of means, real and symbolic. Important armed units have been built within the MVD (secret police); and special measures have been taken to counteract feelings of aloofness or autonomy on the part of the military as against other elements of the bureaucratic elite. Other agencies (Foreign Affairs, the Railway, Administration, and Procurator's Office) have been given uniforms and ranks. Stalin and other members of the Politburo have been given high military rank. Beria and Bulganin are Marshals of the Soviet Army. After the war the successes of the armed forces were attributed to the military genius of Stalin's leadership and the wartime public prominence of certain generals was terminated. Several key military figures were transferred to regional commands, distant from Moscow. An attempt has thus been made to impress on the army that it is a creation of the political regime, operating under its direction as its instrument.

As elsewhere in the Soviet system the regime has employed incentives as well as controls and surveillance. It has sought to establish for the armed forces a sense of prestige and material well-being. The living standards, practical training, and opportunities for cultural development within the armed services have proved generally popular. A conscious effort has been made to develop a sense of elite and to cut the life of the armed forces off from that of the ordinary civilian. The reversion, after 1935, to ranks, saluting, epaulettes, special uniforms, orderlies, and other distinctions between officers and men was also designed both to strengthen discipline and to make the profession more attractive to the commanding personnel. The army is thus both carefully nurtured and carefully watched and hedged about by other chains of command.

It seems probable that the increase in international tension in the past several years, and the increase in Soviet arms production, have tended to bring key professional figures in the Soviet military establishment back closer to the center of policy-making, and, more generally, enhanced their influence within the upper levels of the regime.

6. THE EVOLUTION OF THE SECRET POLICE

The security forces of the Soviet Union, like the army, are, by their nature, instruments for the protection of the regime. The secret police was created, staffed, and vigorously controlled by the Party. In the tradition of the tsarist Third Department and Okhrana, the Cheka and its successors have been a thoroughly disciplined arm of the existing regime—at least since July 1918, when a revolt of security troops in Moscow impressed the Soviet leaders once and for all with the potentially two-edged nature of its weapon. The security agencies have served continuously as principal instruments for the enforcement of the bureaucratizing process, operating in "Special Sections" installed within factories, military units, etc. They have had almost unlimited jurisdiction in combating opposition to the regime. The extent of their actual powers appears to have fluctuated, but the trend has been toward relatively increased authority—a trend supported by the bureaucratization of the Party and, notably, by the Great Purge.

It has already been noted that the Military Revolutionary Committee was entrusted with combating counterrevolution; and that, from a part of its functions, arose the Cheka (the Extraordinary Commission for the Combat of Counterrevolution, Sabotage and Breach of Duty by Officials), created in December 1917 and attached to the Council of People's Commissars. Formed in a period when the new regime was seeking to consolidate its power, the Cheka was given unlimited powers of penal prosecution without judicial procedure, and, in some cases, assumed the right of final decision and control over the courts. Regarded not as a judicial body but as an instrument of "tremendously merciless repression" against counterrevolution, the Cheka was given final decision of life and death with no appeal. It might confiscate property, exile to concentration camps, or shoot; and it endeavored to instill a paralyzing fear in all enemies of the regime, especially during the period of civil war.

Following Russian practice of the nineteenth century, there were set up, outside of the regular judicial system, special courts called Revolutionary Tribunals which were sometimes directly connected with the Cheka and always allowed complete powers of repression. They were guided only by "the circumstances of the case and the revolutionary conscience." With the relative relaxation in the Soviet Union after the end of the civil war, these Star-Chamber courts were merged with the People's Courts in a new judicial system.

The Cheka had fulfilled its initial revolutionary functions by the beginning of the NEP, and had perhaps over-fulfilled them by intruding too vigorously on the operations of the Party and Soviets at lower levels. There is a substantial body of evidence to suggest not only popular resentment of the Cheka during the civil war but also resentment within the Party at the operations of ruthless, poorly disciplined agents, many of whom were former criminals. The Cheka was replaced by a more clearly defined and nominally restricted agency, "The State Political Administration," or GPU, on February 8, 1922. The Cheka had aroused increasing dissatisfaction in agencies on whose jurisdiction it tended to trespass, notably the local Soviets and the Commissariat of Justice. Originally established in the Commissariat of Internal Affairs, the GPU was given independent status in the Council of People's Commissars as the "United State Political Administration," or OGPU. This instrument helped Stalin forge his personal dictatorship over opposition in the Party between 1923 and 1929.

The OGPU was empowered to arrest, execute, or exile to its own "correctional camps," without judicial trial, people charged with brigandage, looting, and illegal boundary crossing; it also acted in case of offenses as elastic in their definition as espionage and counterrevolution. It was, however, formally limited by the Central Executive Committee (CEC) in imposing the death penalty, and was required to indict prisoners within two weeks of arrest. After holding a prisoner for two months, the OGPU had to obtain permission from the CEC for further detention, or transfer the case to the regular courts. The Commissar of Justice held the power, in fact, to transfer all cases to the regular courts at his discretion. In practice, however, with the intensification of the struggle within the Party, (and by stages which may have been more gradual than present evidence indicates) Stalin increased the severity of the instruments used against Party opposition. He resorted to arrest and exile as early as 1927–28, and to imprisonment and execution in the purges after Kirov's death in 1934. In the Great Purge the secret police and its local agents definitively handled cases involving opposition in the Party.

In July 1934 the OGPU was transformed into the Union-Republican People's Commissariat of Internal Affairs (NKVD), with the investigative and *de facto* judicial and punitive powers of its predecessor. It also had functions more normal to an interior ministry, such as control of customs, vital statistics, and civil affairs. Like the OGPU, it administered "correctional camps" and had at its disposal a considerable armed force, independent of the Red Army, to execute its wide functions. The NKVD was to turn offenders over to the courts for trial and major political offenders were to be tried by the Military Collegium of the Supreme Court of the Soviet Union. Nevertheless, when the activities of the NKVD were intensified, notably during the 1936–38 purges, only a few outstanding leaders were tried by NKVD committees. Moreover, the NKVD included a special council (consisting of the Commissar of Internal Affairs, his Deputy Commissar, and the Prosecutor of the Soviet Union) which could send prisoners to corrective camps for periods up to five years or exile them. As in the case of the OGPU, the Prosecutor was empowered to assure the legality of the acts of the NKVD; but the arbitrary power of the regime permitted such flexibility as was desired. In 1946 at the time the other commissariats were transformed into ministries, the NKVD became the Ministry of Internal Affairs, or MVD.

With the expansion of the Soviet Union westward before the German attack (1939–41) and with the intensification of controls during World War II, the work of the NKVD (MVD) grew enormously. Its functions were split up by separating out of the NKVD a Commissariat of State Security (MGB) in 1941. Reunited in the NKVD after the German attack of June 1941, the MGB was re-established separately, in April 1943, as the Red Army offensive got under way. The operations of the MGB were apparently, in the first instance, concentrated on the newly occupied and Far Eastern border regions, although its mandate extends throughout the Soviet Union. From such data on the functions of these agencies as is available it would appear that the MVD retains its forces and the administration of camps. The MGB embraces intelligence and secret-police activities, operating through "special sections" in all other institutions, including the MVD.

The extension of the activities of the several security agencies brought with it a considerable expansion of the prison-exile system which had been a notorious feature of the tsarist regime. The "corrective labor camps" of the early years of the Soviet regime, created as an experiment in penal reform, were transformed into political concentration camps by the beginning of the NEP period and became significant sources of forced labor during the period of the First Five-Year Plan.

The first real corrective labor camp was established by the OGPU on Solovetsky (Nightingale) Island in the White Sea in 1923, and was populated by assorted political and criminal offenders. By 1929 the OGPU had established in the north some seven camps, the occupants of which were employed in lumbering and fishing. With the accretion of population occasioned by the uprooting of peasants in the early 1930's, labor camp activities expanded to include construction notably of transport enterprises (canals, railways). When the NKVD was established in July 1934 it included a new "Chief Administration of Corrective Labor Camps and Labor Settlements" (GULAG), which was soon to handle the large influx of heterogeneous elements involved in the 1936–38 purges. By the end of the 1930's a huge network of camps stretched across northern European Russia and into the far northeast of Siberia, centering on Magadan, the headquarters of the Dalstroi mining and construction enterprises. The population of these camps now constitutes a class of perhaps about 8,000,000 political exiles and civil criminals engaged in forced labor. The existence of an enterprise of this order of magnitude and economic responsibility obviously has created a most powerful vested interest in the maintenance of a police state in the specific sense that without a continuous flow of recruits, chosen on grounds other than their individual violation of rules of civil order, the system of forced labor would atrophy and the powers of the secret police would diminish.

Chapter Four

SOVIET POWER AND
THE ECONOMY

1. INTRODUCTION

THE BROAD lines of economic development of the Soviet Union are well known. Minimum requirements of public and bureaucratic information have resulted in the regular publication of statistical data which, while incomplete and booby-trapped for the unwary user, nevertheless appear to yield a tolerable picture of the over-all rate of growth in Soviet industrial output, the level of output in key sectors of the economy, and (less surely) total real income and (in selected years) the distribution of real national income as between consumption on the one hand and investment and military outlays on the other. The breakdown of expenditures as between productive investment and military outlays is less sure both because it is intrinsically difficult to distinguish basic facilities constructed for general economic (as opposed to military) purposes, and because the scale of the armed forces, their equipment and stockpiles, as well as output rates for military end products are treated by the Soviet Union with extreme secrecy.

For present purposes it is not essential to examine in any detail the course of the Soviet economy. The aim of this section is merely to suggest the interaction between certain key economic problems and decisions, on the one hand, and the policies, economic or otherwise, pursued by the Soviet regime. It is evident that the evolution of Soviet society has been strongly affected by the brute issues of Russian economy which the regime has confronted; by the dynamic consequences of the decisions taken to cope with them, including decisions affecting social and political life; and by the dynamic consequences of decisions taken with respect to the economy but which were motivated by noneconomic objectives.

76

2. KEY RELATIONS BETWEEN POWER AND THE ECONOMY

The complexity of the interaction between the economy and Soviet policy stems from its multiple relation to the power the regime could effectively wield, both within the Soviet Union and in relation to the outside world. At least three major links between power and the economy are evident.

First, a minimum level of economic welfare was required to prevent starvation, preserve the efficiency of the working force, and even, perhaps, to avoid insurrection born of simple desperation. At each period, then, the regime has been forced, with its human and material resources as they are, to undertake arrangements for achieving a level of output and consumption which would provide a basic foundation for its continued rule. This primitive consideration of political economy played a part in Lenin's decision to install the NEP; and it has continued to exert a realistic tempering influence on the inherited ideology of the regime which, in combination with other considerations discussed below, contributed to the formation of a centrally controlled bureaucratized economic structure dedicated to efficiency rather than to the substantive welfare goals incorporated in the Marxist ideological inheritance. More concretely, this first consideration has steadily required an allocation of a substantial proportion of the national income for minimum consumption purposes.

Second, the structure of the economy (e.g., its industrial-agricultural balance) and its form of organization (e.g., private vs. public) had social and political consequences on which hinged in part the degree of effective power the regime could exercise over the society. The loyalty of the Soviet regime to the idea of state ownership and operation of the means of production, and to rapid industrialization, has not been merely an ideological hangover. Socialism commended itself as a means of administration which contributed to the centralization of political power in the hands of the regime. This is a major example of the convergence of the ideological goals of the revolution and the priority of power. Similarly, among the convergent motivations which probably influenced the decision rapidly to collectivize Russian agriculture at the end of the 1920's was the increased immediate political control it would give to the state over the peasantry and the longer-run consequences it would have, both in moving a larger proportion of the population into the already disciplined urban life of the industrial worker and in diminishing the peasant's individualistic attachment to his own land. A higher degree of efficiency in agriculture was, certainly, a technical requirement for accelerated industrialization. The particular form chosen for assuring the Russian food supply with a lesser outlay of real resources appears to have been heavily influenced by power interests of the kind cited above.

Third, the strength of the regime vis-à-vis the external world was believed by Stalin to hinge largely on its military strength in being and, in the long run, on its heavy-industry base. These direct and indirect considerations of military power obviously have had an enormous influence on Soviet economic decisions, notably since the inauguration of the First Five-Year Plan in 1928.

The last two of these three relations—subsuming the link between the economy and the expansion of the regime's internal and external power—have converged in their practical effect. They could not, or were not permitted to come fully into play, however, until about 1928. Until that time the more fundamental practical requirements of minimum welfare and order dominated economic policy. These included the NEP, the bureaucratic organization of the socialized sector of industry (85 per cent by 1928); re-establishment of foreign trade; and the bringing in of foreign technicians and even of limited amounts of foreign capital. The primary energies of the state were concentrated on political tasks within this loose economic setting of economic convalescence and preparation. Stalin was concentrating his attention on the problem of achieving and consolidating his dictatorship, and he used his growing power to restrain accelerated industrialization until his dictatorship was secured. More generally the regime, recovering from the failure of War Communism, was building with more care the administrative and technical foundations for later industrial advance. By the end of the twenties, however, Stalin was prepared to enlarge the extent and strengthen the foundations of his power, ending definitely the protracted debate on economic policy that interwove the struggle for Lenin's succession.

The economic requirements of the drive for increased internal and external power helped justify the transition to a highly centralized bureaucratic structure of economic administration, to a system of income distribution which would offer high incentives to increased productivity, to extreme measures for the mobilization of internal capital resources, to a system of collectivized agriculture, to a sustained emphasis on the creation of basic capital resources.

Within this framework of new (or accelerated) policies and institutional arrangements the management of the economy has raised certain problems for the regime:

1. Its power objectives have clashed with the short-run possibilities of increased welfare, denying the nation, thus far, any substantial welfare benefits from the increase in its per capita national capital and output.

2. The efficient centralized administration of the economy has demanded forms of organization and income distribution which have clashed with the ideals of the Revolution and with longer-run persistent elements in Russian culture.

3. The requirements of military strength, in being judged essential by the regime both before and after World War II, have clashed with the longer-run objective of enlarging the industrial base of the economy, despite some overlap between military and capital requirements—e.g., in transport, steel, and aluminum capacity, etc.

As indicated in Part Two of this analysis, each of these conflicts contributes to current and potential tensions and instabilities within the Soviet political and social structure.

3. THE REAL NATIONAL INCOME AND ITS DISTRIBUTION

It is the unanimous opinion of non-Soviet economists that the official published Soviet national income figures contain a powerful upward bias since 1928, owing to several elements in their method of calculation; and it is almost unanimously agreed that no wholly satisfactory method of correction can be applied. Certain observations, nevertheless, can be made on the over-all rate of growth of the Russian economy.

The revolutions of 1917 came after a period of rapid economic and political evolution, for both phases of which the freeing of the serfs in 1861 constitutes a benchmark. Over the three decades following 1861 the foundations for rapid industrial development were laid; and, in the quarter-century before 1914, a converging set of international and domestic forces yielded an extraordinary rate of growth in Russia's total real income. The increase was notable in the industrial sector, but the advance was closely linked to the agricultural position, domestic and international. In the 1890's this growth rate may have been of the order of 8 per cent per annum, typical of a society catching up with the accumulated world pool of technical possibilities whose application in Russia had been frustrated by its previous low state of social, political, and technical organization. This rate was not sustained in the years 1900–05 because of civil unrest, the Russo-Japanese war, and international cyclical depression; but rapid advance continued from 1905 to 1914. The Soviet effort at industrialization clearly represents, then, the continuation of a longer Russian trend.

The consequences of war, revolution, foreign intervention, civil war, and the regime's initial policy of War Communism brought the national income down to a disastrously low figure by 1921. Official Soviet statistics give a national income of 21 billion rubles (in 1926–27 prices) for 1913; 8 billion rubles for 1921. Output gradually increased from 1922 and reached a figure close to, or only slightly above, that of 1913 by 1928, when the First Five-Year Plan was formulated. The statistical measurement of the Soviet national income and industrial production since 1928 is a matter of speculation, especially for the years 1928–37, over which period considerable differences in opinion exist among Western experts with respect to the rate of economic progress. The figures in the accompanying table are believed to be reasonable, although perhaps conservative, estimates for these two variables.

These figures show the high rate of growth achieved under the First and Second Five-Year Plans; the deceleration caused by increased armaments in 1937–40; the recapture of the 1940 level of output by 1948–49; and the subsequent resumption of a high rate of growth. On the whole, it seems likely that the Soviet Union, having largely overcome wartime setbacks, will move, or has already moved, into a declining-rate-of-growth stage of industrial output and real income.[1] The reasons for this widely agreed judgment (reflected in Stalin's projected economic goals for 1960, as well as the current plan) include a declining rate of increase in the non-agricultural population, the probable requirement for increased investment in long-postponed low-priority categories (notably housing and transport), and the relative depletion of certain high-productivity mineral resources.

The high growth rate of the period since 1928 reflects, in part, the long-term result of the basic reorganization of the society after

[1] *The Economic Survey of Europe since the War* (ECE, Geneva, 1953), p. 40, gives the following figures for Soviet industrial output (gross), each year given in terms of an index in which the previous year equals 100:

1947	122	1949	120	1951	116
1948	127	1950	123	1952	111

1921, including increased literacy and technical training, improved management, and other factors difficult to measure. The Soviet regime in these years had to reorganize or create afresh, within the framework of the new structure, elements which had been generated between (say) 1861 and 1917, but which war, and especially revolution, had damaged, e.g., a class of industrial managers (now state rather than private), a substantial group of technicians, an industrial working force, etc. In addition, it had to go beyond and create a structure which would encourage and permit further rapid growth rates. The high growth rates after 1928 reflect, in part, this fundamental process of human and institutional capital formation in

	Net Nat'l Product *	Annual Average Rate of Growth, Net Nat'l Product	Industrial Output † (Gerschenkron ‡ to 1928; Jasny, § 1928–49)	Annual Average Rate of Growth, Industrial Output	
1885			21		
				1885–89	6.1%
1890			27		
				1890–99	8.0%
1900			61		
				1907–13	6.25%
1913			100		
1916			109		
1920			20		
1928	25.0		132		
		1928–37 8.7%		1928–37	12.4%
1937	53.2		378		
		1937–40 6.3%		1937–40	7.0%
1940	64.0		462		
1948	60.0		426		
				1948–49	15.5%
1949			492		

* In billion rubles, at 1926–27 prices, as estimated by Naum Jasny in *The Soviet Economy during the Plan Era* (Stanford, 1951), p. 22.
† Index, 1913 = 100.
‡ A. Gerschenkron, "The Rate of Industrial Growth in Russia since 1885," *The Tasks of Economic History*, Supplement VII (1947) to *The Journal of Economic History*, pp. 146, 161.
§ *Op. cit.*

the 1920's. They also reflect a rapid rate of growth in population. They were achieved against this background of favorable influences, however, only by a sharp increase in the volume of resources currently devoted to investment. The collectivization of agriculture was designed, in part, to contribute to this result; this measure was reinforced by programs of state finance which succeeded in diverting resources away from urban consumption (by taxation and inflation) and away from agricultural income. Soviet Russia moved from a position in the 1920's where perhaps 15 per cent of the national income was invested to one where investment input has steadily taken about 25 per cent of current resources, except in periods of very high armament outlays.

From 1934, after Hitler's accession to power, there was, in addition, a gradual increase in direct military outlays, which until that time had accounted for only about 2 to 4 per cent of the real national income; this proportionate increase sharply accelerated in the period 1937–41. At the expense of real consumption and the rate of investment, (and, thus, at the expense of the over-all rate of growth), military outlays rose to perhaps 15 per cent of real national income in 1940. In the course of the war the regime succeeded in organizing perhaps 40 per cent of the national income for military purposes. After 1945 there was a cutback in military outlays of about 50 per cent until 1947, at which time rearmament was undertaken.

The upshot of this sequence of events for the Soviet citizen is that at three distinct periods, when the economy has begun to yield a distinct improvement in welfare, decisions have been taken which have drawn resources sharply away from the consumption sector into investment and military outlays. The first such period was about 1928, when recuperation from war and immediate postwar events was about complete. The second came about 1937, when the economy had recovered from the disruptive effects of collectivization and was beginning to feel the consequences, in the consumption sectors, of the large capital formation of the previous decade. This brief phase, marked by the appearance of new consumers' goods, gave way to a rapidly accelerated armament drive as the world power position became increasingly unstable. A third shift in resources away from consumption may now be underway, although the latest Five-Year Plan holds out more promise for the consumer than any of its predecessors, if its goals are, in fact, fulfilled.

Total Soviet output re-achieved the 1940 level by about 1948;

and by 1950 (despite some increase in armament outlays from 1947) there were evidences of an improvement in urban living standards which took them back, perhaps, to the 1937–38 level. Again, the Soviet calculus of the external position in relation to its own external power objectives has led to accelerated armament; although in the present case the policy of the Soviet Union vis-à-vis the external world is a larger determinant of its action than in the 1930's, when the Soviet posture was primarily defensive in the face of a world environment that lay almost wholly outside its control.

Thus the restriction of the living standard of the Soviet citizen to a minimum compatible with efficiency has not been a matter of continuing conscious planning or fixed policy. The regime is probably not dedicated to denying its people an improved standard of living, on principle; although an improved standard of living might set in motion expectations of further increase which might, in turn, clash with the other uses of resources or result in disappointment and accentuated popular discontent. On balance it seems likely that the regime would wish to allocate increased resources to popular welfare if other uses of resources, linked to its believed power requirements, did not enjoy a higher priority. As in other aspects of the regime's policy a relative continuity of result emerges from a series of specific decisions in which the priorities the regime has applied are the primary continuous element. In this case, full and intimate political control over Russian society, rapid domestic capital formation, and Soviet military strength vis-à-vis the external world have held a position of priority over domestic welfare.

Chapter Five

THE EVOLUTION OF
SOVIET IDEOLOGY

1. INTRODUCTION

THE CONCEPT of ideology is exceedingly complex, and it is now widely used to cover a variety of phenomena which require separate analysis. We have already considered in Chapter 1 the manner in which certain elements in Communist ideology contributed to the emergence of the priority of power.

It is evident that the Soviet regime has very largely abandoned the substantive policy goals which inspired those who supported the Revolution in 1917. The Soviet state has moved systematically toward a policy in which the maintenance and enlargement of its own power has become the primary, almost sole, touchstone for the worth of any given course of action. The pursuit of power itself, notably against the outside world, carries its own concepts and even, in a sense, its own ideology, to which the Soviet state has paid its respects by a revival of nationalist symbols and values within Soviet society; by an Hegelian glorification of the state and its leader; and by a pathological concentration of public attention on the alleged aggressive intentions of the outside world.

Nevertheless, a version of Marxist ideology has remained in Soviet society. It has furnished, in the first instance, a common vocabulary and agreed set of concepts. The persistence in the social environment of an ideology, even radically modified, has, however, left also a heritage of value symbols which the Soviet state has continued to employ in defending its public policy. For example it felt impelled, in the 1930's, to incorporate some of the abandoned elements of the revolutionary heritage within the Constitution. And even in the postwar years public discussion has continued on the question of how soon a state of true Communism is likely to come about. Further, this vocabulary, this Marxist prism through which the regime looks out on the world, undoubtedly plays a part in shaping Soviet external relations.

The main thread of the story of Soviet ideology since the Revolution is the systematic modification of the complex and contradictory Marxist tradition to make it serve as a rationale for the pursuit of power by a political dictatorship. It will be recalled that Marx believed he had turned Hegel on his head by making the political and social structure of societies, and their dominating ideas, a dependent function of their material bases and interests. In effect, like the other modern totalitarian states, the Soviet regime has turned Marx on his head by seeking (without complete success) to make political power exercised by a single dominant figure the basis for economic, social, and cultural change. The need of the regime to maintain a surface continuity of ideas has, however, forced it to face this conceptual problem and to elaborate a theory of historical change which makes the role of the key individual's will the central dynamic force.

The pattern of events described in Chapters 1 and 2 is, in one sense, eternal. History from earliest recorded time contains stories of those who have pursued power to the limit. There is nothing new in the story of one individual or group who eliminated others from the exercise of power and then sought to modify institutions so that others could not obtrude upon their handling of power. It is a distinguishing characteristic of men, however, that they appear to require for their actions a rationale which gives them some sense of legitimacy, of communal moral sanction.

As noted earlier, the fundamental authority which Lenin and Stalin invoked was that part of the Marxist tradition which gave those who understood Marx's theory of history special sanctions in the exercise of power, and freed them substantially from the normal human restraints which govern men in their nonpolitical relations to one another. And it is, in substantial part, this kind of legitimacy, stemming from the special wisdom of him who best knows the doctrines of Marx (and Lenin) that Stalin claimed, and which now, in turn, is claimed by the "collective leadership" of Malenkov's regime, through the Central Committee of the Party. Legitimacy plays in Soviet society the same role that inheritance of kingship by family line has played in the past; and, in fact, under Stalin the old and new forms of legitimacy were substantially merged. Stalin made some considerable effort to place himself not only in the tradition of Marx and Lenin but also in the tradition of the historic powerful Russian rulers.

The modification of Marxist doctrine to conform to the dictatorial pursuit of power has been, then, a modification which largely withdrew from Marxism both its substantive goals and its theory of economic determination, but maintained pieces of the doctrine in modified form as a device for legitimacy, as a common vocabulary, and as a living part of contemporary dogma where it converged rather than conflicted with the priority of power. Although parts of the Marxist inheritance of substantive goals still obtrude on the efficient working of the system of dictatorship, it is fair to say that what is left of Marxism is what has been found useful, with or without modification, to support the maintenance and enlargement of power by the regime at home and abroad. Like other fundamental Soviet transitions, the transformation of its ideology took place step by step, reflecting decisions made in response to particular circumstances and problems. In general it may be said that the changes in formal Soviet doctrine have lagged behind events. From time to time Stalin simply brought the official rationale up to date with the *de facto* situation.

2. STALIN AND LENIN'S INHERITANCE

Stalin's contributions to Communist doctrine can, in one sense, be regarded simply as a sustained effort to supply a more or less consistent rationale for the situation he inherited and exploited after Lenin's death. The revolutionary doctrines of 1917 had incorporated within them the necessity for world revolution to occur concurrently with the revolution in Russia; but at Brest-Litovsk Lenin had decided in fact to proceed with socialism in one country. The revolutionists of 1917 had devoted a good part of their lives to attacking the concept of the state and had looked to a variety of devices under the new order which would diminish or eliminate the traditional functions of a national state and its bureaucracy; but, in fact, from 1917 forward, a bureaucratic state machinery was put into operation and had been consolidated. Lenin's rationale for this violation of the revolutionary doctrine had been *ad hoc* and empirical. He did what he did in order to cope with urgent situations while holding on to a precarious power based on minority support. Stalin took it upon himself to supply the Leninist heritage with a more rigorous theoretical foundation.

Two factors affected Stalin's theoretical formulations and gave them a certain urgency. At the time of Lenin's death those who still clung to the doctrine of immediate world revolution—or to world revolution as a high-priority, short-run goal—and those who professed themselves in opposition to the existence of a powerful bureaucratic national state were high in Communist Party councils and were extremely articulate. Stalin by no means relied mainly or preponderantly on his ability to defeat Trotsky and his other rivals in ideological debate. Nevertheless, his formulation of a theoretical rationale for his own position was an urgent political task in the years after the death of Lenin, before his own dictatorship was fully consolidated. The Communist Party at its highest levels was still something of a debating society and still worked formally on the basis of votes. Stalin took ample steps to ensure that votes would come his way; but he was still impelled to articulate a theoretical position. Therefore in April 1924, a few months after Lenin's death, he undertook to deliver a series of lectures at the Sverdlov University—his first major bid for status as leader of Communist thought as well as boss of the Communist Party and state apparatus.

Stalin not only required a theoretical rationale, but he felt a need to demonstrate that it was a formulation continuous with the teachings of Lenin. Lenin's prestige in the Communist Party was unique. At Lenin's funeral, with Trotsky (perhaps maneuvered) out of town, Stalin seized with both hands the role of the loyal follower. In a speech peculiar among Stalin's statements for its emotional quality—a quality notably ironic, given Lenin's final disabused reflections on Stalin's worth among his successors—Stalin made his six famous vows [1] to maintain and extend Lenin's heritage. Stalin evidently judged that only such a claim of continuity with Lenin's teachings would supply a minimum framework of legitimacy, as he moved towards total power.

Stalin's two main tasks, then, in terms of Communist theory, were to supply a rationale, apparently consistent with the theoretical writings of Lenin, for the pursuit of socialism within one country as opposed to world revolution; and to explain why it was that the national state not only showed no signs of withering away under Communism but exhibited a remarkable tendency to grow—in scale, authority, and degree of centralization.

[1] These are worth comparison with Malenkov's six "sacred duties," enunciated at Stalin's bier, both for similarities and differences.

3. SOCIALISM IN ONE COUNTRY

The manner in which Stalin resolved his priority for the Soviet Union with his ultimate Communist commitment for world revolution is indicated in the following quotations:[2]

The goal is to consolidate the dictatorship of the proletariat in one country, using it as a base for the overthrow of imperialism in all countries. Revolution spreads beyond the limits of one country; the epoch of world revolution has begun.

. . . The very development of world revolution . . . will be more rapid and more thorough, the more thoroughly Socialism fortifies itself in the first victorious country, the faster this country is transformed into a base for the further unfolding of world revolution, into a lever for the further disintegration of imperialism.

While it is true that the *final* victory of Socialism in the first country to emancipate itself is impossible without the combined efforts of the proletarians of several countries, it is equally true that the development of world revolution will be the more rapid and thorough, the more effective the aid rendered by the first Socialist country to the workers . . . of all other countries.

Stalin's theoretical reply to Trotsky and the others, then, was that the world revolution could be achieved only by stages and not in a single wave of revolutionary effort. To those Communists abroad or at home who were restless and wished to get on with the task of world revolution, Stalin said, simply: The time is not ripe; your duty is to strengthen the Soviet Union as the ultimate base for future revolution elsewhere. From 1924 to October 1952 this remained Stalin's position, with the apparent exception of the moves in Eastern Europe after 1945 taken in the shadow of the Red Army, and the assistance to Mao in China, from early 1946 forward. But examined closely, these cases disappear as exceptions, for the direct Soviet interest had dominated Moscow's behavior in both cases.

Like Lenin before him, Stalin, in this as in other matters, separated ends from means. He maintained a verbal loyalty to the end, i.e., world revolution. The means he saw as giving, for the time being, an overriding priority to the requirements of the Soviet Union. As in other cases where ends and means are separated, the distinction had its consequences. It was in terms of this doctrine

---

[2] Historicus, "Stalin on Revolution," *Foreign Affairs* (Jan. 1949), pp. 198–99.

that the German Communist Party received such indifferent support from the Soviet Union in its revolutionary efforts in 1923 and the Chinese Communists were guided by Moscow to disaster in 1927. It is still this doctrine which serves as a rationale for the total subordination of the satellite parties and governments of Eastern Europe, as well as the Communist parties of the Western world, to Moscow control.

While Stalin's Communist opponents, both within and without the Soviet Union, could and did argue that his conception violated the aspirations of most Russian Communists and the bulk of the prerevolutionary writings of Lenin, Stalin's theory was in full harmony with Lenin's practice, and he sought valiantly to make it consistent with selected extracts from Lenin's texts.

4. THE PARTY AND THE STATE

Whereas Stalin's views on socialism in one country were expressed firmly and promptly after Lenin's death, his theory of the Party and the State underwent some progression over the years. The brute fact of bureaucratic dictatorship was difficult to square with the revolutionary hopes and myths; and, to this day, the method of dictatorship is concealed beneath elaborate theological and even institutional cover.

To the extent that Stalinist theory has made explicit the emerging role of the Soviet state, it has depended heavily on its prior rationale for "socialism in one country." Stalin's progression on this subject closely parallels events within the Soviet Union and his own policies. Like other aspects of Stalin's theories, his views on the state may be legitimately regarded as an ex post rationale for policy decisions and actions already taken.

In 1926, during the NEP, Stalin wrote as follows, in the course of an argument urging the Party to bide its time before instituting accelerated programs of collectivization and industrialization: [3]

The concept of dictatorship of the proletariat is a state concept. The dictatorship of the proletariat necessarily includes the concept of force. There is no dictatorship without force, if dictatorship is to be understood in the strict sense of the term. Lenin defines the dictatorship of the proletariat as "state power based directly on *force*." (Lenin, *Collected Works*, Russian edition, Vol. XIX, p. 315.) Hence, to talk about dictatorship of the Party *in relation to the proletarian class*, and to identify it with the dictatorship of the proletariat, is tantamount to saying

[3] Joseph Stalin, *On Problems of Leninism* (Moscow, 1940), p. 139.

that in relation to its own class the Party must be not only a guide, not only a leader and teacher, but also a sort of state power employing force against it. Therefore, whoever identifies "dictatorship of the Party" with the dictatorship of the proletariat tacitly proceeds from the assumption that the prestige of the Party can be built up on force, which is absurd and absolutely incompatible with Leninism. The prestige of the Party is sustained by the confidence of the working class. And the confidence of the working class is gained not by force—force only kills it—but by the Party's correct theory, by the Party's correct policy, by the Party's devotion to the working class, by its contact with the masses of the working class, by its readiness and ability to *convince* the masses of the correctness of its slogans.

By 1930, however, with the First Five-Year Plan and forced collectivization in full cry, Stalin was more nearly prepared to define the dictatorship of the proletariat as "state power based directly on force," with somewhat less attention to the requirements of popular persuasion. His pronouncements during the First Five-Year Plan include a positive rationale for the state, and a bold claim that the day when the state could wither away safely was still at some distance. At the Sixteenth Party Congress (1930), he said: [4]

We are for the withering away of the state, while at the same time we stand for strengthening the dictatorship of the proletariat which represents the most potent and mighty of all the state authorities that have existed down to this time. The highest development of state authority to the end of making ready the conditions for the withering away of state authority: there you have the Marxist formula!

With Stalin firmly in control of both Party and State, and with his own canonization as the sole legitimate inheritor of the mantle of Marx, Engels, and Lenin gathering momentum, he moved to a still more explicit rationale for the Soviet state in his report to the Congress of the Communist Party in 1939. Here he links his doctrine of socialism in one country to the rationale for an all-powerful Soviet state, displaying an evident confidence in modifying traditional Communist doctrine which in many fields marked the latter phase of his rule: [5]

. . . It is sometimes asked: "We have abolished the exploiting classes; there are no longer any hostile classes in the country; there is nobody to suppress; hence there is no more need for the state; it must

[4] Quoted in C. B. Hoover, "The Soviet State Fails to Wither," *Foreign Affairs* (October 1952), to which this section of the text is substantially indebted.
[5] Stalin, *op. cit.*, pp. 656–58, 659–62.

die away.—Why then do we not help our Socialist state to die away? Why do we not strive to put an end to it? Is it not time to throw out all this rubbish of a state?"

What could have given rise to this underestimation? . . . It arose owing to the fact that certain of the general propositions in the Marxist doctrine of the state were incompletely worked out and inadequate. It received currency owing to our unpardonably heedless attitude to matters pertaining to the theory of the state, in spite of the fact that we have twenty years of practical experience in matters of state which provide rich material for theoretical generalizations, and in spite of the fact that, given the desire, we have every opportunity of successfully filling this gap in theory. . . .

. . . what if Socialism has been victorious only in one country, taken singly, and if, in view of this, it is quite impossible to abstract oneself from international conditions—what then? Engels' formula [the withering away of the state] does not furnish an answer to this question. . . .

In order to overthrow capitalism it was not only necessary to remove the bourgeoisie from power, it was not only necessary to expropriate the capitalists, but also to smash entirely the bourgeois state machine and its old army, its bureaucratic officialdom and its police force, and to substitute for it a new, proletarian form of state, a new, Socialist state. And that, as we know, is exactly what the Bolsheviks did. But it does not follow that the new proletarian state may not preserve certain functions of the old state, changed to suit the requirements of the proletarian state. Still less does it follow that the forms of our Socialist state must remain unchanged, that all the original functions of our state must be fully preserved in future. As a matter of fact, the forms of our state are changing and will continue to change in line with the development of our country and with the changes in the international situation. . . . We are going ahead, towards Communism. Will our state remain in the period of Communism also?

Yes, it will, unless the capitalist encirclement is liquidated, and unless the danger of foreign military attack has disappeared. Naturally, of course, the forms of our state will again change in conformity with the change in the situation at home and abroad.

No, it will not remain and will atrophy if the capitalist encirclement is liquidated and a Socialist encirclement takes its place.

Here is where Communist theology left the matter down to the time of Stalin's death.

Stalin's crude theoretical abstractions were linked, of course, to acts of substance. Taking Lenin's mixed, partially formed heritage, he developed from it a one-man dictatorship, operating an immense bureaucratic national state, with an increasingly powerful industrial and military base. As will be indicated in the next chapter, he not only altered the Marxist concept of the state to conform to this circumstance but he reshaped the whole pattern of Soviet social cultural life, including its operative standards of value. The instrument by which these massive changes were achieved was the most powerful state we have seen in recent centuries. Marx's materialistic interpretation of history had regarded the state as the servant of a ruling class, whose primacy, in turn, resulted from the workings of "historically objective" conditions. Stalin evidently regarded himself and the state he created as the maker of "historically objective" conditions. His reversion from Marx to Hegel was, in this sense, complete; but the philosophic basis for his view was clearly an extension of Lenin's 1902 conception of a disciplined party that would be prepared to struggle for power, in the name of the proletariat, against the stream of history and, if necessary, against the will of the working classes. Lenin's party was an instrument—a means—for achieving power; Lenin regarded (or believed he regarded) state power as a means for achieving Communism's substantive international, human goals. Stalin's concept of the role of the Soviet state continued and extended this separation of ends and means. With a peculiar single-mindedness he built Russian national power and the authority of the Soviet state to a new high point in the name of goals which day by day receded, but whose ultimate attainment remains to this day the sole overt rationale for the Soviet dictatorship, as Malenkov's, Beria's, and Molotov's speeches on the occasion of Stalin's death attest.

5. THE MEANING OF IDEOLOGY IN CONTEMPORARY SOVIET SOCIETY

The dramatic alteration in Soviet policy away from the substance of the initial revolutionary goals is well attested and hardly a matter for debate. It may well be asked, then, why Stalin clung, and his successors apparently cling, to the tattered framework of Marxism, straining to present a line of continuity with a past that was buried, at the latest, during the Great Purge of 1936–38. Put another way, why did Stalin, a political operator of some talent, but with gifts for abstraction of a low order (and a profound lack of respect for intellectuals in general) present himself to the Communist world as a great theorist?

The answers to these questions must be sought in the functions served by ideology in the organization of societies and in the nature of those different elements which we tend to group together in the word "ideology" itself.

There are several related but distinguishable functions which ideology may perform. Ideology may furnish a society with a set of basic moral values which are held up as touchstones for the worth of any given action by individuals and by the community. Particular actions or public policies may be justified by persuasive association with these values. The term "ideology" is also used, however, to describe not a basic minimum value system but a specific set of institutions, goals, or programs. Finally, ideology can be interpreted as a set of concepts and terms by which men interpret the world around them and communicate with one another. Ideology serves as a common vocabulary, usually built up over considerable periods of time and encrusted with evocative associations, which gives a certain order to the chaotic experiences confronted by men. The fate of each of these elements in the revolutionary ideology of 1917 has differed; and the residual elements of that ideology play different roles in current Soviet society.

It can be maintained that, in its ultimate values, Soviet ideology has not changed since 1917 or, in fact, since the turn of the century when the Russian Communist Party was shaped by Lenin. At its core, the basic element in the ideology derived from the notion of a single, correct, and, therefore, good course of history, capable of appropriate interpretation only by him who is the best Marxist. This was Lenin's moral sanction as leader of the prerevolutionary Party; and it was on this basis that Stalin sought to create the legitimacy of his succession to Lenin. From this concept of the correct interpreter of history in Marxist terms arose also the rationale for the absolute unity of the Communist Party and the inviolability of the Communist Party line. Legitimacy, in terms of the authoritative interpreter of scientific Marxism, plays in the Soviet state a role comparable to the passing of kingship by blood in a monarchy. The deeper roots of this requirement for legitimacy we need not seek here. What can be said is that even the most cynical of rulers, acquiring power for the most self-seeking of motives, appears to feel the need for some such mantle of respectability in the face of the citizens of his own society.

This acceptance of overriding primacy for the single authoritative interpreter of history clashed, of course, with much of the substance of the revolutionary program. As detailed elsewhere in this essay, the whole humanistic baggage of the Revolution, its belief in the power of the industrial working class to generate spontaneously appropriate policies, its hopes for human welfare, its reliance on good environment as the maker of good men—all of that has gone in favor of the program and policies of a dictatorial, bureaucratic state concerned, at highest priority, with the maintenance and enlargement of its own power. In his essay on "Dialectical and Historical Materialism," published in September 1938, Stalin allowed himself a succinct restatement of Marxist materialism. He said: [6] ". . . to put it more crudely, whatever is man's manner of life, such is his manner of thought." And, indeed the sanctioned manner of thought in the Soviet Union has been accommodated to its manner of life, producing a system of incentives and restraints and a culture widely at variance with that envisaged at the time of the Revolution by the Bolsheviks themselves. The ideological enthusiasm which marked the generation of revolutionaries and even the early days of the First Five-Year Plan has given way to standards of bureaucratic efficiency and conformity. The implications of Stalin's changes in fundamental theory, and especially his theory of the role of the Soviet state, have been projected down into the structure and working standards of the society. The function of Stalin's theory of the state under conditions of socialism in one country is, then, to serve as a rationale at the highest level for the pattern of life and policies which have, in fact, emerged in the USSR.

But it is the role of ideology as the medium for relating individuals to each other and to their environment which is probably its most important residual function in the Soviet Union. The function of Marxism and Communist ideology as a means of perception is, in itself, complex. In the first place, this ideology governs the way men look at the world and interpret it. The Soviet leaders were trained in a Marxist vocabulary; they talk and think, especially about the world abroad, in terms of economic interests, class groups, and class struggles. It is very doubtful, because it is wholly outside their direct personal training and experience, that they understand the ethical, and even religious, foundations of Western societies or the conception of politics as the arena for the settlement of differences among individuals and groups within rules which are designed to protect the individual as well as the community, the minority as well as the

[6] *Ibid.*, p. 607.

majority's right to govern. They do know, of course, a very great deal factually about the outside world and about the mechanics of its operations. Practical experience and ample sources of intelligence have certainly made them modify their ingrained judgments on many aspects of the external world. They are capable, as a matter of tactics, of producing such sophisticated "Western" documents as the reply to President Eisenhower's speech, published in Moscow on April 25, 1953. But this modification in a crude Marxist view of the external world has probably been made piecemeal and *ad hoc*, not by a basic reappraisal of Western society and its foundations.

Men do tend to be taken in by their own magic, and part of their magic consists in the concepts they use to describe and interpret the world around them. In this sense it seems likely that Marxist ideology is still alive and vital in the higher reaches of the Soviet regime. And it may be dangerous, because, to the extent it operates, it limits and distorts the regime's perception of the external world and the probable manner of the rest of the world's response to situations it confronts, including its response to aggressive Soviet initiatives.

In the second place, the Soviet ideological vocabulary serves as an indispensable overt medium for conducting conflicts over power and policy substance without revealing their true basis. As noted earlier, Stalin's struggle for power after Lenin's death with his opponents on the so-called Left and the so-called Right, was conducted overtly not in terms of power but in terms of differences in interpretations of Marx and Lenin as they applied to next steps in Soviet policy. And so it has been with virtually every shift in the Party line down through the years. The early phase of collectivization was presented in ideological terms as was the slowing up of its pace in the mid-1930's. One strand of the ideological heritage was invoked to rationalize the Popular-Front phase of Communism in the middle and late 1930's; another was invoked in order to explain the 1939 pact with Hitler. In the postwar years it would appear likely that Malenkov and Zhdanov conducted a bitter feud at the secondary level of power both for status and on the substance of policy, all of whose overt manifestations took the form of arguments for the ideological correctness of one or another position, usually assumed by their respective protégés.[7] And, most recently, from mid-January 1953 to Stalin's death, the "doctors' plot" was presented to the

[7] Boris Nicolaevsky, "Malenkov, His Rise and His Policy," *The New Leader* (New York, Mar. 23, 1953).

Soviet public as evidence of the need for increased vigilance against capitalist encirclement; whereas, in April, when the plot was declared a hoax, the ideological sanction of the Soviet Constitution was invoked to explain the sudden access of official rectitude. Thus the ample, conflicting arsenal of ideological terms and concepts constitutes a verbal and conceptual screen for the harsher realities of Soviet life.

Third, and certainly most important, the ideological heritage of Marx and Lenin serves as a steady rationale for the state of both internal tension and hostility to the external world which has marked Soviet life since November 1917. Stalin's concept of the Soviet Union as a base for future world revolution, surrounded by an encircling capitalist world, has proved an invaluable foundation for continuing to justify at home an indefinite postponement of improvements in welfare, a massive secret police, and Russia's cultural and human isolation from the Western world. From the time of the immediate postrevolutionary days, when many of Lenin's opponents rallied to his regime in the face of foreign intervention, the Bolsheviks came to appreciate the practical value to them of a hostile external world. They have never wholly relaxed this mood although they have tempered it from time to time, notably in the period of alliance with the West during World War II. Moreover, they have, since the mid-1930's, systematically buttressed the ideological conception of capitalist encirclement with memories of external hostility drawn from pre-Communist Russian history. Despite these fluctuations and alterations in content, perhaps the only indispensable function of ideology in the Soviet Union is a rationale for the acceptance of a state of internal siege—required, in fact, for the maintenance of the regime's domestic authority, but explained to the Russian peoples in terms of the external world's implacable designs on Russia.

What can we say, finally, of the sincerity or lack of sincerity of Stalin and his successors, with respect to the ideology they profess? As a psychological concept the notion of sincerity is, itself, not wholly clear; and the authors of this essay lack both the evidence and the technical knowledge to reconstruct the state of mind of Stalin, Malenkov, Beria, Molotov, and the others who have manipulated the instruments of Soviet power. It can be said, however, that all available evidence points to the domination of Stalin's mind (during his lifetime) and that of his colleagues by an ideology derived from their own experience in the pursuit and maintenance of power. Its effective touchstones of good and bad are the consequences of any given act for their own power. If other elements enter into the rationale for their action, they are now likely, on the whole, to be based increasingly on Russian nationalism rather than on Marxism. Nevertheless, the leaders may still believe, in some part of their beings, that they represent correctly the Marxist revolutionary heritage. They most certainly are loyal to the institutions they have built in Russia and take pride in the material progress of the society to whose guidance and control they have devoted their mature lives. And this institutional loyalty may be associated, in no very strict way, with their ideological heritage. They may thus have successfully and, in some sense, sincerely identified their own success as a ruling group in Russia with the ultimate goals of Communism. It can be asserted, however, with reasonable confidence that such an obscure residuum of ideological faith is not likely to have appreciable effect on policy when it conflicts with the short-term interests of the regime with respect to the maintenance of internal stability or the enlargement of external power.

Chapter Six

THE BUREAUCRATIZATION OF SOCIAL AND CULTURAL LIFE

1. INTRODUCTION

THE CONVERSION by historical process of the Soviet state into a personal dictatorship, whose primary effective concern was the maintenance and enlargement of its direct institutionalized power, as opposed to the pursuit of specific political, social, and economic goals, had important effects on the policies pursued in the fields of Soviet social and cultural life. In these areas the heritage of Marxism and the Revolution carried with it certain specific lines of what might be called, in the Western sense, radical policy. As Stalin's dictatorship crystallized, the criteria for cultural and social policy changed. What was required, above all, was a social policy which, whatever its content, might sustain and justify an enlarged power for the State.

In particular, the requirements of efficiency and discipline made for modification in the Marxist heritage in three directions. First, the regime found itself increasingly prepared to abandon those forms of social policy inherited from Marxism and the Revolution which conflicted with the requirements for efficiency, discipline, and stability in the behavior of the population. Second, and more positively, the regime sought to use social policy as an instrument for strengthening its control over the peoples of the Soviet state. Third, the Soviet regime came to regard social policy as a field in which it could make concessions of a minor kind to the popular wishes of the people.

Although the extent to which the first and third directions of change are identical cannot be firmly established, it seems probable that the motivating interest of the regime in most instances was increased efficiency rather than a placating of popular sentiment for political purposes. It should be noted that an action designed to increase the efficiency of a population, taking into account intractable or slowly changing characteristics, tastes, and prejudices, may come, in practice, to much the same thing as action designed to diminish popular resentment. On balance, these changes have made for a pattern of policy more conservative, more nearly linked with the Russian national tradition, than might have been envisaged in the early days of the Revolution. This reversion in substance has, however, been accomplished by a regime which has at the same time maintained a residue of those elements in Marxist-Leninist doctrine (either in their original form or modified) which are judged useful to the regime for other purposes.

2. SOCIAL STRUCTURE

There has been no more dramatic clash between revolutionary aspiration and Soviet practice than with respect to the goal of social equality. Throughout the world, but notably in tsarist Russia, the radical movement had thrived before 1914 on evidence of gross inequality in income and opportunity as among men. Soviet history in this matter, as in others, begins with a tactical modification in the revolutionary program, to meet urgently felt practical requirements, and ends with a full ideological rationale for the situation which progressively emerged in consequence of the means the regime chose to exercise its rule. As noted earlier, Lenin's program in the first instance had envisaged not only the elimination of the landed aristocracy and the commercial and industrial middle class, but also the crushing of the old bureaucracy. The *de facto* recognition of the need for maintaining inequalities of income for technical specialists retained in their prerevolutionary functions begins the story of the Soviet transition to its present "organized inequality." [1] This exception was soon widened by the practical experience of operating industry under the system of War Communism. By 1920 industrial payment in relation to results was laid down by the Party as the rule; and the general loosening of central economic controls which marked the period of NEP widely extended the fact of unequal distribution of income. By 1930 the Soviet pattern of real income distribution recognizably approximated that in capitalist societies.

Nevertheless, in two respects, some substance of the revolutionary

[1] A phrase from Barrington Moore, Jr., *Soviet Politics—The Dilemma of Power*, p. 238, on whose work this section of the text draws substantially.

program remained: until 1929 a fixed maximum income for members of the Party was apparently in force; and more important, a systematic effort was made to increase equality of opportunity in the society by giving special privileges in education and social service to the citizens of the industrial working class, and, especially, to their children. There is no doubt that, over the first two decades of its history, Soviet society was marked by a high degree of social and economic mobility. Moreover, during the 1920's, the ideal of equality was often reiterated and lapses were regarded as a temporary deviation on the road to a communism which would emerge in the foreseeable future, if it was not just around the corner.

Under Stalin's rule, in the period of the First Five-Year Plan, the pattern of inequality hardened. In 1931 Stalin repudiated equality of income as a Left deviation, petty bourgeois in character, and laid down the operative rule: "From each according to his abilities, to each according to his labor."

The rapid development of industry in the 1930's, within this rule, as well as the expansion of the police and armed forces, created a new and increasingly self-conscious class of bureaucrats: industrial managers, police and army officers, artists, scientists, teachers, and lawyers, with substantial claims on Soviet resources, not only in the form of money income, but also in a wide range of privileges which distinguish them from the peasants and industrial workers. This new and significant middle class—called "the intelligentsia" in Soviet terminology—comprised about 14 per cent of the population in 1939; and it has certainly not diminished since that time.

The foundation in high policy for the elevation of the technician-bureaucrat was stated most clearly by Stalin in a speech delivered in 1935—significantly enough, to the graduates of the Red Army academies: [2]

Formerly . . . we used to say that "technique decides everything." This slogan helped us to put an end to the dearth in technique and to create a vast technical base in every branch of activity for the equipment of our people with first-class technique. That is very good. But it is not enough, it is not enough by far. In order to set technique going and to utilize it to the full, we need people who have mastered technique, we need cadres capable of mastering and utilizing this technique according to all the rules of the art. Without people who have mastered technique, technique is dead. In the charge of people who have mastered technique,

[2] Central Committee of the C.P.S.U.(B.), ed., *History of the Communist Party of the Soviet Union* (New York, 1939), p. 337.

technique can and should perform miracles. If in our first-class mills and factories, in our state farms and collective farms and in our Red Army we had sufficient cadres capable of harnessing this technique, our country would secure results three times and four times as great as at present. That is why emphasis must now be laid on people, on cadres, on workers who have mastered technique. That is why the old slogan, "technique decides everything," which is a reflection of a period already passed, a period in which we suffered from a dearth of technique, must now be replaced by a new slogan, the slogan *cadres decide everything.* That is the main thing now. . . .

The trend in Soviet policy over the past decade has been to reinforce the stability in status of the new middle class that has "mastered technique." [3] At the Eighteenth Party Conference in Moscow in 1941, in one of his few major public statements, Malenkov enhanced the authority of the managerial class and undercut the criterion of proletarian origin as a standard for promotion in the Soviet hierarchy. The Soviet income tax of 1943, with its flat rate of 13 per cent for all incomes above 1000 rubles per month, is certainly easier on the middle class than the tax system of any other major industrial society.

There is some evidence that this dynamic evolution is having its logical consequence, that is, in the third Soviet generation advantage is being passed along by income and family and the high social mobility of the earlier years is being slowed down. The progressive inheritance tax of 1926, which took up to 90 per cent of an estate, was supplanted in 1943 by a law which set an upper limit of 10 per cent. A combination of labor draft and school fees has tended somewhat to restrict access to higher education for the youth of poor parents. This trend toward the passing of privileges by family status is confirmed obliquely in the Soviet press and by that sensitive social index, popular humor. It is, however, merely a trend whose future course and consequences cannot now be predicted with confidence.

What can be said is that Soviet society has emerged in the post-1945 years confirmed as a hierarchical structure, with its standards and privileges built around the higher levels of the bureaucracy—a class thoroughly different in values and objectives from the group of professional subversives and revolutionaries, the more or less

[3] See, especially, the authoritative analysis of A. Inkeles, "Social Stratification and Mobility in the Soviet Union: 1940–1950," *American Sociological Review* (August 1950), pp. 465–79.

idealistic thugs who seized power in 1917, dominated Soviet society over its first decade, and were mostly eliminated in the Great Purge.

3. THE LAW

The evolution of Soviet law, like many aspects of its social and cultural transition, can be broken down into four reasonably well-marked stages embracing the periods of War Communism, NEP, the early years of the Five-Year Plans, and the bureaucratic crystallization of the mid-1930's. This last stage came, for law, in 1936-37 with the repudiation of the doctrines of the revolutionary legal theorist Eugene Pashukanis and the promulgation of new legal codes, which simultaneously embraced the disparate phenomena of the new Soviet Constitution and the Great Purge.

The brutal revolutionary optimism of the period of War Communism saw the tsarist legal structure set aside. In Marxist theory, law was a part of the state superstructure by which the fact of class power was imposed on society. With the coming of the dictatorship of the proletariat, law became Communist Party policy—an instrument for consolidating the Revolution and crushing the opposition. The goal of "the withering away of the law" was held up as a proximate goal, along with the withering away of the state in general.

With Lenin's acknowledgment of the errors of War Communism and with the installation of NEP, Soviet legal theory and practice sharply diverged. The revolutionary theorists continued to discuss the law in traditional Marxist style. As late as 1927 the President of the Supreme Court, Stuchka, wrote: [4] "Communism means not the victory of socialist law, but the victory of socialism over any law, since with the abolition of classes with their antagonistic interests, law will disappear altogether."

In fact, however, NEP saw a considerable revival of traditional European law, notably that covering economic relationships. The impact of revolutionary thought and aspiration could still be found in some areas, notably in marriage law and the formal bias of the courts in favor of the industrial worker. And, above all, the secret police continued to operate largely outside the formal framework of law. On the whole, however, in law as in economics, the period of NEP was regarded frankly as a tactical throwback to bourgeois techniques.

The coming of the First Five-Year Plan was, at first, regarded by

[4] H. J. Berman, *Justice in Russia* (Cambridge, Mass., 1950), p. 21, on whose work this section of the text draws substantially.

Soviet legal theorists as a resumption of movement forward toward the revolutionary goal. The advent of socialism in the form of enforced collectivization and accelerated industrialization under state ownership and control, was hailed by the authoritative legal theorists as, at last, providing the Marxist basis for a true withering away of bourgeois law. In 1930 Pashukanis wrote: [5]

We have a system of proletarian politics and upon it law should be oriented. Once we even wished to arrange the curriculum so that, for example, the course in land law would be replaced by a course in land *policy* and law, because among us law can play no independent and final part: this was the design when War Communism was going out. During the years of the New Economic Policy and of the rehabilitation period, the system of codes was introduced and began again to develop, and at the same time attempts to pack and to tie all law into a system were renewed. Now, when we have passed to the reconstruction period, the utmost dynamic force is essential. . . . Revolutionary legality is for us a problem which is ninety-nine per cent political.

On this view the Plan superseded the Law.

All of this, like so much else in Soviet ideology, was finally reversed in the mid-1930's. In his Report on the Draft Constitution in 1936, Stalin said: "We need stability of laws now more than ever." Vishinsky, whose previous pronouncements had been wholly orthodox, within the Pashukanis school, was assigned the task of implementing Stalin's new perspective and administering the *coup de grâce* to Pashukanis. Vishinsky's text, evidently derived from Stalin's 1930 pronouncement on the Soviet state, was: "History demonstrates that under socialism . . . law is raised to the highest level of development." Since 1936 the teaching and practice of law have been rehabilitated, new codes have been promulgated, and a tone of positive legalism has suffused Soviet society. This was recently demonstrated, in April 1953, by the reversal of the mysterious case of the doctors.

What does all this emphasis on legality amount to? What is its substance? It is evident that the new Soviet legalism has little or nothing to do with the protection of civil rights in the Western political sense of setting limits to the state's ability to encroach on the individual citizen; it may, however, come to have some such substance in the future if the bureaucracy can succeed in asserting its rights against the secret police. Soviet law leaves a large and

[5] *Ibid.*, p. 34.

elastic area where "enemies of the state" may be dealt with outside the law and the courts. As Berman has written: [6]

Where the stability of the regime is threatened, law goes out the window. No fundamental legal opposition is tolerated. Where real opposition is even suspected, it is dealt with by "suppression and the use of force." The Soviets have the delicacy at least not to call this law. Yet the line is not always easy to draw, and the inherent conflict between law and force results in some strange paradoxes. The law punishes discrimination on the basis of nationality, yet the Ministry of the Interior removes and disperses whole national groups which have been considered insufficiently loyal—the Volga Germans, the Crimean Tartars, the Chechen and Ingush in the North Caucasus. Anti-Semitism is a crime in law, but Zionists are sent to labor camps as counterrevolutionaries. Legal guilt is purely personal, but political guilt may be avenged against relatives and friends.

Having left himself ample scope for extra-legal operations, Stalin sought bureaucratic order and discipline in Soviet society and chose to rehabilitate the law as one instrument for this purpose. The complex relations that developed within the administrative arms of the state as they embraced agriculture and an expanding industry, and the emerging role of the citizen as an instrument for effecting state policy in the setting of this increasingly industrial society, demanded an area of law and order for the foreseeable future. The earlier legal theorists had held up with an inappropriate vigor the vision of a society where law was no longer required; and their post-1929 rationale for economic and administrative planning as a substitute for law under socialism simply did not meet the case. A vast array of conflicts of interest arose in which the state's interest lay merely in prompt and orderly settlement. In this area law has developed rapidly over the past two decades, as an extension of bureaucratic practice.

The extent to which legalistic habits of mind characterize the second generation of Soviet bureaucrats has been amply revealed in postwar diplomatic negotiations, where Soviet virtuosity in the manipulation of texts, the exploitation of rules of procedure, and the other devices of international order has become legendary.

4. PSYCHOLOGY, EDUCATION, AND THE FAMILY

The transitions in Soviet theory of the state, social hierarchy, and the law were paralleled by related changes in psychological

[6] *Ibid.*, pp. 48–49.

theory. In turn the transition in psychology has been accompanied by important shifts in the character of Soviet education and in the official conception of the appropriate nature and functions of family life. Concerned as it is with the nature of human action, psychological theory dramatizes with peculiar clarity the underlying values which suffuse the society where it obtains. As Professor Bauer has recently demonstrated with skill,[7] this is peculiarly true of the modern Soviet state, where psychological theory became, in its day, a matter of high public policy, and so remains down to the present.

Soviet psychology proceeded after the Revolution along what might be called academic, deterministic Marxist lines. The dictatorial developments in Communist political practice—first within the Party, then in the Russian state—were not reflected in psychology or in the closely related field of education. Man was viewed as the product of his heredity and, especially, his material environment. This materialistic emphasis pushed the psychologists, in the first instance, toward a reliance on physiology, an area in which distinguished work had been done in Russia even before World War I, notably by Boldyrev and Pavlov. As the postrevolutionary generation of Soviet psychologists developed, their doctrines closely resembled behavorial psychology concurrently developing in the West. The child, inherently good, was to be shaped by a natural reaction to his environment; and, in general, the life of the new socialist society would itself, without elaborate institutional intervention, educate its citizens appropriately.

These doctrines were linked to the development in the 1920's of a Soviet school system in which great reliance was placed on spontaneous and uninhibited reaction of the child to his setting. It was not accidental that, in the course of his visit to the Soviet Union in the 1920's, John Dewey found the atmosphere congenial. Progressive education was practiced almost to the point of the "withering away of the school."

The Soviet philosopher of this approach to education was V. N. Shul'gin, director of the Marx-Engels Institute of Pedagogy, until its dissolution in 1931. He wrote: [8]

In my opinion, there will be no school in the future communist society. The child will go immediately into social work. There he will find no pedagogues, but a work director, who will be a sufficiently cul-

[7] R. A. Bauer, *The New Man in Soviet Psychology* (Cambridge, Mass., 1952), to whose work this section is substantially indebted.
[8] *Ibid.*, p. 44.

tured person, and one who knows how to handle children. More correctly, we will all be pedagogues. The child will go directly from social work to industrial work, and from there to the library, where he will find answers to all the questions which interest him. We are approaching closer and closer to this all the time.

The early stages of the First Five-Year Plan saw a radical revision of deterministic notions in Soviet psychological theory, as in other areas. There was an obvious clash between a national program designed, by conscious state policy, to alter swiftly the economic foundations of the society and a psychological and educational theory which regarded the individual as the reflex of his heredity and environment. Moreover, since the Soviet state was taking responsibility for a major change in the environment of its citizens, it was somewhat awkward to have in currency psychological conceptions in which human behavior could, in a sense, be blamed on the environment. Stalin's purposiveness with respect to the evolution of the Soviet economy was soon translated into new theoretical models in psychology and new theories of education.

The new theoretical line did not emerge immediately and full-blown. There was a period of confused criticism in the early 1930's, which gave way, by about 1936, to a sharp alteration in educational practice, which itself was only rationalized in succeeding years. A turning point in this transitional process was a decree of July 4, 1936, of the Central Committee of the Party, "On Pedological Perversions of the System of the People's Commissariat of Education," —pedology being the science of child education. This decree attacked certain experimental practices in the schools; more basically, it condemned the notion that the fate of children was fatalistically conditioned by biological and social factors, by the influence of heredity and the environment. The decree held that this passive view of the individual was reactionary and "stands in flagrant contradiction to Marxism and to the whole practice of Socialist reconstruction which successfully re-educates men in the spirit of Socialism and liquidates the survivals of capitalism in economics and in human consciousness." It took some four years satisfactorily to work out the implications of this line, the benchmark of the consolidation being, according to Bauer, the publication in 1940 of Rubinshtein's *Foundations of General Psychology*.

The conception of the new man in Soviet society can best be understood by analogy with Stalin's conception of his own role in relation to history. Stalin viewed himself and the state he commanded as the instrument for driving history in the right direction, at the right pace, at the right time. The flow of Soviet policy was the reflection of this correct and purposeful interpretation of what should be done, in the light of Marxist-Leninist-Stalinist science of society. Within this framework, the function of each man in Soviet society was not simply to respond passively to his environment, but, rather, consciously to govern his actions so as to fulfill his part in the execution of the correct historical line. Theoretically, within his own narrow orbit for action, the New Soviet Man would choose the alternative which would correctly fulfill his role in history.

This conception had its basis, also, in the practical problems of administration confronted by the Soviet regime from the launching of the First Five-Year Plan on. Goals and policies could be defined from above; their execution, however, required that men act with both vigor and technical skill. A Party line or a target in a production plan did not fulfill itself automatically. The new conception of Soviet man was, at its simplest level, the heroic worker who overfulfilled his production target: the Stakhanovite.

At a higher level, as reflected, for example, in Soviet literature, the ideal Soviet citizen was the local or regional Party boss who successfully resolved the material and human problems he confronted to fulfill his own area's production targets. From these practical foundations there has developed a psychological theory which emphasizes the need and responsibility of men consciously to control their actions in line with a higher purpose. What Soviet psychological theory projects, then, is the notion of men who, in the language of the behavioral sciences, "internalize" the Party line; who, like ideal bureaucrats, execute with energy and competence whatever tasks are set for them from above.

In terms of educational practice, the practical meaning of this revolution in psychological theory is quite clear. The old progressive slogans of "learning by doing" have largely been abandoned and have given way to a strict, conservative training in useful techniques and methods. The technically competent engineer, the man capable of observing all the facts in a given situation and acting correctly upon them, is the new model.

The substitution of a purposefulness in harmony with the state's policy for a spontaneous reaction to the environment was paralleled by a reversal, equally distinct, in attitudes toward sex and marriage. The more ardent Communists in the postrevolutionary period (but in this matter, definitely not Lenin) looked to the withering away of the traditional family, as a pillar of the bourgeois society which had been definitively overthrown in Russia. Divorce was made easy, and "free love" was widely taken as the mark of an authentic revolutionary spirit. At this stage, in Trotsky's formulation,[9] "the complete absorption of the housekeeping functions of the family by institutions of the socialist society, uniting all generations in solidarity and mutual aid, was to bring to woman, and thereby to the loving couple, a real liberation from the thousand-year-old fetters." But, as Trotsky also notes, "it proved impossible to take the old family by storm. . . ."

It was, almost certainly, the problems and circumstances of the first phase of the Five-Year Plan which led to a fundamental reconsideration of what family policies should be under the purposeful dictatorship of Stalin. Rapid industrialization had brought with it the movement of millions of people, to the cities from the farms and from one urban area to another. Against the background of the laxity of family life as it had developed over the previous decade, those responsible for Soviet development found the social habits of the Soviet citizenry at cross purposes with the orderly requirements of an efficient working force. More profoundly, the high degree of individualism implicitly encouraged by radical attitudes toward sex and the family did not jibe with the frame of mind desired in the Soviet population.

Moreover, the Soviet birth rate was tending to fall off; and, with Hitler's rise and the possibility of war, the regime might well have been looking to the future size and age composition of the Soviet population.

The crystallization of the new attitudes can be dated, roughly, from 1935–36. Earlier social radicalism was denounced as a "Leftist" deviation, and the whole pattern of policy and of approved standards of behavior altered. Virginity was reinstituted as a virtue, as was respect by the young for their parents; co-education was abandoned. The importance of stable family life was emphasized as a requirement for the effective functioning of the state, and divorce was made more difficult and expensive. Tax incentives were provided for the development of large families. And, in an act made notable because of a brief period of public discussion—which demonstrated that it was unpopular—abortion on other than medical grounds was made illegal in June 1936.

[9] Leon Trotsky, *The Revolution Betrayed* (New York, 1937), pp. 144–45.

The mood of the new approach to the family is well caught in these two quotations, the first from *Pravda* in 1935, the second a letter from the wife of a worker, published in *Rabotnitsa* (The Woman Worker) in 1936: [10]

. . . a bad family man cannot be a good Soviet citizen and social worker. An activist and social worker who at meetings bangs down his fist in defence of women's rights and at home treats his wife and children swinishly, is not an activist but a hypocrite and a bigot. . . . Only the hopeless muddlers, the petty-bourgeois leftists can assert that the family and care of the family is petty bourgeois. On the contrary, irresponsible and caddish treatment of the family is refined petty bourgeoisie. (*Pravda*, June 26, 1935).

We must help our husbands, fathers, sons and daughters to become Stakhanovites. We must live for their interests and help them to put into effect the suggestions of the great Stalin, help them master the technique and heighten the productivity of their work. This we can do by taking constant care of our relations. Friendship and peace at home, comfort, sensible entertainment, cleanliness and tidiness everywhere, well-brought-up children—these will help to keep up the spirits of our relatives, will help them to work and study in peace and with redoubled energy. The Stakhanovites' wives cannot remain uneducated, undeveloped: we, too, must learn. . . . Some may ask: When? Here we must approach the matter in Stakhanovite fashion. We must arrange our work in such a way that we have time for everything—for housework, for study and for rest.

Thus, as he had with law and education, Stalin came, in the mid-1930's, to the view that the operation of a Soviet society which would minimize the problem of domestic control by the regime and maximize its power base required that large areas of Soviet life be governed by an institutionalized discipline. What appeared to Stalin to be the shapeless (if not dangerously individualistic) presuppositions of Soviet psychology, education, and family life needed to be put into a mold which would maximize the virtues which he wished to see cultivated. The emergent pattern of Soviet virtues is quite familiar to the West: they are, essentially, the middle-class virtues of mature Victorianism, when industrial society had taken shape. They are not qualities of the great entrepreneur or builder of empire, but rather those of the stable bureaucrat: orderly, conservative, competent, unimaginative, and above all, loyal to instruc-

[10] Rudolf Schlesinger, *The Family in the U.S.S.R.* (London, 1949), pp. 336–37 and 327, respectively.

tion from above. It is thus no accident that these related and mutually consistent changes came about piecemeal over the same years that industrialization was accelerated, when the new bureaucracy was being installed in place of the purged older generation, and its status as the privileged instrument of Stalin's power was being confirmed.

5. LITERATURE AND THE ARTS

The evolution of Soviet literature (and the arts in general) is well summarized by the chapter headings in Gleb Struve's *Study of Soviet Russian Literature, 1917-1950:* [11]

> Literature in Transition: 1917–21
> Revolutionary Romanticism: 1921–24
> The Emergence of a New Literature: 1924–29
> Literature Puts on Uniform: 1929–32
> Literature in the Doldrums: 1932–41
> Literature on War Service: 1941–46
> Toeing the New Party Line: 1946–50

The range of freedom accorded Soviet literature and the arts in the postrevolutionary period was wider than in most other aspects of Soviet life. While anti-Communist writers and artists had either left Russia or were silent, a substantial number of artists remained behind without becoming Communists. These "fellow-travellers," as Trotsky designated them in a phrase of historic momentum, wrote about the life around them as they perceived it, limited in only a general way by the need to avoid overt criticism of the regime.

From early Soviet days, however, there was a school of Communists who wished to bring literature under a stricter discipline. This school consisted of certain more ardent supporters of the regime, known as the On Guardists, after the title of their magazine. Their position, enunciated in the first issue of *On Guard,* in June 1923, included the following: [12] "In a class society, imaginative literature, just as everything else, serves the objects of a specific class, and only through that class, of the whole of mankind; hence, that literature is proletarian which organizes the psychology of consciousness of the working class and of the wide toiling masses towards the final aims of the proletarian as the reorganizer of the world and

[11] Gleb Struve, *Study of Soviet Russian Literature, 1917–1950* (Norman, Okla., 1951), on which this section of the text draws substantially.

[12] *Ibid.,* p. 73.

the creator of Communist society. . . ." In terms of substance, then, these Communists called for writing which would explicitly reinforce the doctrines of revolution and help push the Soviet people into a full Marxist class consciousness.

In the light of later developments, however, it is notable that even those who regarded the prime function of Soviet literature and the arts as the heightening of the workers' class consciousness, and therefore as an agent for increasing the support for "dictatorship of the proletariat," left open to the writer the artistic form of his material. And since, at this stage, the state authorities refrained from using their powers to enforce a monopolist position for the On Guardists, the fellow-travellers continued to write in their own ego-centric way. The literary life of Russia up to 1929 was full of recognizable left-wing intellectuals—in the Left Bank, Bloomsbury, Greenwich Village tradition—who experimented with form (and, inevitably, substance) along lines recognizable in the West and not wholly divorced from Western artistic currents. This range of tolerance was formally reinforced in 1925 by a special resolution of the Central Committee of the Communist Party which, while denying the possibility of neutral art, recognized the difficulty of composing rules to govern the form of art in general and literature in particular. This resolution included the following statement: [13] "If the proletariat possess already the unfailing criteria for evaluating the socio-political content of any work of literature, it lacks such ready-made answers to all the problems of artistic form."

Within this framework Soviet literature, art, cinema, and the theater enjoyed a lively and not unproductive existence. The scope of this freedom at its most articulate is well illustrated by extracts from the diary of the novelist Pilnyak, written in 1923: [14]

. . . I am not a Communist and therefore do not admit that I must be a Communist and write as a Communist, while I admit that the Communist power in Russia is determined, not by the will of the Communists, but by the historical destinies of Russia, and, inasmuch as I want to trace those destinies (as best as I can and as my conscience and my intellect prompt me), I am with the Communists, that is, inasmuch as the Communists are with Russia I am with them, too. . . . I admit that I am much less interested in the fate of the Russian Communist party than in the fate of Russia, the Russian Communist party being for me only a link in the history of Russia. I know that I must be ab-

[13] *Ibid.*, p. 83.
[14] *Ibid.*, p. 215.

solutely objective, must not bring grist to anyone's mill, must not delude anyone, and I admit that I may be wrong in everything, but I also know that I cannot, nor know not how to, nor ever shall, write otherwise than I do, even if I wanted to do violence to myself. . . . In recent years our state has been setting up incubators for Party literature, providing them with food rations, and nothing came of it, or rather bad things came of it, for when these people touched art they stopped being politicians, without becoming artists. . . . Hence another conclusion: I believe that a writer must care only about his manuscripts, about their being *good*, and the honesty and validity of his Party-school-social membership card is his own personal business which has nothing to do with literature."

It should be noted that Pilnyak was one of the more abject of the repentent sinners in the early 1930's, at the time when the artistic fellow-travellers were being brought firmly into line.

With Stalin's launching of the First Five-Year Plan, the criteria for literature and the arts became, simply, those of short-term propaganda. That work was encouraged which was believed to assist in the most direct, literal, and immediate way, the achievement of the Plan. The On Guard position at last became official doctrine and, more than that, it was institutionalized in an organization called RAPP (Russian Association of Proletarian Writers). In 1929 this organization was given the power to dictate literary policies which had to be followed if the writer was to survive. A literary dictator emerged in the person of Leopold Averbach. The literary themes became, overwhelmingly, the tasks, difficulties, and triumphs of the Five-Year Plan. This was the huckster period of Soviet culture.

The gradual process of the Stalinist settlement in social and cultural life, which in general can be dated from the mid-1930's, began early in literature. In a Central Committee decree of April 1932, RAPP and the dictatorship of Averbach were ended by the creation of a Union of Soviet Writers. More than that, a new literary policy was laid down, in opposition to the literal and rather abstract propaganda which had marked the RAPP dictatorship. This was the policy of "socialist realism" which, when its meaning had been sorted out in the course of the next several years, came to be the ruling style of Soviet culture down to the present.

The repudiation of the RAPP enthusiasts had, apparently, two converging sources. In the first place, certain major Soviet literary figures, notably Maxim Gorky, were shocked by the low literary quality of the RAPP products. It is unlikely, however, that this purist judgment would in itself have led to the reversal of 1932, had it not also been judged that RAPP's work was bad and ineffective propaganda. The new approach under the Union of Soviet Writers maintained the dictatorial framework for Soviet literature created by RAPP, but provided a wider formula in the ambiguous concept of "socialist realism," whose object was, according to the 1932 statute of the Central Committee: [15] "The creation of works of high artistic significance, saturated with the heroic struggle of the world proletariat and with the grandeur of the victory of Socialism, and reflecting the great wisdom and heroism of the Communist Party . . . , the creation of artistic works worthy of the great age of Socialism." It took some time before the meaning of Socialist realism as a norm for Soviet artistic creation became clear. What has emerged, in fact, is a flow of novels, short stories, and plays in which traditional and conventional human situations are related to the policies and achievements of the Soviet regime in an optimistic setting. Experimentation in literary and artistic form was, by the mid-1930's, brought to a firm and rather dramatic end. The texture of Soviet writing over the past twenty years has a distinct popular flavor, not very different from the literature generated in the Western world for mass consumption. A mediocre Hollywood script writer might feel himself quite at home in modern Russia, insofar as story line, dialogue, and happy ending were concerned. Socialist realism in literature has thus proved to be extremely conservative in form and designed to interest what the Soviet rulers believe to be a mass market. It has carried, however, the additional requirement that its themes glorify the Soviet regime and its achievements. Thus, Soviet literature has retained its high propaganda content, although more dilute and less Marxist than in the days when Averbach rode high.

In music, Socialist realism has meant that composers are enjoined to send their audiences out into the streets whistling memorable tunes. Folk music and folk melodies woven into somewhat more sophisticated musical settings enjoy official blessing. In painting and sculpture "socialist realism" has meant the development of a calendar art strongly reminiscent of that encouraged by Hitler in Nazi Germany.

During the war the artistic restrictions under which Soviet creative artists operated were lifted in the sense that, so long as the themes put forward stimulated national patriotism, a greater degree

[15] *Ibid.*, p. 239.

of flexibility in form was permitted than in the decade which followed the formation of the Union of Soviet Writers. There is no doubt that the patriotism reflected in Soviet wartime poetry, novels, plays, and war reporting represented a more authentic expression of the artists' insights than anything which had come forth in the previous decade. And there is also little doubt that Soviet artists, along with the populace in general, looked in the postwar years to a long-term relaxation of the rigors of Stalin's dictatorship. They felt they had served their country and even the regime well during the war and that a new-found increase in mutual confidence might be (and certainly should be) perpetuated in the postwar years.

Against this background the tightening up in Soviet literature and the arts which began in 1945, and which took decisive form in the resolution of the Central Committee on August 14, 1946, was a serious blow. This resolution, associated with the period when Zhdanov dominated the Party under Stalin, reinstalled tight ideological direction for both form and content in Soviet literature and the arts. Typical of such Soviet initiatives, it singled out a few specific cases, focusing in particular on Zoshchenko, described as "scum of literature" and Akhmatova, "a typical representative of empty poetry which is devoid of ideas and alien to our people." In general the resolution proclaimed that: [16]

. . . Our magazines are a powerful weapon of the Soviet state in the task of educating the Soviet people, and especially of the young, and must therefore be guided by that which constitutes the essence of the Soviet order, namely its politics. The Soviet regime cannot tolerate the education of the young in a spirit of indifference to Soviet politics, in a spirit of pooh-poohism and of ideological neutrality. . . . All preaching of ideological neutrality, of apoliticalness, of "art for art's sake," is alien to Soviet literature.

With this decree the area of freedom regained during the war disappeared and Soviet arts lapsed back into the sterile mediocrity of the prewar decade—with an additional official requirement to dramatize the hostility of the external world, especially the evil represented by American life and America's alleged intentions toward the Soviet Union.

In the dreary story of Soviet cultural life since 1929 there is one tempering element which may prove in the long run to be of great importance. As part of the social and cultural consolidation of the mid-1930's, Stalin's policy not only rehabilitated Russian national-

[16] *Ibid.*, p. 330.

ism and the great historical figures of the Russian past, but it encouraged (on a selective basis) a respect for the Russian literary classics. An effort was made to present the new products of Socialist realism as continuous with the great achievements of the Russian past. This has meant that Soviet citizens, who remain by all accounts omnivorous readers, have had available to them the writings of Pushkin, Tolstoy, Chekhov, Turgenev, Gogol, and sporadically (but now out of favor), Dostoyevsky. Mr. George Denicke, in a perceptive statistical analysis,[17] has demonstrated the substantially greater popularity among Soviet citizens of prerevolutionary classics over the current output of the Soviet literary mill. Despite all manner of official efforts to push current approved writing, the number of copies of the classics sold far outweighs the newer products.

Denicke's hypothesis about Russian literary taste is strikingly corroborated by the evidence he has gathered on the relative popularity of plays produced in the Soviet theaters. By a decree of March 4, 1946, all Soviet theaters were ordered to become self-supporting. The system of direct or indirect subsidies was abolished. This test of consumer preference has resulted in a marked rise in attendance at prerevolutionary Russian plays as opposed to the Soviet plays. As a result of this unmistakable trend various *ad hoc* measures appear to have been taken in recent years to increase attendance at the current Soviet theatrical products.

One can even discern certain trends in public taste as among the Russian classics, notably a recent rise in popularity of Turgenev. The increasing vogue of so thoughtful and perceptive a writer, with his humane concern with the problems of the individual, is a fair indication that the cheap and superficial optimism projected in the works of socialist realism had not in fact come to dominate the outlook of Soviet citizens. More than that, perpetuation of the works of Russia's great creative period of the last century has undoubtedly kept alive, in one form or another, a knowledge of human values shared between Russia and the West which, in the long run, may prove an important solvent.

6. RELIGION

The evolution of Soviet policy with respect to religion demonstrates not only the general pattern of departure from initial revolu-

[17] "Links with the Past in Soviet Society," Series 3, No. 84, External Research Staff, Office of Intelligence Research, Department of State (Washington, D.C., Mar. 21, 1952).

tionary objectives but also the limitations of even modern totalitarianism in eradicating the more profound cultural foundations of
a society. Soviet policy begins with the clear objectives of (1) de-
stroying the power of organized religion; and (2) removing the hold
of religion over the minds of Soviet citizens. The story ends with
an uneasy acceptance of the fact of religious belief among large
sections of the Soviet populace and with an effort to harness this
intractable faith to support for the regime, notably through the
Orthodox Church.

Although its antireligious purposes did not figure among the
major slogans of the Bolshevik revolutionaries in November 1917,
Marx's and Lenin's views of religion as an instrument for sustaining
feudal and bourgeois societies were well known. In January 1918
the regime took over, without compensation, church properties and
soon instituted bans on religious education. Marriage and divorce
became monopolies of civil policy. Further, the members of the
priesthood were given the lowest possible position of status and
privilege in Soviet society.[18]

In the course of the NEP period, the churches managed to survive,
although they were subjected not only to sustained and well-
organized antireligious propaganda but also to sporadic guerrilla
warfare by the state in the form of tax policy, censorship of sermons,
etc.

The early phase of the First Five-Year Plan saw further incursions
on the churches, notably in rural areas during the phase of enforced
collectivization. Churches were closed on a large scale and substantial numbers of priests were sent to forced labor camps. The Militant Atheists League, the principal arm for propaganda and other
attacks on religion, reached a high point in its officially sponsored
power in these early years of the First Five-Year Plan.

From about the end of 1930 on, there appears to have been a
gradual reconsideration within the regime of what Soviet policy
toward religion and the churches should be. The crude ideological
attack of the Party, through the Atheists League, had destroyed
neither the churches nor their ministry; and it left at least half of
the Soviet population still regarding themselves as believers. Moreover, it may well have been that the association of collectivization
with attack on the church in rural districts had complicated the
practical problem of achieving collectivization. In any case, the

[18] See N. S. Timasheff, *Religion in Soviet Russia, 1917–1942* (London,
1944), p. 22 ff., on whose work this section draws substantially.

Militant Atheist League was curbed in its activities in the course of 1935 and 1936. On Christmas of 1935 the population was once more allowed to light Christmas trees, an act previously forbidden. In 1936 the manufacture of wedding rings resumed and the Constitution of 1936 ended the disenfranchisement of priests.

Symbolic of this period was the suppression of a version of one of Borodin's operas, *The Knights*, in which a burlesque of baptism was performed on the stage as a drunken farce. The Central Arts Committee closed the opera with an announcement which appeared to link a new respectful view of religion as part of Russian culture, with a new respect for prerevolutionary Russian history: [19]

It is well known that the Christianization of Russia was one of the principal factors in the rapprochement of the backward Russian people of Byzantium and later with the peoples of the West, namely with peoples of higher culture. It is also well known what a big part clergymen, particularly Greek clergymen, played in promoting literacy in the Russia of the Kiev period; thus from a historical standpoint Byedny's libretto is an example not only of anti-Marxist, but also of a frivolous attitude towards history and a cheapening of the history of our people.

The apparent dispensation for the Orthodox Church which emerged in 1936 was quickly violated from a direction more serious even than the Atheist League. Among the groups systematically attacked in the course of the Great Purge were ministers of various faiths who, like the others involved, were accused of a range of specific crimes allegedly designed to overthrow Stalin's regime with support from abroad. According to Timasheff,[20] during the year 1937, 1100 Orthodox Churches, 61 Protestant prayer houses, and 110 mosques were closed.

With the ending of the Great Purge, however, a more purposeful effort was made not merely to tolerate the continuance of formal religion in the Soviet Union but to harness it to the purposes of the regime. In 1939, as the danger of war became increasingly great, an informal concordat was arranged with the Greek Orthodox Church which, after the German attack on the Soviet Union of 1941, took on some importance. In the face of war the Soviet regime tried to harness every possible source of authentic resistance against the enemy, and religion, along with the Great Russian nationalist spirit to which it relates, was given an accentuated positive respectability

[19] *Ibid.*, p. 47.
[20] *Ibid.*, pp. 52–53.

in the regime's propaganda. Acting Patriarch Sergius, head of the Orthodox Church, played his part in this effort, stating at the time of the German attack: "We will not desert the nation now." Soviet propaganda against the Germans included the charge that they sought to end "the very existence of Christianity. . . ."

Since the war there has been something of a stable settlement between the regime and the Orthodox Church. The association of the regime and the Church was strengthened by government decrees in 1945 and 1946 which granted the right of corporate personality, for the holding of property, and relieved monasteries from taxes on land and buildings.[21] The Soviet regime under Stalin appeared to have been satisfied with the *de facto* arrangement which emerged just before and during World War II. The Church has, so far as we know, kept strictly away from anti-Communist politics and devoted itself to keeping alive the habits and substance of religious worship. As in the case of Great Russian nationalism, it was, apparently, Stalin's judgment that on the whole the continued existence of the Orthodox Church would strengthen his chances of mobilizing Great Russian nationalism as a force on the side of the regime; and, in addition, the vitality of the Church in Russia may be considered necessary to bind certain of the Eastern satellites to the Soviet Union. As Timasheff concludes: [22] "Both parties hate the compromise imposed on them by the force of circumstances, but do not see any way to modify it. Both continue hoping that the future will be theirs."

This has meant, however, that the other forms of religious worship carried on within the Soviet Union (excepting, perhaps, the Armenian Church and the Baptists) have not enjoyed the toleration under which the Orthodox Church now operates. Catholic, Protestant, Moslem, and Jewish believers have continued to suffer one form or another of chronic attack or harassment which is to be linked, in general, to the nature of the Soviet nationality policy in recent years.

7. HISTORY

In the first instance, Marxism is a theory of history. It is, therefore, peculiarly relevant to examine briefly the evolution of historiography under Soviet rule. The subtitle of such an exercise

---

[21] See N. S. Timasheff, "Religion in Russia, 1941–1950," in W. Gurian, ed., *The Soviet Union, A Symposium* (Notre Dame, Indiana, 1951).

[22] *Ibid.*, p. 194.

might well be "The Rise and Fall of Professor M. N. Pokrovsky." [23]

In the immediate postrevolutionary years Pokrovsky, who was Assistant Commissar of Education from 1918 on, played a role similar to that of the On Guardists in Soviet literature. He was the leader of an ardent Communist group of historians at a time when the Soviet system tolerated, side by side with its positive followers, an even larger group of historians who, while not positively anti-Bolshevik in their writing, were non-Communist in politics and linked to Western traditions of historical writing and method.

Professor Pokrovsky founded the Institute of Red Professors and the historical section within it designed to train Marxist-Leninist historians. In the period between 1925 and 1931 he built up the society of Marxist historians to a membership of 800; and, at the time of his death in 1932, he was honored as a major intellectual leader of Stalin's regime. He was buried with fanfare within the Kremlin wall.

It was only in 1929, however, that he achieved something like the intellectual dictatorship in his area that Averbach did through RAPP in literature. In that year the Institute of History was largely cleared of its "bourgeois" personnel. Historical writing began to show the lines of cultural policy in general, that is, it was, in substantial part, devoted to justifying and glorifying the First Five-Year Plan.

In the case of Pokrovsky's history this task—of using history to back the First Five-Year Plan—led to a considerable intellectual problem. Pokrovsky had been as pure and literal an economic determinist as one could find. He had even faced up to Engels' second thoughts on the possibly independent role of ideas in determining the course of history and had disposed of them by judging Engels unsound, since ideas themselves were the product of past economic facts and relationships.

The history which emerged under his hand and guidance was little more than an elaboration of the crudest Marxist historical sequence as laid out, for example, in the Communist Manifesto. Pokrovsky presented the history of Russia in the five classic Marxist stages: primitive Communism, slave-holding, feudalism, capitalism, and socialism. His economic determinism was, at times, even more

[23] This section is substantially indebted to the account of "M. N. Pokrovsky and the Impact of the First Five-Year Plan on Soviet Historiography," a paper delivered by Paul H. Aron before the Russian Research Center at Harvard in 1950, and used as background, with his kind permission.

literal. Aron indicates that Pokrovsky was quite prepared to interpret the major movements, during the nineteenth century, in Russian policy toward land and the peasants as a simple reflex of movements in the grain price. How, then, could he cope with the notion of a Five-Year Plan, instituted as a conscious act of history, by a great leader, and representing a purposeful effort to create the historical sequence out of which Communism itself might ultimately evolve. In the language Pokrovsky had been using over the course of his professional life, the First Five-Year Plan represented an outrageous initiative by the political superstructure designed to alter the economic base of society.

The work of Pokrovsky's school over this period represented an *ad hoc* compromise. It continued to purvey a mechanical deterministic conception of history covering the past, but dealt with the Five-Year Plan in the terms of current propaganda, as an independently initiated heroic act by the Party and its leader.

The anomaly of an economically determinist history being written at a time when the state and its rulers sought to behave like a Hegelian hero was not fully resolved until January 1936, when Pokrovsky was posthumously denounced as a "vulgar determinist" and Soviet history, along with the rest of its social and cultural life, moved into a new stage judged more consistent with and helpful to the bureaucratic dictatorship which had, in fact, emerged over the previous years. As in the case of literature, it took some time before the historians fully adjusted themselves to the new criteria of what was historically correct. The Soviet history that has emerged preserves a Marxist surface and a Marxist vocabulary but represents, in many ways, a reversion to the norms of history as written and taught in Russia before 1914. Russian history itself is now presented with more attention to its unique features and less attention to rigid historical stages. The special problems and destiny of Russia and its peoples have the stage in a sense in which they did not when Pokrovsky was in the saddle. Above all, the role of great individual figures in shaping Russian history—notably Ivan and Peter the Great—was revived. One of the tasks of recent Soviet history has been to place Stalin not only in the sequence of Marx, Engels, and Lenin, but also in the sequence of Russia's great national rulers.

In accord with this process of revision, Stalin himself undertook to direct the preparation of a "Short History of the Communist Party of the Soviet Union," in 1938. This document, of which some 31 million copies are officially stated to have been printed by 1946, presents the evolution of the Russian Communist Party from 1883, when the Social Democratic Party was created, down to the Great Purge (1939 English edition). Stalin is systematically presented as a key figure, second only to Lenin. The book as a whole seeks to make Stalin's personal dictatorship and his theories of the state consistent with the Communist ideological past on the one hand, and the ultimate attainment of a true Communist state on the other. It launched an extraordinary phase of history-rewriting, with gross falsification of evidence, which has spread out now into the satellite states and must absorb a high proportion of the time and effort of modern Communist historians.

Like the modern Soviet theory of the state and current theories of psychology and education, Soviet history has become increasingly a glorification of the deeds of men who, by a combination of will and an understanding of correct historical laws, pushed history along its proper paths. The true ancestry of modern Soviet historiography lies elsewhere than in the writings of Karl Marx.

Chapter Seven

THE ROLE OF RUSSIA IN THE EVOLUTION OF THE SOVIET STATE

1. THE RUSSIAN HERITAGE

IT IS the burden of this essay that the current state of Soviet society is to be understood in terms of the complex interaction over time among the sectors of that society, consequent upon the creation of a bureaucratized dictatorship dedicated to the maintenance and enlargement of its power within Russia and vis-à-vis the external world. The nature of this interaction and, therefore, the precise forms which Soviet society has taken, have been partially determined by an inescapable historical continuity imposed on the regime. This continuity arises, simply, from the fact that the whole process occurred in a specific country, Russia, at a particular stage of its long history, under specific conditions and in relation to certain cultural forces not susceptible to rapid change. This chapter seeks to summarize briefly the nature and mode of operation of such distinctively national elements. It aims to account for certain Russian aspects of Soviet society and Soviet policy. In particular the discussion seeks to focus on the manner whereby those physical and cultural factors which have determined the nature of Russian civilization in general have also had their influence on the policies, techniques, and mannerisms of the Soviet state.

Even the extremely powerful instruments which a twentieth-century dictatorship has at its command leave largely outside the control of the state certain important aspects of the life of people. In fact, one of the weapons which dictatorships exploit is the fact that the priority of motivations among ordinary citizens places politics and the exercise of political power relatively low on their scales of interest.

In most societies human beings appear to be concerned, in the first instance, with the adequacy of food and shelter for themselves and their families, with their personal lives, and with their security. A modern dictatorship can, indeed, interfere with these intimate human pursuits; and such interferences contribute to the tensions which exist within Soviet society and which can be noted in other modern dictatorships. Nevertheless, any general evaluation of Soviet society must recognize that it is made up for the most part of people who continue to talk; to live; to govern their marriage, family, and home lives, and tastes along lines which remain largely continuous with a past much longer than the Soviet regime.

This fact has contributed significantly to the social, cultural, and intellectual policies which the Soviet regime has come to regard as efficient instruments for dealing with its peoples. The criterion of efficient short-run operation, in a given society, imposes on its dictatorial rulers a discipline which is similar to, but distinguishable from, the discipline involved in societies where the identification of the ruler and the people's interest is more direct.

There has been in recent years some speculation as to the relationship between certain elements in Russian culture and the present dictatorship. Hypotheses have been advanced which would imply that extreme Russian individualism may be, somehow, linked to a requirement for absolute authority. Russian habits with respect to the swaddling of infants have also been advanced as basic to a predilection for dictatorial rule from above. These hypotheses— modestly advanced as clues rather than conclusions and by no means accepted generally by anthropologists—have not been developed in such a way as yet to make a persuasive link between the cultural characteristics asserted and the Russian political process. In particular, it is evident that many societies, in the past and at present, have found themselves under political dictatorship. In each case, looking backward from the existence of dictatorship, it is possible to isolate a good many factors in the history of the society which made it likely and possible, if not inevitable, that some form of political dictatorship would emerge. It is also evident that the political outcome might have been different if forces less profound than those rooted in the society's culture had not been what they were. In short, there is as yet no firm basis for moving directly from observations about real or alleged aspects of the Russian culture, in its anthropological sense, to its recent political experience.

It is clear, however, that certain aspects of the Russian position as of 1917, less significant than its cultural foundations, but, perhaps, ultimately related to them, contributed to the possibility of violent revolution and to successful Bolshevik exploitation of it. There were, in the first instance, the setbacks in the field of the tsarist armies and the incapacity of the tsarist regime to adjust to the forces set in motion by these defeats. Secondly, the antitsarist, non-Communist groups were split among themselves and were incapable of unifying or of mobilizing enough power to defeat the Bolsheviks in the cities where power was seized. Thirdly, those who led the civil war were incapable of offering any alternative except anti-Bolshevism at a time when the Russian people apparently felt the need for fundamental changes in the objectives and organization of their society. As a contemporary observer of the civil war has recently written: [1] ". . . there was no reason to suppose that any substantial part of the population desired a return to the pre-revolutionary order. That is the primary reason for the failure of the 'White Guardist' movement which offered the people no better prospects than return of the discredited Tsarist regime."

It may be concluded, then, that the weakness and narrowness of the democratic tradition in Russia as of 1917 significantly contributed to the possibility of the Bolshevik *coup d'état* and to ultimate Bolshevik victory in the civil war. No realistic alternative was effectively crystallized out of the diverse non-Communist majority interests and offered to the Russian people.

2. THE IMPERATIVES OF THE PURSUIT OF POWER IN TWENTIETH-CENTURY RUSSIA

Having seized power, the Soviet regime soon confronted a range of forces which strongly influenced the real possibilities open to it. These fundamental facts of Russian life helped determine the forms which an effort to consolidate and enlarge the regime's power would assume. The Bolsheviks were operating, in the first instance, within the physical boundaries of the Russian Empire. The natural resources available were given, as were the existing agricultural and industrial potential. The level of education and the skills of the peoples under their control were at a stage determined by prior Russian history. Put another way, the exercise of power from the

[1] From an unpublished manuscript on German-Soviet relations by Gustav Hilger and Alfred G. Meyer.

geographical, social, and economic base of Russia as of 1917 (and the several decades thereafter) determined largely the forms which the pursuit of power would take both at home and abroad.

At home the enlargement of power meant an acceleration of the industrialization process which had been going on rapidly in Russia for some decades before World War I, notably since the mid-1890's. It meant seeking increased productivity in Russian agriculture and coping with the aspirations of the peasantry for their own land, problems long familiar in prerevolutionary Russian history. It meant coming to terms with the nationalities question which, as in the case of the peasantry, Lenin did by making important concessions in 1921 with the installation of the NEP. And it required making some sort of policy toward the heritage of Russian culture, including religion. As described earlier, this was ultimately accomplished by abandoning, to a degree, the substantive radicalism of the Bolshevik Revolution and making important compromises with the persistent facts of Russian cultural life. Repeating an old tsarist pattern, the general formula adopted has been to permit a degree of cultural and religious latitude while insuring not only that the political power of the state has not been obstructed, but also that if possible, it has been strengthened by the presence of traditionalist strands.

To some extent, however, the regime has sought to change the patterns of Russian culture at its roots. Populations in the nationalities areas—notably the Ukraine and the Caucasus—have been moved, and they have been diluted by the Great Russian immigration; antireligious propaganda has been sustained; extraordinary efforts have been made to project and imprint the image of the New Soviet Man, energetic, disciplined, unquestioningly loyal to the state. But the New Soviet Man is, after all, a version of the ideal tsarist subject, placing loyalty to the state above any other standard for action, although transplanted into a changing industrial society where energy and an ability to adapt have been added to the continuing and overriding criteria of discipline and loyalty to the state. In a throwback to deterministic Marxism the regime has flirted in recent years with the notion that the moving of the peasant to larger more urbanized concentrations might diminish his attachment to the concept of private ownership of land and other traditional aspirations which have resisted two decades of preponderantly collectivized life. On balance, however, the regime has tended to recognize increasingly its incapacity to alter radically the anthropological foundations of Russian life; it has sought, rather, to neutralize them or to put them positively to its use.

Geographically, any regime seeking to maintain and, if possible, enlarge its power from the Russian base would be confronted with similar, if not identical, concrete issues. Russian history and, in a wider sense, Russian civilization have been profoundly influenced by the problems of organizing internally a coherent state over a vast area and defending that state from external assault along its extensive and vulnerable frontiers. From the Muscovite Grand Duchy forward the physical problems of governing, in the primitive sense noted above, have obsessed the Russian state.

Externally, toward the West there was the problem of the European balance of power and especially of relations to Germany. Any Russian regime attempting to increase its power vis-à-vis the outside world in the years after 1918 might well have explored the possibilities of agreement with Germany with a view toward sharing of power in Eastern Europe. Any Russian regime might well have confronted also the danger that Germany, in its pursuit of power, might encroach on Russian spheres of influence and might even be tempted to conquer and annex important parts of the Russian Empire. Similarly, increased power over the Dardanelles and in the Baltic might well have emerged as part of the substance of the pursuit of power for any Russian regime; and so also in the Far East, with Manchuria, Korea, Sakhalin, etc. Whatever the motivations or techniques employed, the maintenance and pursuit of power from certain geographical bases leads to similar forms of enterprise. As indicated at the end of this section, however, it is, in our judgment, incorrect to draw from these observations the conclusion that the Soviet regime is simply another example of Russian autocracy.

3. THE PATTERN OF RUSSIAN AUTOCRACY AND SOVIET RULE

The national characteristics of a society, created by a very long process, are bound to leave their mark on its political techniques—even when political rule is arbitrarily imposed. The extent of historical continuity in Russia is indicated by comparing the operative character of the Soviet regime with the main characteristics of tsarism over the years 1500–1900, as summarized by B. H. Sumner: [2]

(a) The semi-sacrosanct personification of authority in a supreme ruler whose power, though closely circumscribed by the weight of

[2] B. H. Sumner, A Short History of Russia (New York, 1949), pp. 84–85.

custom and dependence on the landed and military classes, never became explicitly limited by clearly formulated or regularly operative checks of a legal or institutional kind, and frequently was of decisive consequence.

(b) The conception of service to the state to be enforced in some form or other, first from all land, later from all groups of subjects, a conception that was never fully realized in practice, though it was more and more effectively applied until the middle of the eighteenth century.

(c) The application of this conception of service to the landed class in such a way that not only must no land go out of service, but all land must be in service, with the result that all land came to be regarded in the last resort as under some control of the Tsar.

(d) The linking up of the idea of service with that of the omnipotence of the state, of its unlimited range of action (except, prior to Peter the Great, in regard to the church), of the state as the creator and not merely the regulator of all associations within it, other than the church.

(e) The lack of differentiation between legislative, administrative, and judicial functions and the development of a centralized bureaucracy on an exceptionally large scale, corresponding to the exceptionally wide range of state control and extent of the empire.

(f) The paramountcy of the military needs of the state, which made the army, directly and indirectly, the first concern of tsarism and intensified the use of force and arbitrary police action in government.

These six characteristics inevitably took on various hues in the course of four hundred years, and in the nineteenth century a seventh appeared —the attempt to impose uniformity in the greater part of the vast and polyglot Romanov empire.

There is no doubt that the prevailing formal tradition of Russian government over the past five and a half centuries has been autocratic. The Soviet regime is, in an important sense, in the direct line of succession to Muscovite rule. Mobilization, in the context of an unstable world balance of power, of wide-spread resources and a heterogeneous population (including self-conscious nationality groups) has helped make chronic in Russian history highly centralized regimes which have demanded the subordination to their needs of the interests of all elements of society.

Despite persistent efforts by various powerful elements of Russian society to decentralize authority, grand dukes and tsars were proved able to effect their claim to ultimate authority. No competing institution could gain sufficient sustained support. Through councils and assemblies, the bureaucracy, the military, and various strata of the nobility shared considerable authority from the sixteenth century on. They legislated and even designated who the autocrat would be; but they were never able to control him for long or to overthrow the principle of autocracy.

At times—usually in periods of weakness or crisis—the ruling family and various elements of the nobility in the Royal Council, the Assembly of the Land (Zemsky Sobor), the Privy Council, and Senate shared the authority of the state. The Assembly, which legislated infrequently and appointed tsars, was without juridical foundation and had lost all real authority before Peter arbitrarily abolished it. The Ruling Senate, like the bureaucracy, was never more than a consultative administrative and judicial body. In the eighteenth and early nineteenth centuries the nobility, through its strategic control of the palace guard, was able to designate the autocrat; but it was unable to maintain its control. It failed signally, in the revolt of December 1825, to achieve fundamental change in the structure of the state.

In the half-century before 1914, however, pressures increased for a system of government with greater distribution of power. It is misleading to identify governments autocratic in conception and form with the substance of autocracy, i.e., the effective centralization of key decisions and the predominance of the state's own interest in the content of those decisions. In these terms there is little doubt that, while the forms of autocracy remained virtually to 1917, deeper Russian trends ran strongly in the other direction. The substance of autocracy has varied over Russian history; and, even at its peak, as Sumner notes, it was tempered by "the weight of custom and dependence on landed and military classes."

In general, the ninteenth-century Council of State enjoyed only a consultative influence, but in 1905 that body was transformed into a controlled upper house along the lines of Prussia's parliamentary system. The increasing influence of liberal Western ideology in court circles, the nobility, and intelligentsia was reflected in the designation of local authority to the Zemstvo organizations. The acts of these organizations were always subject to the veto of the provincial governor, and their authority was progressively restricted by the bureaucracy. Nevertheless, in them an element of grass-roots democracy had taken limited hold on the Russian scene. The spread of the concepts and values of Western liberalism and socialism, as well as the appearance of a small but growing industrial and commercial middle class, had evident consequences. The new groups demanded a greater influence on national policy; but they evoked, at first, only a firmer insistence by autocracy on its divinely ordained absolutism. The growing antagonism between these Western-oriented elements, backed by growing peasant discontent, and the central authority, with its swollen bureaucracy (staffed largely with the declining nobility), contributed to and provided leadership for the 1905 upheaval and its achievement of a Western parliamentary structure in the Duma. This body, too, however, was subject to increasing restriction and the imperial veto, and could not influence cabinet appointments or other decisive acts of government. Thus the actual operation of the autocratic machinery persisted much as before 1905 until its patent incapacity to deal with the war crisis swept it from the scene in 1917.

The parliamentary tradition dating, somewhat arbitrarily, from the French Revolution, had evidently grown rapidly in Russia in the pre-1914 decades. But it had struck insufficiently deep roots in the popular consciousness to dominate the chaos of 1917. Its liberal and socialist leadership was split and indecisive in the face of peasant and worker demands released by the March Revolution and the urgent requirements of either fighting the war effectively or making peace. In these circumstances the Bolshevik minority of about 25 per cent, with a positive program, a unified command, and a keen sense of power tactics, won support among key urban groups, as well as elements among soldiers and peasants, and took over power with comparative ease. The balance of forces represented in the Constituent Assembly certainly reflected the aspirations of Russia more nearly than did the Bolsheviks. The majority simply proved incapable of making itself effective in the anarchy of 1917.

There is an important sense, then, in which the Soviet state is a reversion, in Russian history, away from a historic trend. The half-century before 1914 had seen the rise of ideas and reluctantly-granted institutions which moved Russia away from the deeply imbedded autocratic tradition. The Zemstvos, Zemgor (a popular institution which more or less took upon itself certain important aspects of military provisioning during World War I), and the Duma were in being and were demonstrating their ability, in a limited way, to meet and especially to articulate popular needs. Widening elements of the population were becoming aware of the meaning of democratic ideas.

Evidently, the strength of this evolving democratic pattern of thought and behavior was inadequate to master the situation in

1917. Russia reverted to an extreme version of autocracy. The verbal concessions of the Soviet Constitution reflect, nevertheless, the underlying popular vitality of elements in the democratic tradition. It is by no means unthinkable that, in the long run, the trend of the pre-1914 decades will resume and triumph over the older tradition of absolute centralized state power in Russia, although the timing, the process, and the vicissitudes of such an evolution can not be predicted. The analogies between Stalin, Peter the Great, and Ivan the Terrible are real enough. It is partly because Soviet rule is a throwback that such analogies are so persuasive. But Russia's history has not been static. The evolution of Russia from 1861 to 1917 resulted from forces which the Soviet regime has contained or distorted but not eliminated from the operative determinants of Russia's future.

4. RUSSIAN NATIONALISM AND THE SOVIET REGIME

The written record of Russian history reveals a long tradition of awareness of nation, or at least of common culture. This strand of national attachment was associated with and developed by the long struggle for national security, internal and external, and by a reaction against, as well as an acceptance of, Western cultural infiltration. Russian nationalism has persistently incorporated a profound, primitive attachment to the Russian land. The expansion of education and the growing influence of Western ideology in the nineteenth century gave modern Russian nationalism a fairly broad popular base by the outbreak of World War I.

The practical significance of Russian national feeling was made evident to the Soviet regime during the period of foreign intervention after the Revolution; and by the mid-thirties the Party leadership revealed a determination to transform it into an asset of the regime. The force of this feeling was made apparent by the reaction of Russian troops and peoples both before and after German policy in Russia had defined itself in 1941–42. The large-scale defections in the first phase of the war and the initial reaction of certain nationality groups were matched by the profundity of the nationalism (and notably Great Russian nationalism) which asserted itself as Hitler identified himself as perhaps the most ruthless in the long succession of foreign invaders. The regime apparently made an appraisal along the following lines:

1. The Russian peoples are quite unprepared to fight for a Communist regime as such, and they might even be prepared to defect

in large numbers to a foreign enemy in the hope that the Soviet regime might be overthrown and an alternative Russian government installed.

2. On the other hand, the Russian people appear prepared to rally around a strictly nationalist effort to overcome a foreign invasion when the foreign power fails to offer a dignified national alternative to the Soviet system.

3. Of all the peoples of the Soviet Union those of Great Russia are, in the national sense, the most reliable.

Major and dramatic concessions were thus made to Great Russian nationalism in the course of the war. The conclusions drawn concerning popular motivations, which were continuous with the line of thought underlying Stalin's policy since 1934, appear to have been carried over into the postwar period, despite the re-assertion of ideological conformity which has also marked the past several years. Efforts to identify the regime with Russian nationalism in the face of a hostile world have been accentuated, even as compared with the mid-1930's. This has involved in particular a systematic effort to portray American purposes with respect to Russia in the image of Hitler's actions. Finally, a decision has been made to rely heavily on the nationalism of Great Russia. A purposeful appeal to this majority element has been made, and such costs as may be involved in exacerbated feelings among the nationality groups have been accepted.

5. THE RUSSIAN HERITAGE AND THE PRIORITY OF POWER

The human and physical materials of Russia have thus strongly affected the content of Soviet policy. They have helped alter almost beyond recognition the character of the regime's ideology. They have helped determine the concrete objectives, internal and external, which the regime has sought in its efforts to consolidate and enlarge its power.

There is, moreover, a significant interweaving of Russian elements with the patterns of Marxist thought. Three major points of convergence between Marxism and the Russian heritage can, in particular, be noted.

First, the concept of conflict between the socialist state and its capitalist environment links well to the history of Russia's awkward relations to the Western world, with its differing religious and cultural foundations, periodic conflicts and invasions. It is notable that, while both Marxist and national elements are invoked in Soviet

The divorce of the regime from the nation it governs is firmly crystal-lized in attitudes and institutions whose change now would consti-tute virtually another revolution.

A similar foundation exists for the maintenance of a relation of extreme and persistent hostility to the outside world. In the first instance, important elements in the Bolshevik regime regarded its victory as merely a tactical phase in a world revolutionary uprising. This view of the matter was appreciated abroad and led to a certain amount of ill-feeling toward the Bolsheviks as well as to counter-revolutionary intervention in Russia. The reaction of the Soviet state, in turn, was a compound of ideological and national feeling. The success of Soviet resistance at this early stage dramatized the value of an external enemy as a rationale for the internal policy of the regime. And thus the external enemy came to be virtually in-stitutionalized as a permanent feature of Soviet policy.

The Russian mannerisms of the Soviet regime are, then, to be regarded as the consequence of the tactics of pursuing power from a Russian base; they represent more nearly the long-run infiltration of an occupation regime by the area and society it rules than a direct national phenomenon determined by the aspirations of the Russian peoples or by an emotional identification of the rulers of the state with those peoples.

To put this conclusion another way, Russian geography, culture, and its historical position as of 1917 certainly set limits within which any regime would have had to operate over the succeeding three and a half decades. Forces were at work that any regime would have had to cope with and, in one form or another, reflect if it were to re-main effectively in power. The Soviet regime is deeply marked by certain stable or slow-changing elements in the cultural life of Russia. But it appears analytically important to remember that Russian life had and has the capability of producing, from the same limiting foundations, other forms of government and societal organ-ization. And it appears important in the making of policy toward the Soviet Union not to confuse the operative motivations of the regime toward its own peoples or the outside world with the national mannerisms it has acquired.

Chapter Eight

SOVIET FOREIGN RELATIONS

1. INTRODUCTION

SOVIET relations with the external world have, in general, come to be governed by the same empirical criteria for the exercise of power which evolved in Soviet internal policy. One can observe in the immediate postrevolutionary years a similar struggle between inherited ideological notions and the raw limitations which the historical environment imposed on the new Soviet state. From 1917 to 1923 Lenin made a series of foreign policy decisions which were governed by short-run practical power considerations. As in internal policy, these set the format which Stalin more fully elaborated. After an ineffective rear-guard action, those who clung to an ideological basis for Soviet foreign policy were eliminated from effective power by 1929 and, for the most part, were physically eliminated by the end of the Great Purge a decade later.

On balance, the foreign policy techniques of the Soviet state have been generally conventional and its performance similar to that of other ambitious national states with the following important exceptions:

1. As in internal policy, a residue of what might be called "ideological rationale" for foreign policy has been maintained and applied in those circumstances where it has been judged empirically to be useful or where it has not conflicted with the maintenance and enlargement of Soviet power.

2. In particular, the Soviet state has, with a few recent exceptions, maintained direct control over Communist parties abroad and has manipulated their policies, on an ostensibly ideological basis, to conform to changing judgments concerning the power needs of the Soviet state.

3. An ideological residue has combined with the needs of internal

135

policy to maintain the Soviet state in a posture of almost continuous hostility to the external world; this hostility is aggressive in the particular sense that, within the limits imposed by its prime goal of protecting its control over Soviet domestic society and the perhaps unconscious limits imposed by the techniques it is prepared to use, the regime seeks, as opportunity may offer, to expand indefinitely its external power.

4. The status of direct authority acquired in Eastern Europe by the Soviet regime after World War II has led to a progressive imposition of a system of total control which has reflected fully the patterns of contemporary Soviet internal policy.

5. The system of internal controls, including information controls, has permitted the Soviet regime, notably since 1929, to alter its foreign policy tactics more sharply than is possible in societies where governments are dependent on the understanding and consent of public opinion.

There is no evidence that before 1939 Soviet foreign policy was governed by a serious long-range plan, as opposed to long-run hopes and ambitions. It appears to have responded to problems, threats, and possibilities thrown up by the course of events outside the Soviet Union which it was, for the most part, incapable of determining or controlling. Its response took the form of such actions as were judged most likely, on a short-range basis, to maintain or expand the national power of the Soviet regime. Further, over this period the Soviet regime chose in general to forego an enlargement of its external power on occasions where such enlargement was judged to involve major risks to the internal stability of its national base. Similarly, in the conduct of its relations with Communist parties abroad the Soviet regime has chosen to maintain absolute control over their policies, and to govern those policies on the basis of the believed short-run interest of the Soviet Union rather than permit the parties abroad those forms of organization and policy which would maximize their effective power in their own areas. Although the post-1945 status of the Soviet regime in Eastern Europe and the development of Communism in Asia and the Middle East have given the Soviet regime a new and more promising environment in which to operate, there is no evidence that the foreign policy criteria of the regime have changed.

2. THE CASE OF BREST-LITOVSK

The first great issue of foreign policy confronted by the Soviet regime in November 1917 was the issue of war or peace with Germany. It evoked a searching conflict between ideology and the short-run requirements of Soviet internal power, which was decided in favor of the latter. In a sense the decision foreshadowed much of future Soviet policy, internal as well as external.

Failure to carry out either a successful war or an effective peace policy had been largely responsible for the weakness of the Provisional Government, and immediate cessation of hostilities had been a cardinal point in Bolshevik appeals throughout 1917. At the same time, the idea of a world revolutionary struggle was prominent in the minds of many Bolshevik leaders and imbedded at the core of their ideology. Yet Lenin, and gradually more of his followers, insisted at every turn on the priority of attainable interests, first among which was the maintenance of the Soviet position in Petrograd and Moscow. This view could, of course, be argued within the Party as a necessary means to achieve the ultimate purposes of world communism; but, as generally, the end actually attained was heavily determined by the means, and the priority of the Russian base has conflicted at every turn with the cause of world Communism and given that peculiar movement its present cast.

On November 8, 1917, Lenin read to the Congress of Soviets a "Decree of Peace" proposing immediate negotiations with all belligerent powers for a "just and democratic peace," without annexations and without indemnities.[1] A separate peace, with the conception of a Russian Communist evolution in isolation, was definitely not yet part of the Bolshevik platform, based as that program still was on the anticipation of an international workers' revolt. But when it became clear that the Allies were not favorable to peace talks, the Bolsheviks made formal application (November 26) to the German High Command for an immediate armistice for the purpose of concluding peace. Two days later a cease-fire order went out to all Russian troops, and on December 15 a four-week armistice was concluded with the Central Powers.

The Russian delegates did not come to the conference at Brest-Litovsk as old-style diplomats. They used every opportunity to spread revolutionary propaganda and to ridicule their German an-

[1] Cf. J. W. Wheeler-Bennett, *The Forgotten Peace, Brest-Litovsk, March 1918* (New York, 1939), p. 69.

tagonists before the outside world. Their two-fold purpose was to advance the cause of world revolution at the same time as they were bargaining for terms for Soviet Russia. But it is significant that Lenin realized as early as January 1918 that his expectation about the rising proletariat of Europe, particularly of Germany, was wrong, and that his principal attainable, though by no means assured, goal was the consolidation of the November Revolution in Russia.

Fortunately for the unity of the Bolshevik Party, plans for the delayed world revolution and for the consolidation of the Soviet regime were not yet in conflict. Both aims called for a "breathing space" at this time, and Trotsky the spellbinder was sent to replace Joffe at Brest-Litovsk, with instructions to prolong the discussion as much as possible.

The details of the peace negotiations need not be rehearsed here. The Allies continued to be unresponsive, Europe's industrial workers did not rise, and the German High Command rejected Trotsky's "no indemnities, no annexations" proposals. In answer to the German counter-proposals Trotsky requested an adjournment and returned to Petrograd for consultation.

In spite of continued accusations of being a German agent, Lenin insisted on immediate peace. In his famous "Twenty-one Theses" he put his position very simply:

The Russian Socialist Government is confronted with a question which requires an immediate solution: either to accept the annexation- ist peace or to start at once a revolutionary war. . . . The question whether it is possible to undertake at once a revolutionary war must be answered solely from the point of view of actual conditions and the in- terest of the Socialist Revolution which has already begun. . . .

Bukharin, however, led an enthusiastic group within the Party in favor of immediate revolutionary war; and Trotsky hit upon the formula "no war no peace" by which the Soviet government would simply declare the war ended without accepting any terms in antici- pation that the German Command would not then order its troops to advance—a formula perhaps not forgotten by recent Communist negotiators in Korea.

In the winter of 1918 control of policy was more directly depend- ent on opinion within and without the Party than it later became, and thus Lenin had to compromise. With great misgivings he yielded to Trotsky's formula, with which the latter returned to Brest-Litovsk. As Lenin had feared, the slogan was no more effective than its predecessors had been; less than a week after the formula had been pronounced, General Hoffmann ordered his troops to advance. Chastened by the failure of its first attempt at revolutionary orthodoxy on the international scene, Soviet policy now had to follow the line urged by Lenin, who had enough of that "very pretty fairy tale"—World Revolution.

German terms had stiffened. In fact, they now proposed what the Bolsheviks regarded as a "shameful peace." But there was no Russian army, and the Revolution in Russia had to be saved. And so, although he was called "traitor," "Judas," and "German spy," Lenin won the fight within the Party. The German peace terms were accepted. The priority of the Soviet Russian Revolution and the priority of actual over potential circumstances were established.

3. THE ELABORATION OF PRACTICAL INTERNATIONAL POLITICS, 1918–33

With few exceptions the primacy of domestic power considerations established in the discussion over Brest-Litovsk has remained paramount in Soviet foreign policy decisions. In terms of the maintenance of power, the principal need in the spring of 1918 was to save Petrograd and to preserve the regime's base. Therefore Brest-Litovsk had to be signed. In the next few years the general aims of the Soviet government were equally obvious and practical: to preserve itself, the regime required termination of foreign intervention, noninterference in Russia's domestic affairs, and lifting of the blockade and the trade restrictions imposed by the victorious Allies.

The Versailles Treaty, though annulling Brest-Litovsk, deliberately isolated Russia and created a *cordon sanitaire* of buffer states. The Soviets, in riposte, initiated a series of bilateral agreements with the Baltic countries (February–August, 1920), recognizing their independence and establishing diplomatic relations. Similar agreements were concluded with Finland, Persia, Afghanistan, China, and Turkey. Eventually, after a seesaw military struggle, Russia also made peace with Poland. By 1921, about the same time that the civil war ended, the Soviet government had attained the primary initial aim of its external policy, that is, freedom from outside disturbance. While the Soviet state was still diplomatically isolated from the major powers, there was no longer a military threat; and all the neighboring states had resumed relations. Principles such as the inevitability of world revolution and self-determination were applied where they were judged useful in terms of the real possibilities and disregarded where not. By the time fighting ended, the Soviet government controlled the Ukraine, Georgia, and most of Northern Asia, but not the other states formerly belonging to the Tsar.

At the same time the Soviet leaders forced the establishment of the Communist International (Comintern), on the assumption that revolutions outside Russia were necessary for preservation of the Soviet Revolution. After the fall of Bela Kun in Hungary and the failure of the various German Communist attempts, this consideration seems to have become ever less important in the minds of those Soviet leaders who dominated the Party. Nevertheless, the Comintern provided a convenient means for keeping in contact with the outside world despite the isolation implicit in the Versailles settlement, and it afforded, as well, a limited instrument for exercising a degree of Soviet power abroad. The Comintern's usefulness in these secondary roles was judged sufficient to justify its maintenance on practical grounds, although its interests have been systematically overridden when they conflicted with those of the Soviet regime.

In the period of the twenties the main concern of the Bolshevik leaders was the consolidation of their domestic political base and the economic reconstruction of the country they now effectively controlled. Although the Revolution was secure in the sense that Russian territory remained more or less intact and no immediate alternative to Soviet rule was in sight, problems of internal economic and political management demanded enormous efforts and presented a primary threat to the regime. The failures of War Communism had revealed the administrative inadequacies of the Soviet state. The building of an efficient bureaucracy occupied a considerable proportion of the energies of the leadership as did, of course, their internecine struggle for the succession to Lenin.

Russia was under further pressure to establish reasonably conventional international arrangements in order to acquire foreign economic assistance. However distasteful this was to the Bolshevik leaders, Lenin's Party was determined not to be bound to "revolutionary phrases." As early as 1919 there had been tentative proposals for Anglo-Russian trade talks; and by 1922 Soviet Russia had already concluded trade agreements with Turkey, the Balkan countries, Norway, Austria, and Italy. When the opportunity came to capitalize on the disunity of the Allies and their hostility to Germany, Soviet diplomacy took full advantage, broke up the Genoa conference, where the powers had been discussing questions of recognition, economic aid, and the repudiated tsarist debts with Soviet representatives. The USSR then proceeded to conclude with Germany the Treaty of Rapallo, whereby the two powers ostracized by the European concert agreed to political and economic co-operation. The German and the Russian diplomat skilfully played cat-and-mouse both with each other and with the Versailles powers in a thoroughly traditional manner; and both emerged with highly favorable agreements on reparations, secret military collaboration, and economic assistance. Thereafter one nation after another, except the United States (until 1933), accorded recognition to the Soviet government. The political regime of the foreign country never deterred the Bolshevik leaders—even Fascist Italy signed a pact with the Soviet Union in 1924. The Soviet Union began to frequent international economic and disarmament conferences, though still denouncing the League of Nations in principle.

Within this developing framework of conventional arrangements, the Comintern continued to operate, often to the embarrassment of Russian policy. The fall of the British Labour Government in connection with the Zinoviev affair (1924), continued nonrecognition by the U.S., and the general distrust with which Europe viewed Russia are doubtless traceable to fear of Comintern activity. But certainly after the abortive rising in Germany in 1923, the Soviet regime accorded a low priority to the encouragement of European Communism. The debacle in China in 1927 completed the practical isolation of Communism and confirmed the primacy of Stalin's already enunciated doctrine of "socialism in one country." It is significant that the Comintern held only one World Congress between 1924 and 1935, and held that one (1928) to give its blessing to what was in effect an act of Russian isolationism—the decision to proceed with accelerated industrialization on a strictly national basis.

So long as no power seemed to be a direct threat to Russia's development, it was in the interest of the Soviet Union to support generalized antiwar and disarmament proposals, given the dominant concern of the regime with internal problems. Major allies were neither needed nor available, and disarmament could have no disadvantage for the least armed and economically weakest power. Moreover, the more Chicherin or Litvinov talked peace and took pains to dissociate themselves from the Comintern, the more likely the Soviet Union was to receive favorable treatment from the West.

Thus Litvinov announced Russia's adherence to the Kellogg Pact in 1926 and proposed total disarmament to the League's disarmament commission in 1927. Early in 1927 he proclaimed the Litvinov Protocol whereby Russia, Poland, Esthonia, Latvia, and Rumania accepted the Kellogg Pact and renounced war. Finland, France, Persia, and Italy were added in the years 1930–33 to the Russian system of nonaggression pacts.

The extent of the regime's concentration on domestic affairs was shown during the world economic crisis of 1929–33. What would seem to have been a partial vindication of the Marxist prophecy of increasingly severe capitalist crises, and a first-rate opportunity for Communist agitation, found Communist parties the world over futilely engaged in obstinate struggles with other parties which showed, in part at least, socialist aspirations. Principal Soviet diplomatic efforts were directed, not to helping these parties or furnishing them with positions which would maximize their possibilities for developing effective local leadership, but rather to taking advantage of the crisis to secure economic agreements to tide over the First Five-Year Plan.

4. MANEUVER AND BANKRUPTCY, 1933–39

The German Communist Party constituted the most flagrant example of energy dissipated in contest with other parties of the Left, although its activity can hardly be called without consequence in view of its substantial contribution to Hitler's rise to power. What the motivations were for the Kremlin leaders who gave orders to the German Communists is not clear. This is one of the few major instances in the history of Soviet foreign policy for which no obvious rational explanation in terms of Soviet power interests can be supplied. To the extent that Soviet leaders believed that German Communists could attain power alone, or that Fascism was merely a transitory precursor to Communism, they can be said to have been prisoners of some version of Marxism. But the realism that Lenin and Stalin had demonstrated since Brest-Litovsk and the peculiarly ambivalent relationship of the Soviet government to the German Communist Party indicate that this is an insufficient, if not completely incorrect, answer. Apparently the Politburo, with its attention centered on the Five-Year Plan, collectivization, and other internal problems, simply misunderstood the German situation and underestimated the danger of Nazism, a mistake not uncommon at that time in the council chambers of Europe.

The accession of Hitler and the earlier attack by Japan on Manchuria induced the Soviet Union to make changes in its foreign policy, or, perhaps more accurately, to invent a new foreign policy. The principal aim remained, that is, the safeguarding of the security and integrity of the Soviet state. But the period of idyllic, utopian foreign relations in which one dealt in nonaggression pacts, outlawing of war, and disarmament, and in which the principal immediate concerns were foreign trade and loans, was clearly past.

Under these circumstances the regime judged that it now required positive alliances to protect its security. Since the buffer states set up at Versailles to protect Europe from Bolshevism could serve as a buffer to a potential German advance, Russia could now wholeheartedly support the League, collective security, and maintenance of the *status quo.*

Formerly the League had been denounced as an "international organization of the capitalists for the systematic exploitation of all the working peoples of the earth," and as "the holy alliance of the bourgeoisie for the suppression of proletarian revolution." But the overriding priority of security interest and the complete control of public expression enabled the Soviet regime to accomplish its change of position with comparative ease. Soviet Russia entered the League as a permanent Council member in September 1934.

By 1935 Soviet declarations such as those on the "advisability of peace," and the rising power of Nazi Germany had overcome Western suspicions sufficiently to bring about mutual-assistance pacts between the Soviet Union and France, and the Soviet Union and Czechoslovakia. England, led by a conservative government, refused to join in a defense pact with Russia despite considerable popular support, including that of the then-dissident Winston Churchill.

The continuing growth of Fascism confronted the Soviet leaders with a dilemma. They could either suppress the internal revolutionary tradition and try to work with conservative governments within and without the League in order to build defenses against Hitler, or they could try to use their still extensive Communist network as a skeleton around which to build a united anti-Fascist front. They tried to follow both policies.

The Seventh Congress of the Communist International in the summer of 1935 proposed "the establishment of a united front for the purpose of combating the capitalist offensive, capitalism, and war." Comintern activity took on new life, and all talk of "social fascism" was given up in favor of the new policy of co-operation with bourgeois governments and Social-Democratic parties. Again it was the requirements of Russian security that determined Soviet policy, and again the change in the Party line was made with comparative ease at home and with Communists abroad, to whom the new dispensation gave enlarged scope for action and maneuver.

For a time the new anti-Fascist allies appeared to be quite successful, and both France and Spain elected "Popular Front" majorities. But the stronger and more vocal Popular Front movements became, the more distrust was aroused by both local and Moscow Communist activity. In the eyes of the conservative West, Communists could not wholly live down their character as revolutionaries and Russian agents. The rise of Popular Front governments in some ways inhibited the possibilities of cementing more formal security links between Russia and the West.

The first test of anti-Hitler strength came in March 1935 when Hitler occupied the Rhineland. Russia's pleas for countermeasures went unheeded. The Spanish Civil War brought out even more fully the disunity of Europe. Stalin's initial hesitancy, followed by his policy of intervention and exploitation, did not enhance the confidence of the Western powers. The British policy of vacillation and nonintervention, French dependence on Britain, and the bad impression made on the West by the purges of 1936–38 served to complete the defeat of Russia's collective-security policy, and may have strengthened that element in the Kremlin's thought which led toward an alternative and simpler means of assuring Soviet security.

In November 1936, Germany and Japan signed the anti-Comintern Pact, which Italy soon joined. Then the Popular Front government fell in France. The spread of the Great Purge to the army made Russia appear to be an even more uncertain factor on the international scene. The rebel forces in Spain had increasing success. By the time Hitler was ready to begin his expansionist campaigns in 1938 it was evident that the Soviet Union had failed to gain the confidence of the Western powers. At the same time, the Kremlin had lost such confidence as it may have had in the strength of the Western powers as a result of their performance over the Rhineland and Spain. If there was any united front by the autumn of 1938, it was the Fascist and not the anti-Fascist front.

Stalin's motivations in the matter of the Spanish Civil War are not wholly clear. Conceivably he thought the protection of France's southern frontier and the prevention of another Fascist government justified intervention. The prospect of gaining influence over the

Spanish government, of furthering a possible revolution, and of testing the tactics and weapons of the new Red Army may all have appealed to him. But the half-hearted way in which the intervention was conducted and the obvious fact that Soviet policy in Spain only antagonized those countries on whose support Russia would have to depend in case of German aggression, make these explanations somehow deficient. On balance, it seems most likely that the tying down of Italian and German energies in Spain, far distant from the Soviet frontiers, had sufficient appeal to justify an intervention of limited resources and limited liabilities. Whatever Stalin's purposes, it is evident that the gambit failed and he cut his losses.

The crisis of 1938 exhibited the utter collapse of the Soviet anti-Hitler policy. On March 17, less than a week after the *Anschluss*, Litvinov called for joint action among the European states to insure against further German aggression; but the British Cabinet rejected the proposal as "premature." By the time of the Czech crisis in September, Russia had definitely been excluded as a partner by the Western countries and was pointedly not invited to Munich, though she had been a guarantor of the Czech frontier. There is no doubt that the Chamberlain government wanted to keep Russia out of any European settlement; and that, if a war had to come, the Western nations would have preferred a German-Russian struggle.

After Munich, which had shown France and Britain to be incapable of making an effective front against Germany, Russia was left in a position of relative diplomatic isolation, with no firm allies, no assurance of co-operation in case of attack, and facing a growing menace in Germany. Perhaps the traditional Communist fear of a bourgeois coalition led to a disproportionate emphasis in the Soviet leaders' minds of the possibility of a German-English-French alliance. Yet it was a fact that the Western nations had treated directly with Hitler, without Russia's participation. The Soviet reaction was to seek to protect itself as well as possible. This aim was furthered by European developments in the next few months.

Hitler, ignoring his Munich promises, occupied Czechoslovakia and the Memel Territory in March 1939. Thereupon Britain and France hastily pledged aid to Poland, and both the Western Allies and Germany began negotiating for Russian support. It is not certain whether it was Germany or the Soviet Union which took the initiative in the talks between the two powers. Apparently both nations had been extending feelers since the summer of 1938, and a German-Russian trade agreement was promptly renewed (for a year) in December 1938. In the latter half of the year the domestic propaganda of each country began to ease off its attacks on the other. In the spring of 1939 these preliminary overtures began to be taken seriously in Berlin, notably after Stalin's speech of March 10 to the Eighteenth Party Congress. In any case, Russia suddenly became no longer the outcast of Munich but rather the balancing element in the European power structure, for whose support both sides in the coming struggle were prepared to bid.

The dismissal of Litvinov in May was an overt sign that Russia was prepared to change her policy of the past five years, to jettison, if necessary, her anti-Fascist ideological framework and to accept that offer which promised the best short-run chance of security. Negotiations for both possible combinations were conducted simultaneously in the spring and summer of 1939, and Stalin, in the historical manner of European diplomats, took full advantage of this situation. Particularly in the latter stages of the negotiations, Stalin was able to bargain hard, although clearly he needed an agreement as much as anyone.

Britain and France had pledged aid to Poland; but Poland was not prepared to offer the Russian Army passage through its territory. Furthermore, though the Western powers desired Russian support, they were not willing (in contrast to the Germans) to compromise third parties such as Poland and Rumania. Therefore an understanding between the Western powers and the Soviet Union was difficult to attain. What the Allies demanded of Russia, it appeared, was active collaboration, that is, an agreement to fight against Germany in any war that might develop with Hitler. Hitler, on the other hand, required merely a promise of neutrality, to which end he was willing to concede large pieces of Europe and Asia to Russian influence.

Since the immediate danger of an unopposed frontal attack upon Russia had been averted by the precipitate guarantee to Poland, and since the Allies had shown themselves by no means eager to accept Soviet terms, Hitler's seemed to be the better short-run offer. As Stalin trusted neither party, he prolonged the negotiations up to the last possible moment before the weather-set deadline for the German invasion of Poland, September 1. But when the time came for decision, Soviet policy disregarded world opinion, disregarded the ideological battle with Fascism, even disregarded, perhaps, long-range considerations of power politics as they were in fact revealed by the course of World War II. On August 23, 1939,

Molotov and Ribbentrop signed their Non-Aggression Pact. Ten days later there was war.

Just what Stalin expected after the Pact and after the outbreak of war is not certain. Apparently what he anticipated, or at least wished for, was a long-drawn-out struggle in which Germany and the Allies would slowly exhaust each other, leaving to Russia the role of arbiter at some later date. Certainly Stalin expected neither the quick collapse of the Poles nor the even more surprising collapse of France. What he would have done had he known of the overwhelming initial German superiority cannot be told.

While the Soviet Union was living in the precarious security of 1939–41, it continued the dual policy of strengthening its own forces while appeasing Hitler. Russian trade enabled Germany largely to overcome the effects of the British blockade, and Communist movements throughout the world, with less relation to their own national needs than ever, condemned the Allies for starting the war, undertook sabotage, and campaigned against lend-lease and military-preparedness legislation wherever possible. At the same time, Russia's own mobilization was given top priority, and its foreign policy was clearly designed to secure all possible strategic advantages. Thus the Soviet Union initiated new mutual-assistance pacts with the Baltic states almost immediately after the partition of Poland (October 29), and tried unsuccessfully to reach an agreement with Turkey. When Finland balked at a similar offer of a defense pact, Russian troops marched in (November 30). Once again, though probably with less success than ever, revolutionary jargon about "liberation of the workers," "crushing the Mannerheim clique," and so on, was used to explain a maneuver of a primitive strategic character.

German and Russian interests began to clash in the Balkans in the summer of 1940, and relations between the two countries gradually cooled after that point, although economic relations were continued to the outbreak of war in June 1941. On the eve of Hitler's invasion of Yugoslavia in April 1941 Stalin signed a treaty of friendship with Yugoslavia in an ineffective gesture to avoid the impending German move, or, perhaps, to impress Hitler with Russia's intent to draw a line at some point in Germany's movement to the East. At the same time the Soviet Union signed a treaty with Japan ensuring, so far as diplomacy could, the security of its Far Eastern position. When Germany attacked Russia in June the very event whose prevention had been the chief aim of Soviet policy for eight years apparently found the Russian forces tactically unprepared, though specific warning—including the time and place of the German invasion—had repeatedly been offered to the Soviet government by Britain and the United States. There is some evidence that Stalin found it difficult to believe that the strong short-run power interests which were shared by Germany and Russia would not sustain the pact of 1939 and override Hitler's impulse to pursue his ambitions in the East. To his cost Stalin discovered that Hitler gave to *Mein Kampf* more serious status, as a plan for action, than he himself accorded to Communism's sacred texts.

5. SOME GENERAL OBSERVATIONS ON THE POSTWAR POSITION

The course of Soviet foreign policy since 1945 is so close upon us that it is difficult to view it in a firm historical perspective. In general it would appear that Stalin saw in the aftermath of World War II unique opportunities for extending the power and influence of the Soviet regime. The ground-force positions attained or negotiated in the course of the war, the temporary elimination of Germany and Japan as independent elements of power in the world political arena, the weakness of Western Europe, the rise of powerful nationalist movements in Asia and the Middle East, and especially the success of the Chinese Communists have all presented possibilities of some attraction to the Politburo. These possibilities have been exploited within a framework set by the Soviet appreciation of American military strength and weakness. Stalin avoided the risk of U.S. strategic air attack; but he exploited to the full U.S. postwar demobilization and the inhibitions on the use of U.S. military force imposed by American and Western coalition politics.

In their determination to make the most of the practical possibilities available, the ideological background and, perhaps more important, the historical experience of the Russian Communist leaders have probably played a part. The theories of Marx and Lenin place a peculiar importance on war as a historical instrument for creating the conditions for revolutionary advance. More particularly, it has not been forgotten in the Kremlin that the Bolshevik opportunity to seize power in 1917 arose directly from a situation of weakness created by a protracted war. In addition it has probably not been forgotten that anti-Communist forces proved capable of rallying and re-establishing themselves to a degree which proved disappointing to the Bolsheviks in the years after World War I. It seems likely that these elements of ideology and remembered history joined with the long institutionalized posture of Soviet hostility to the external world to produce a policy of aggressive exploitation of opportunities after World War II.

In keeping with previous performance, the Soviet regime has pursued what it has believed to be its power interests in various parts of the world on an *ad hoc* basis, adjusting to potentialities and limitations as they have emerged. The fundamental facts about the postwar world, as opposed to the position before 1939, would appear to be:

1. The potentialities for the extension of Soviet power were vastly increased.

2. The increase in Soviet (as in U.S.) power has placed the Soviet Union in a position where its own actions are of such influence on the world environment that they help significantly to determine the environment and the issues which confront the Soviet Union.

It is no longer rational for the Soviet Union (or the U.S.) to behave as if the world environment it confronts is independently determined, and to construct its foreign policy on a series of specific reactions to events as they arise. There is, however, no conclusive evidence that the criteria for Soviet foreign policy have altered or that a systematic plan is serving as the touchstone for day-to-day Soviet foreign policy decisions.

Nevertheless, the shifting from the essentially defensive pursuit of power from a relatively weak base, which characterized the Soviet position from 1918 to 1941, to its offensive posture after 1945 in a world arena in which the Soviet Union is a major power base constitutes an enormous historical transition. It has raised, in particular, the following fundamental issues:

1. The degree to which major war should be risked by the Soviet regime in pursuit of its objective of enlarged external power.

2. The extent to which reliance should be placed on conventional diplomacy in expanding Soviet power, as opposed to the use of Communist parties and other instruments of subversion and internal interference abroad.

3. The manner in which relations should be conducted with Communist regimes abroad, whether indigenously generated or installed in power by the Soviet Union.

4. The shielding of the internal Soviet control system from the impact of enlarged relations with the non-Soviet world.

A full view of postwar Soviet foreign policy in the light of these central issues lies outside the scope of this essay, involving, as it would, Soviet actions throughout the world. In general it may be said that, under Stalin's direction, the Politburo has:

—firmly disciplined its pursuit of external power within the limitation that major war be avoided;

—attempted, as in the inter-war years, to use both diplomatic and subversive techniques simultaneously, shifting the relative weight attached to each in different areas at different periods of time, and accepting the political costs of this evident ambivalence;

—accepted, with the possible exception of China (up to the present), the political losses consequent upon the continued exercise from Moscow of direct absolute power in Communist areas abroad, rather than permit the development of partially independent Communist regimes;

—taken extraordinary measures to limit the direct knowledge and experience of its citizens concerning the outside world, and heightened its effort (begun before 1939) to associate the regime with historic xenophobic Russian nationalism.

It is a theme of this essay that, while the external expansion of Soviet power holds a priority second to the maintenance of the regime's internal control, the maximization of external power over time is a persistent goal of the Soviet rulers. What, then, are the roots of this posture of aggression?

First, it is doubtful that the Soviet regime is operating by a schedule or timetable of world domination or has so operated from the moment it abandoned its hopes of detonating world revolution through the catalytic agency of Russia's November Revolution. However, Marx's and Lenin's analysis of the course of future world history still exerts, after a fashion, a hold on the minds of Soviet leaders. It will be recalled that, while Lenin made his peace with Germany at Brest-Litovsk, and while the new regime was unprepared to take major risks to aid the later revolutionary efforts of German Communists, still the notion of world revolution was not wholly or cleanly abandoned for the long run. More important, perhaps, than its persistence as an ideological residue, this conception became institutionalized in the ties of the Soviet regime to the

Communist parties of the world by means of the Comintern. These ties have been used in the interests of the Soviet national state— often at the expense of the progress of Communism abroad. Nevertheless, the ingrained habits of thought of the regime have steadily looked to an expansion of its world power, even though this expansion is not an overriding priority nor governed by a fixed plan; and these habits of thought have their origins in the original ideological conception of Communism's world triumph. This conception constitutes in its present modified form, like government ownership and operation of industry, one of those ideological elements which converged with the pursuit of Soviet power, and thus it has survived.

Second, and more important, the internal stability of the regime has come to be judged dependent on the maintenance within the Soviet Union of the view that the external world is hostile, which, in turn, justifies Soviet hostility. Even if this Soviet hostility were a pure position of propaganda disassociated from aggressive Soviet moves abroad (which it has never been), it would tend to set in motion reactions which would, in turn, give an element of substance to the propaganda. Chronic hostility and the insecurity that goes with it lead to actions of aggression. Psychologically, in part, it may be that Soviet aggression is defensive rather than offensive, based on fear as well as hope. In the end, for practical purposes, and notably in the context of the residuum of ideological aggression discussed above, Soviet hostility is to be judged positively aggressive, even if partially based on an insecurity which in the end stems from overriding concern with the maintenance of the regime's domestic base. For there is no evidence that any action of assurance or appeasement by the external world is likely to give that sense of security to the regime which would lead its present leaders to settle down; and there is considerable evidence that weakened positions in the external world will be fully exploited by the Soviet regime. If this analysis is correct, the ultimate source of the regime's insecurity lies in its relation to its own peoples, and this relationship is not easily susceptible to reconciliation by initiatives from the outside world.

Third, the habits, now firmly bureaucratized, for handling power within the Soviet Union condition the external behavior of the regime. The exercise of domestic power is based on attitudes and methods of as nearly total control as modern techniques permit. These attitudes and methods make it difficult if not impossible for the present regime to operate comfortably in the situations of diffused or shared authority which a firm structure of world order demands. In Germany and Eastern Europe, notably, as well as in disarmament negotiations in the United Nations, the somewhat musclebound stage of Soviet internal evolution has certainly contributed in recent years to behavior which, by any objective test, is to be judged aggressive.

The picture which thus far emerges, then, is of a regime which is prepared to exploit fully such possibilities for expanding its power as the world scene may offer but which is limited consciously in its pursuit of power by the desire to avoid major war and limited unconsciously by the institutionalized methods to which it is attached both in conducting its foreign relations and in controlling its own society. How these now deeply ingrained methods and responses have combined with the altered power position of the postwar world is illustrated by the evolution of events within the European satellites since 1945.

Chapter Nine

THE EUROPEAN SATELLITES: EXPANSION OF THE SOVIET SYSTEM AND THE PROCESS OF TAKE-OVER

1. INTRODUCTION

THE MILITARY evolution of World War II presented the Soviet Union with immense opportunities to extend its power westward. The immediate postrevolutionary dream of a communized Europe came alive again. After the success at Stalingrad (if not earlier) the Soviet leaders, despite their preoccupation with the winning of the war, turned their thoughts to postwar possibilities for Soviet-dominated Communism. Not only Marxism itself but their own experience had engraved on their minds the potentialities offered them in war-weakened societies.

Even the quite specific question of Soviet Russia's relations to a Communist Eastern Europe was not new. Stalin, in 1918, against the background of the nationality problem about which he was then in correspondence with Lenin, had written from Tsaritsin: [1]

For the nations constituting the old Russia, our (Soviet) type of federation can and must be regarded as of the greatest assistance on the road towards international unity. The reasons are obvious: these national groups either had no state organization in the past or had long ago lost it, so that the Soviet (centralized) type of federation could be grafted on without any special friction.

The same cannot be said of those national groups not included in the old Russia as independent formations but having developed a specific

[1] J. Stalin, letter to Lenin of June 12, 1920, quoted in Lenin, *Collected Works*, 3d Russian ed. (Moscow, 1935), Vol. 25, note 141, p. 624.

state organization of their own, and which, if they become Soviet, will perforce have to enter into some State relation with Soviet Russia. Take for instance a future Soviet Germany, Poland, Hungary or Finland. It is doubtful whether these nations, who have their own State, their own army, their own finances, would, after becoming Soviet at once agree to enter into a federal relationship with Soviet Russia of the Bashkir or Ukrainian type . . . they would regard federation of the Soviet type as a form of reducing their national independence and as an attempt against it.

I do not doubt that the most acceptable form of rapprochement to these nationalities would be confederation. . . . I am leaving out the backward nationalities, e.g. Persia, Turkey, in relation to whom or for whom the Soviet type of federation and federation in general would be still more unacceptable.

Bearing all this in mind, I think that it is indispensable to include at some point in your minutes on the transition forms of rapprochement between the workers of the various nations the mention of *confederation* (alongside federation). Such an amendment would lend your proposals more elasticity, enrich them with one more transition form of rapprochement as described, and would render State rapprochement with the Soviet easier to the national groups which did not previously form part of old Russia.

It would be wholly unwarranted to assume that the Soviet Union simply decided, as a matter of fixed plan, to implement Stalin's "confederation" policy of 1918 after 1945. There were complex problems of Allied negotiation over Germany in which the Soviet Union exhibited, for a time, some evident uncertainty. There was the question of the strength of U.S. postwar armaments and its rate and degree of demobilization. The regime had to establish the degree of importance the United States would attach to maintaining Eastern Europe outside the Soviet orbit. There was the question of Western Europe's political evolution, with its potentialities, in 1945–48, for an extension of Communism far beyond the limits reached by the Soviet armies.

As in the other cases of Soviet policy examined earlier in this essay, the clear-cut result over time probably emerged from a series of particular short-run decisions, the upshot of which was a policy of absolute and intimate Soviet control over the areas where such control could be established. It may emerge, when evidence is more complete, that 1948 marked a distinct stage in the process, where the long-run implications of the emerging position were faced and crystallized in actions and institutions difficult to reverse. The controlled areas have, in the end, come down to those where Soviet or Soviet-dominated troops were present or where their weight could be made felt without incurring the risk of a major war. The transition to a pattern of control, in the image of the present internal Soviet system, from different initial positions, is, looking backward, remarkably uniform.

2. THE PROCESS OF TAKE-OVER

Soviet Russia proclaimed itself the liberator—in fact the only liberator—from the scourge of Nazism in Eastern Europe. Nazi collaborators who were also judged potential enemies of the new regimes were ruthlessly denounced wherever possible, as were certain other actual or believed enemies; all recollection of prewar conditions was branded as reactionary; the "right people" (not necessarily old Communists but rather those considered most pliable) were installed in key positions of power, often by direct order of the Soviet military command; and certain popular measures, such as land reform, were credited to the Soviet liberators and the parties sympathetic to them. Gradually the East European countries acquired controllable police and military forces and began increasingly to resemble their "liberators" in administrative structure.

At the same time the cultural, social, and economic transformation which had been crystallized in the Soviet Union during the prewar decade was imposed by the newly powerful governors with the confidence of a long-established firm opening branch offices. The familiar features of post-1928 Russia appeared: purges, shock troops, forced collectivization, rapid increase in heavy industry, "kulaks," "economic sabotage," "deviation," mechanically uniform propaganda, and so on. And, within a relatively few postwar years, the familiar instruments were employed to yield, under forced draft, a kind of copybook version of modern Soviet society.

The most striking feature of Eastern Europe since the war has been the uniformity of its development. Although the tempo of sovietization varied with the conditions of the several potential satellites, all went through more or less the same three stages. Only in Yugoslavia, which up to 1948 had appeared the model state of the new Soviet Empire, has the result deviated significantly from the standard form.

The first stage was a period of real coalition governments. Yugoslavia, which was not liberated by the Red Army as such, and which had the nucleus of a national government organization on the spot at the end of the war, went through this stage almost imperceptibly; Czechoslovakia, closest to the West both geographically and culturally, remained in it for nearly three years.

In every case several political parties combined in a government, based on Western parliamentary institutions, to form a coalition dedicated to a program including a purge of Fascists and collaborators, fairly radical social reforms such as the break-up of large landed estates, political freedom, and a foreign policy friendly to both the Soviet Union and the Western Allies.

During this first stage real freedom of speech and assembly prevailed except in the matter of criticizing the Soviet Union or its policies. Over other matters there was generally no censorship. Within the coalitions, however, the Communists managed to secure certain decisive positions from which they were able to exert power in the most effective way. With these levers of power—in general the key posts in the interior ministry (for the security police), the army general staff, and the information ministry—the Communists, aided by the threat of the Red Army, were gradually able to remove their strongest enemies, to make opposition to themselves increasingly impotent, and to build up a largely dependable administrative staff.

The second stage in the sovietization of Eastern Europe was a series of bogus coalition governments in which non-Communist parties were still represented in the government but only by members chosen by the Communists, not by the parties themselves. The peasant and bourgeois parties were driven into opposition which, though not yet illegal, became increasingly difficult. Newspapers could still be published, but their distribution, particularly in rural areas, was restricted. Sometimes the government would censor a newspaper; more often the printer's union would "indignantly refuse to print the reactionary calumnies against the peoples' authorities." Riots were frequent, meetings were broken up while the police preserved its "objective attitude," and government by intimidation, if not yet terror, prevailed. The end of stage two (which only Czechoslovakia seems to have skipped) marked the end of the transition to the full-fledged "People's Democracy," i.e., the stage of total control by Communist regimes approved by Moscow.

In the third stage, attained in all the East European states by 1948, all opposition was suppressed, its leaders were either exiled or arrested, and a completely disciplined united front control was achieved. Where there was a Social-Democratic movement, it was forcibly fused with the Communists in some kind of united party. Features of stage three have been purges, liquidations, spy trials, and forced labor.

The countries of Eastern Europe which fell within the Soviet Union's orbit after World War II differed in their political, social, and economic history and current structure. Poland had been the joint victim of Germany and Russia, and had, throughout the war, maintained a strong independent underground. Yugoslavia had fought Hitler before the Soviets were in the war, and the partisans of Tito had developed into something like a mass movement. Hungary and Rumania had fought on the German side; and Bulgaria had been allied to Germany though not at war with Russia. Czechoslovakia had been split into the Czech state, occupied by the Germans, and Slovakia, ruled by a semi-independent German sympathizer. But in the end Soviet policy has come to impose its system, with comparatively little variations, upon all of the states—allied or conquered, industrial or agrarian, monarchical or republican, Catholic or Orthodox.

Poland presented perhaps the most difficult task of absorption for the Soviet regime. On top of a centuries-old tradition of Polish-Russian animosity, Soviet Russia had amassed a record of atrocities against the Poles, beginning with the Hitler-Stalin Pact, and including the probable murder of the flower of the Polish officer corps at Katyn. The tragic razing of the city of Warsaw (July–August 1944), while the Soviet army stood outside and watched the Germans destroy the rebels and their city, was not forgotten. The burning hatred of Germany in postwar Poland, and its desire to industrialize, were, perhaps, the only major political assets the Russians had in dealing with that country. The manner in which the Soviet regime has implemented its control of Poland is, therefore, instructive of the pattern of domination everywhere.

On December 31, 1944 the Soviet-sponsored Lublin Committee declared itself the Provisional Government of Poland. It was recognized five days later by Stalin. After long wrangling among the Big Three, and finally after a Hopkins mission to Moscow (June 1945), the Western Allies compromised on a coalition government of five separate parties, with Mikolajczyk, the former exile leader, as one of the vice-premiers. But the period of "Red Army liberation" had been skilfully used by the Lublin government not only to occupy key positions in the administration but also to infiltrate the other parties as well.

The Ministry of the Interior was divided in two at the start, with Public Administration (routine bureaucratic matters) under Kiernik, a follower of Mikolajczyk, and Security (secret political police, internal security corps, and militia) under a Communist, Radkiewicz.

What was left of the army was also controlled, at least at the top, by Communists, and included many who had served in the Red Army.

The third crucial position occupied by the P.P.R. (Polish Workers Party—Communist) was the Ministry of Regained Territories (the Oder-Neisse territory), set up under separate administration under Gomulka, out of the hands of Kiernik. Since the territory was comparatively rich in industrial and agricultural opportunities, and since a complete resettlement was called for after the Germans were expelled, enormous possibilities for patronage and subjection were available to Gomulka, who was also at that time Secretary of the Polish Communist Party.

The regime was confronted in the early stages of its rule by some guerilla actions by unreconciled members of former underground groups. Later, when the police forces had been organized, the existence of guerilla bands was exploited as a justification for general repressive measures. After Mikolajczyk's original Peasant Party had been taken over by the Communists, two leaders of the new Polish People's Party, which he then established, were murdered. Mikolajczyk's protests and demands for investigation showed his "lack of confidence in the Minister of Security." A subsequent trial brought a suitable confession from an underground agent.

Mikolajczyk was able to hold a Party congress in January 1946, and resisted pressure to join the government bloc. Though Mikolajczyk's Polish People's Party (P.S.L.) was nominally in the government, delegates were arrested, meetings broken up, and party offices raided. The press continuously denounced Mikolajczyk as a British agent, and the P.S.L.'s own paper rations were cut drastically. In the plebiscite of June 1946 the government announced a majority of 68 per cent on the one disputed question—but according to Mikolajczyk the results would have been 83 per cent in his favor had there not been arrests and falsification.

From this time on the government moved quickly. To prepare for the parliamentary elections of January 1947, the "safe" western territories were given excessive electoral representation. Mikolajczyk and his followers were incriminated by the confessions of certain political prisoners who asserted they were foreign agents. Two bogus parties were set up to drain off the peasant vote toward Communist-controlled groups, thousands of P.S.L. members were (at least temporarily) arrested, and "voluntary open voting" took place in many districts. The resulting parliament, overwhelmingly backing the government bloc, passed a new provisional constitution in February 1947. Finally in the fall of 1947 Mikolajczyk, informed that he was about to be arrested, gave up the uneven struggle and left Poland secretly. The only other "independent" party left in Poland, the satellite Socialist party, completed the operation in 1948, when, in response to a demand for "workers' unity," it merged with the Communists to form a Polish United Workers' Party, purged, in the mean time, of all unreliable elements. By the end of 1948 all effective power was concentrated in this United Party. Poland was an almost completely communized state, operating with fully unified police and other controls.

In Hungary the Soviet task was easier because there was no large non-Communist underground and because potential rivals could simply be treated as former enemies in the light of their recent Nazi connections. Yet the occupying forces and their Communist allies actually sponsored the establishment of four differing parties, which would govern in a National Liberation Front. In Hungary, where land reform was a major factor, the Agriculture Ministry was a crucial lever of power for the Communists. Soon, too, they managed to gain control of the economic and political police, though the Minister of the Interior himself was only a sympathetic member of the National Peasant Party.

There was a free election in Budapest in the fall of 1945, resulting in a large anti-Communist majority. But eventually, with the interference and threatened interference of the Russian Commander, Marshal Voroshilov, a four-party bloc was maintained with a Communist in full control of the Interior Ministry. Thereupon the bureaucracy, widely regarded as overstaffed, was purged; the Communists managed to use this opportunity to conduct the purge on criteria of political reliability. Denunciation of peasant leaders and suppression of their journals began in earnest.

The detailed story of Hungary need not be rehearsed here. Pressure on nonconformists, including Premier Nagy, increased as the police was strengthened, and trials and confessions became more common. Early in 1947 Kovacs, the Secretary General of the Small Farmers Party, was mentioned in connection with activity against the Soviet Union, and was seized by Russian soldiers. In May, Nagy was denounced on the strength of alleged testimony of Kovacs and was forced to resign.

An election in August 1947, conducted under police supervision, gave the Communist party 22 per cent and their dummy-party allies another 38 per cent. By June of 1948 the government, now fully in Communist hands, felt strong enough to nationalize Catholic schools, and six months later Cardinal Mindszenty was arrested. After fusion of the two "proletarian parties" had taken place in 1948, the Hungarian Workers' Party had undisputed control and was able to stage a 90 per cent election in April 1949.

Rumania and Bulgaria deviated only in detail from this pattern. In Rumania Vishinsky asserted Russia's will as early as February 1945, and the broadening of the government's base, in accordance with the Moscow Conference of the Big Three Foreign Ministers (December 1945), made no substantial difference in the degree of Soviet control. Ministries of Interior, Justice, and National Economy remained in trusted hands. The first manipulated election took place in November 1946 and, though opposition was not yet illegal, trials, purges, and confessions were common thereafter. In the fall of 1947 the Social Democratic Party was absorbed into the "United Workers' Party"; then King Michael, who had in any case wielded virtually no power, was forced to abdicate; and in March 1948, the renamed People's Democratic Front won its parliamentary election—405 to 9.

In Bulgaria, the first stage was over by the spring of 1945, when the Agrarian and Social Democratic parties were captured by Communists. The first terror-ridden election was held in November 1945, and throughout 1946 parties other than the Fatherland Front were terrorized. One by one, opposition leaders were tried and sentenced, and in 1948 the fusion of workers' parties took place. By the time of the Tito-Cominform split, Bulgaria claimed to be the most advanced of the Peoples' Democracies, as indeed it was in terms of the stages through which it had passed toward "confederation."

Yugoslavia and Czechoslovakia present the two extremes of variation in the pattern of sovietization of the satellites. Yugoslavia, which had its own indigenous National Liberation Front during the war, never passed through the first stage of real coalition government; while Czechoslovakia, possessing strong cultural links to the West, remained in the first stage until the coup of February 1948. But even the special features in these two countries do not substantially alter the essential uniformity of Soviet operations in Eastern Europe—until, that is, the Titoist break in the summer of 1948.

The Communist Party of Yugoslavia chose to hide its identity behind the People's Front, of which it was merely the directing nucleus, and to assign the Interior Ministry at first to an Orthodox priest. But by October 1945, the last opposition paper was suppressed, and a month later a 96 per cent election was held. Beginning with Mihailovic's trial in the spring of 1946, "treason," and not opposition, became the standard Yugoslav crime.

In Czechoslovakia the Communists, though aided until December 1945 by the presence of the Red Army, did not attempt to seize power immediately. The popular strength of the Communist Party (38 per cent at the free elections of May 1946) may have led to the decision to seek real popular support, and no doubt Gottwald, the Communist chief, sought to pose as a patriotic democratic leader.

Yet despite the freedom enjoyed in Czechoslovakia in 1945–48 (only the uranium mines were Soviet-controlled), the actual power position of the Communist Party was extremely strong. Finance, Interior, General Staff, Information (including the Union of Czech Youth and Radio Prague), Agriculture, and Border Areas (controlling confiscated German holdings) were directed by Communists in the provisional government; and, after the 1946 elections, Gottwald became Premier.

The rule of law and absence of serious abuses prevailed up to the summer of 1947, though popular tension was great, and acute internecine warfare was conducted between the Communist and non-Communist ministries. The Czech reaction to the Marshall Plan and the growing (but still secret) crisis with Tito probably were decisive in determining Stalin's decision to enforce more direct control by means of a *coup d'état*. The power at the disposal of the Czech Communists was ample to overcome the divided and unsure opposition of Beneš, Masaryk, and other Czech democratic leaders; and in February 1948, with a rather limited effort, the Gottwald regime was able to transform itself into a stage-three satellite government. Communist gangs, armed factory workers, and police occupied "opposition" ministries; resisters were arrested or fired upon, and all parties, newspapers, and unions were instructed to "cooperate" with the regime. Less than a month after the start of the coup, Jan Masaryk, former foreign minister and bearer of a great Czech name, was found dead in a courtyard. New elections yielded the customary 90 per cent majority in May, and on June 6, President Beneš, seeing that he could do nothing amid the series of purges, arrests, and new laws, resigned. Just as the first Bolshevized state, Yugoslavia, was breaking away from the Soviet bloc, the last was bolted securely into place.

3. INSTITUTIONS IN THE SOVIET IMAGE

By the summer of 1948 the pattern of political seizure had been evolved and carried out in all the East European satellites. At the same time, an economic and institutional framework, modeled ever more closely on that of the Soviet Union, had been taking shape. Because of the varying degrees of Communist control up to 1948, this transformation did not correspond precisely to the stages of political development. But the pattern of economic changes in Eastern Europe illustrates how the historical experiences of the Soviet regime were consolidated, telescoped, and applied in the Soviet Union's first large-scale foreign venture.

In general, the economies of all the satellite states were made to conform as much as possible to the needs of the Soviet economy, and those countries upon whom the Soviet Union had reparations claims were harshly exploited. Roughly, those countries which had the most inequitable distribution of land before the war, such as Hungary, went through the greatest agrarian transformations, while those which had been most industrialized—for example, Czechoslovakia—suffered the least economic dislocation. In this transformation Russian confiscation of German property played a major part, the Soviet Union taking over and enlarging the positions of economic power the Germans had held.

Among the peasants the standard plan in all the states comprised, first, a distribution of large landed estates among the peasantry, then a kind of transitional "NEP" stage, during which the main aim was to organize a more efficient system of exchange between town and village; and finally large-scale collectivization and liquidation of substantial landowners (kulaks).

The first step, expropriation of large estates and German property, took place in all the countries by legislative decree. Where there were large Church holdings, however, as in Hungary, land reform was not completed until 1947–48.

The second stage presented the Soviet regime with the same problems that it had faced at home in the 1920's, i.e., the factories, now concentrating on capital goods, could not produce unless the workers were fed; and the farmers were reluctant to sell their crops without being able to buy the products of industry. The solution was generally the same as it had been in Russia: fixed crop quotas which had to be delivered to the state at low prices, and allowance of a margin, dependent on the size of the harvest, which could be sold on the free market. In contrast to Russia, however, machine tractor stations were introduced before large-scale collectivization, both to increase production and to increase control over the peasantry.

Warned by the terrible experiences of the Soviet Union, the satellite planners seem to have proceeded slowly thus far on the third agricultural stage. That collectivization is definitely a part of the program for Eastern Europe has been shown, however, by such moves as the establishment of "Centralized co-operatives" and "Peasant self-help," particularly on redistributed lands.

Industrial planning has also been based largely on the Soviet model. All the satellite countries adopted short recovery plans and then embarked on Five- or Six-Year Plans for industrialization. Yugoslavia undertook its plan in 1947, Czechoslovakia and Bulgaria in 1949, and Hungary and Poland in 1950. Although private property was not outlawed as such, industry, banking, and wholesale trade had been effectively transferred to government control by the end of 1948.

In all the satellites planning seems to have been more ambitious than expert, and more in the nature of production targets than precise schedules. The rate of investment to national income sought has been high everywhere, but has not always been attained. Consumer-goods production in general has been reduced absolutely as well as relatively. Trade unions have been introduced even where they were comparatively unknown before the war, but these have had only the characteristic Soviet functions of stimulating productivity, increasing the size of the labor force, and disciplining the workers. The familiar Russian "heroes of labor," "shock workers," medals, Stakhanovite movements, and "socialist competition" are common in Eastern Europe, notably since 1948, when longer-term efforts to integrate the area into the Soviet economy became more general and explicit.

The whole structure of the satellite states cannot be examined here. Where Soviet examples were available, as in the organization of propaganda, police, or military institutions, they were closely followed by the satellite governments. Where there was no easily applicable model, as in the Church question, action seems to have been hesitant and uneven from country to country, although in general the attempt has been made to win Orthodox support for the regime and to suppress or intimidate the Catholic Church. What can be observed over-all is a remarkably unimaginative application of the bureaucratized techniques developed out of the Soviet evolution and applied by force—in defiance of popular feeling, in defiance of Marxist doctrine of history, and, in the end, in defiance of such authentic national Communist movements as existed within the area.

4. THE COMINFORM, TITOISM, AND THE DYNAMIC CONSEQUENCES OF THE TAKE-OVER

In the summer of 1947 the Kremlin chose to organize its satellite Communist parties, plus the French and Italian Communist parties, into the Communist Information Bureau. In part the Cominform was a response to the Marshall Plan, in that it promised increased economic integration to the East European states. In part it was an additional technique for binding the subject nations closer together by a means which appeared other than Soviet fiat. Certainly it constituted notice that Eastern Europe was not to be regarded as a group of separate states but rather as part of a unified power system.

This decision to tighten still further the degree of Soviet control met actual or believed opposition from a group of relatively strong Communist leaders whose loyalty to Moscow was unquestioned but who had held to, or were believed to have held to, the conception of nationally oriented Communist states. They were judged inappropriate agents for the stage of bureaucratized control over the satellites into which Soviet policy moved in 1948. Whether, or in what proportion, this stage represents a reflex to gathering Western strength, an instinctive desire to tidy up on the part of habit-dominated bureaucrats, or a conscious transition toward full incorporation of the satellites into the Soviet Union it is impossible to say on present evidence. In any case, this new phase has been marked by Tito's successful defiance in 1948, and by the unsuccessful, abortive, or suspected resistance (or dissidence) of Gomulka in Poland, Kostov in Bulgaria, Patrascanu in Rumania, Rajk in Hungary, and Clementis and Slansky in Czechoslovakia. While there have been some substantive policy disagreements between the satellites and Moscow (for example, on East-West trade, the idea of

Balkan Federation, and the rate of collectivization), it is evident that all real conflicts have been over the degree and character of Soviet control. Both sides, particularly in the case of Yugoslavia, built up after the event ideological differences to justify their positions on this issue of power distribution. Here again the politics of postwar Soviet Europe has followed the model of prewar Soviet internal politics.

The Cominform has been, essentially, a sideshow in the latest stage of satellite control. Its central feature has been more or less direct control by Moscow over the armed forces, secret police, and party bureaucracies of the individual states. Moreover, it has become clear, at least since 1948, that even in matters of local Balkan policy, such as negotiations between Bulgaria and Yugoslavia, Soviet Russian interests are made paramount.

In Yugoslavia Tito was strong enough politically and militarily within his country, and so located geographically, that he could hold out against the power, short of invasion, that Stalin could mobilize against him. In these circumstances, but not in his motivations, Tito was unique among the Eastern European postwar Communist leaders. For Tito the issue became one of his own life as well as that of his regime; and the correctness of his decision to resist Soviet control has been borne out by the fate of other potential or alleged Nationalist Communists who "recanted."

It is evidently now the bias of Soviet policy to choose virtually complete direct management over such areas as it controls rather than wider, more dilute influence. In terms of this bias, the loss of Yugoslavia was perhaps inevitable and even proper. Though the Titoist defiance has certainly injured the cause of world Communism, the advantage to the Kremlin of retaining the impression of absolute vigor in enforcing its will and tolerating no insubordination or even institutional variety in the region it still dominates may have, thus far, outweighed the loss of one satellite. Tito, continuing within the Cominform on his own terms, might well have disrupted the coherence of Soviet control. His elimination was essential to the new stage of which the placing of a Russian Marshal, Rokossovsky, in command of the Polish armed forces, in the fall of 1949, and his subsequent (1952) elevation to the post of Vice-Premier, is perhaps the most striking symbol.

In the short run the Soviet regime can clearly impose such policy decisions as it may wish to impose. By the successive elimination of independent and strong men it may, on the other hand, have weakened the structure of effective administration and may therefore be forced into an increasing degree of direct responsibility, if its policies are to be implemented.[1] Certainly the Kremlin faces the problem of finding new reserve strength to replace purged party leaders. On the other hand, if the present situation can be maintained for a few more years, the new products of the Communist education and propaganda system may be ready to inherit satellite leadership, or at least posts in the satellite bureaucracy, much as men in Russia move into the internal bureaucracy.

In general it may be said that the complex of controls over and incentives offered to the satellite peoples has produced a widespread political apathy. The degree of acceptance of the present state of affairs is, however, for a variety of reasons, considerably less than in the Soviet Union. There is no equivalent to Great Russian nationalism which the regime can exercise, except the fear of Germany; and Soviet German policy, as it has evolved, is by no means reassuring to the peoples of Eastern Europe. They are, on the whole, acutely dissatisfied and eager for liberation, but with no clear picture of an alternative for themselves that lies within their power to bring about.

[1] The East German riots of June 1953, the impotence of the German Communist administration, and the consequent Soviet reliance on the raw power of the occupation army illustrate this problem forcefully.

Part Two

COHESIVE FORCES, INSTABILITIES, AND TENSIONS IN CONTEMPORARY SOVIET SOCIETY

Chapter Ten

THE PATTERN OF SOVIET SOCIETY IN GENERAL

1. INTRODUCTION

THE TASK of this portion of the analysis is to draw up, on a cross section rather than a dynamic basis, a balance sheet of the forces tending to hold contemporary Soviet society together and those tending to create instability and tension. In essence, this is an effort to judge the net contemporary impact of the regime whose evolution has been described in the preceding pages, on the lives of various kinds of individuals and groups within the society it controls, and to assess the secondary, and not wholly controllable, impact of the Soviet system on the institutions it has created to meet its needs. It should be emphasized that even in a cross-section analysis of this type the dynamics of Soviet society cannot be forgotten or set aside. The cohesive forces, instabilities, and tensions all take their meaning from the paths which the Soviet system has followed and from the alternative future courses it may follow. The aim here is, simply, to examine the balance of forces within a moving society as they interplay with the expectations of men, and the workings of certain key institutions.

It will be recalled that the central characteristic of the Soviet regime is believed to consist in an extraordinary degree of unification of power at the top of the structure. The instruments for the exercise of this power include the armed forces, the state administration, the secret police, and the Communist Party. To these must be added Soviet information policy, the positive aspect of which is propaganda, and the negative the denial of information except as selected and interpreted by the regime.

Projected down into the lives of individuals and groups, the purpose of the system is to induce them to behave in such a way as to carry out those actions believed required for the maintenance of the internal power and the maximization of the external power of the Soviet state. For each group the specific tasks believed necessary for the execution of this aim, the context in which it is carried out, and the frictions to which it gives rise are likely to differ.

2. COHESIVE FORCES

Broadly speaking, the technique of the Soviet state is to offer to each group a pattern of incentives and restraints designed to deny to it any realistic alternative to carrying out the will of the regime. In order to induce men to execute with reasonable efficiency the tasks believed required, the Soviet regime recognizes the need for their deriving from their roles in the system certain minimum satisfactions. These satisfactions constitute, in a sense, the positive cohesive forces which tend to hold the regime together. On the sound assumption that these positive incentives may not suffice, the regime provides ample restraints designed to maintain the efficiency and stability of the system, and, notably, to prevent the effective crystallization of dissatisfaction in any form of independent political activity. The policing function is supported by Soviet information policy, both positively in the form of propaganda and negatively in a limitation on the facts or ideas made available. Soviet information policy thus seeks to deny to men the data and concepts required to formulate an alternative to the system. Police and Party control are designed to prevent men from crystallizing effective action should they formulate an alternative.

On the side of incentives, the Soviet regime provides sufficient real income to maintain life, and, more important, it provides the possibility of a rising scale of real income for those who work harder or who are prepared to accept more responsible tasks on the regime's strict terms. The process of bureaucratization has been accompanied by a wide spread in income distribution. Its range would certainly appear wider than statistical measurement allows if due weight could be given the non-monetary perquisites of higher bureaucratic positions, e.g., superior resort hotels, cars, housing privileges.

In general it may be said that in allocating its national income for purposes of consumption the Soviet system has followed an approximation of Ricardo's and Marx's "iron law of wages." In a typical series of piecemeal decisions taken in the context of particular circumstances, the regime has, on balance, allocated resources to consumption, as opposed to capital investment and military end products, on that minimum basis required to permit the working force to survive and to function efficiently. In part since its beginnings, and completely since 1929, the increase in economic welfare has not been an independent goal of Soviet policy. Within this "Iron Law" system of consumption allocations, however, it has been necessary to adjust the distribution of income in such a way as to maintain significant material incentives for hard and steady work in priority fields.

A second positive incentive has taken the form of public prestige for efforts believed to be in the interest of the state as a whole. Not only is there the Stakhanovite movement, but also an elaborate gradation of awards and prizes which has been developed to supplement material incentives with the almost universal desire of men for communal approval. In general the regime does not frustrate those ambitious to acquire prestige or to exercise authority over their fellows, but their power, in turn, is hedged about by orders from the top and surveillance from various lateral directions.

A third range of incentives to loyalty can be grouped under the general heading of security. This term is designed to embrace not merely the material security (at a low real income level) which the system affords, but certain basic needs of the individual in relation to society which the Soviet system more or less adequately fulfills. Although there are many conflicts between the concepts publicly projected by the regime and the facts which men confront in their lives, the existence of an ideology which claims inner consistency and continuity, and which, in particular, tends to give to individual men an explicit place in a larger communal organism, exerts a cohesive influence on society, as does an institutional structure of a markedly hierarchical character. These ideological and institutional values are capable of engaging the loyalty of men, partially at least, and on a basis such that they function effectively within the system. This is notably the case because the whole system of Soviet education is designed to accentuate that general quality of men which seeks the security of a communal connection.

It has been a prominent characteristic of Soviet defectors that, in their process of adjustment to more individualistic societies, they have appeared to miss, for a time, the sense of direct connection with society which the Soviet system afforded, even when this aspect of the system was far outweighed in their later evaluation by other faults. Soviet defectors tend to be anti-Communist, but also somewhat anti-individualistic. They do not at first find the notion of a relatively atomistic society quite comprehensible, let alone attractive.

Finally, as noted earlier at length, the regime has permitted and even encouraged the continuance of powerful elements of nationalism in the society, not only in the form of a xenophobic patriotism, but also in the maintenance of certain lines of cultural continuity with the Russian past. From all the evidence we have it would appear that prerevolutionary Russian and foreign literature, implicit with values different from those of the regime, is widely popular; and, in the long run, this fact may be of importance to the reorientation of Russian society on lines more consistent with those of the Western world.

While the efforts of the regime to associate itself with nationalist elements of Russian life have by no means been wholly successful, it must be recognized that the regime has acquired a degree of legitimacy in consequence of its material, military, and diplomatic achievements of the past several decades. Defectors who exhibit, in general, a profound hatred for Stalin and his system appear, nevertheless, to reserve a certain grudging respect and national pride for the extent of Russia's successes under Stalin.

Although it is important to appreciate that some considerable positive forces operate cohesively in Soviet society, it is evident that these alone do not determine its present shape. There is a heavy reliance on what might be called negative cohesive forces, i.e., forces designed not to induce but to compel the individual to behave in the manner desired by the regime. Of these the most powerful and pervasive is, of course, the centralized structure of the institutions within which Soviet citizens normally work. The process of bureaucratization, described earlier, has gradually developed a set of institutions organized on the principle of rigid hierarchical discipline. Almost all sectors of Soviet life are permeated by structures of organization in which each individual is subservient to those above in a detailed, formal, virtually military manner. This system not only results in a maximum of direct control, but also places an automatic premium, in the process of advancement within the society, on the precise effective execution of orders from above.

But this is not all. In addition to standing within his own chain of command, the citizen is under surveillance, with relatively few exceptions, from lateral directions. The Soviet administrator in industry, for example, does not look in one direction for orders, criticism, or opposition but, rather, in three. He is responsible to his own superior, but is watched by the Party organization from one side and by the secret police from the other. The Party and police organizations themselves are impregnated with techniques of surveillance as well as command. Although rough areas of responsibility have evolved and have been allocated to the Party, the police, and the administration, they substantially overlap and are meant to overlap in such a way as to give no man a sense of security. The gradual abandonment, at a high level, of the substantive goals of revolution has been accompanied by a diminution of reliance within the society on idealism and good will as motivating forces. The Soviet regime appears to rely on incentives to material advance, power, and prestige on the one hand, and on disciplined organization, surveillance, and fear on the other.

The suspicion of human beings which this mode of operation implies extends, apparently, to the very top of the regime. It is only at the level of Stalin himself that the administration, the Party organization, and the police were really identified. There is ample evidence that from the level below Stalin down to the local levels of Soviet organization the three elements of direct control were in uneasy and even purposeful conflict, a conflict kept in equilibrium only by their ultimate unification in Stalin's hands.

Among the negative aspects of cohesion must be included one function of the system of propaganda. As noted earlier, propaganda is designed to do what it can to make persuasive the regime's rationale for its policy, and to minimize the dissatisfactions which might arise in the minds of men in confronting the reality of their day-to-day life. It is also designed to deny to men the information and concepts which would permit them to formulate an alternative to the lines of policy which they are meant to implement and to support.

Over and beyond these functions of propaganda, however, there appears to be another. The system of Soviet propaganda is apparently designed, in part, simply to exhaust the intellectual and political energies of men. Almost all levels of Soviet (and satellite) life appear to provide for special, required forms of indoctrination. These take an important part of the time of hard-working people after their work hours or otherwise in their free time. Whether or not these propaganda dosages are meant to convince men, as that term is normally understood in the West, they certainly have the effect, which is undoubtedly known, of exhausting their intellectual and political energies. Propaganda carried to surfeit helps produce, within the whole environment of Soviet life, a political apathy which, with this generation of Soviet rulers, may be judged as useful as, or more useful than political enthusiasm.

Very roughly, then, we can group the cohesive forces in Soviet society under the following headings:

Positive Cohesive Forces
1. Real income incentives.
2. Public prestige.
3. Limited power.
4. Positive propaganda.
5. A linking of the individual to the community by ideology and institutional structure.
6. Fear and suspicion of outside world.
7. Russian nationalism and culture, including pride in certain Soviet achievements.

Negative Cohesive Forces
1. Disciplined bureaucratic organization.
2. Surveillance and arbitrary power of secret police.
3. Pervasive control of Party.
4. Denial of knowledge and exhaustion of political energy by information policy.

3. INSTABILITIES AND TENSIONS IN SOVIET SOCIETY

The Soviet system, as it has emerged, is a form of political organization designed to function with reasonable efficiency in the face of widespread dissatisfaction. Dissatisfaction is here taken to arise from a clash between the realities men confront and the expectations created by their cultural setting, including, in the present case, expectations encouraged by residual humanistic elements in Marxist ideology still alive in the Soviet Union. From its initial seizure of power in November 1917, the Soviet regime confronted its people with policies and situations contrary to those they had been led to expect. Its subsequent methods produced increased opposition. While the system makes some effort to persuade and satisfy the people who live under it, the regime has by no means counted on the creation of what would be regarded as majority support within a democratic society.

The existence of dissatisfactions, therefore, cannot be equated with instability. As a general rule it may be said with some confidence, on the basis of existing evidence, that the instruments of negative cohesion available to the regime are amply fitted to cope with the dissatisfactions in Soviet society—so long as the instruments themselves remain effectively unified at the top of the structure.

This does not mean, of course, that the tensions and dissatisfactions in the society are without meaning for the future of Russia or for American policy toward Russia. It does mean, however, that they are unlikely to become politically significant in changing the shape of Soviet society, except after a split among the instruments of force at the top. In general, men are prepared to act to relieve their dissatisfactions only when a realistic alternative is open to them. The Soviet system has purposefully suppressed, by inducement and constraint, any realistic alternative to conformity to the regime. Under these circumstances the average man becomes apathetic, lowers his horizons of self-expression, and retreats to those areas of life into which the regime is least likely to intrude. Modern totalitarian regimes do not generate heroic opposition among their citizens, but instead inspire confusion and withdrawal to those areas still left for some form of human self-expression. When, however, history offers to the Russian citizen the possibility of an alternative course which better suits his aspirations, it is altogether likely that he will seize it, as indeed considerable numbers of Russian citizens did under the unpromising circumstances of German invasion.

But it should be strongly emphasized that, on present evidence, the desire for an alternative course, and the shape of that course, are matters which men within the Soviet system hardly articulate to themselves and rarely to each other, even to their closest friends.

Despite the limited significance of popular dissatisfaction, it is not impossible that the tensions in Soviet society may play a role in the alteration of the present system in two other respects:

First, it may be that those who hold the instruments of force may ultimately differ sufficiently to damage their unity on an issue of policy which involves one or another form of internal dissatisfaction.

Second, having split at the top, those who hold one or another instrument of power within Soviet society may well look to popular groups in Russia for support in their effort to defeat their rivals for power—if the split degenerates into an open, protracted crisis.

In the light of these observations, and in the light of the analysis presented in Part One of the dynamics of Soviet society, the instabilities and tensions may now be grouped as follows:

1. The instability of executive power, notably the problem of the succession.

2. The long-run instability of relations between concentrated executive power and the higher bureaucracy, notably as between the executive power and the armed forces.

3. Dissatisfactions general throughout Soviet society, created by the gap between expectations and reality, and related to
    (a) The role of police power
    (b) The standard of living
    (c) The position of religion
    (d) Popular distrust of official propaganda
    (e) The lack of popular participation in government

4. Group dissatisfactions, created by the gap between expectation and reality with special meaning for:
    (a) The peasant
    (b) Nationality groups
    (c) The intellectual
    (d) The bureaucracy
    (e) The industrial worker
    (f) Prison and forced labor

Broadly speaking, it is the present view that it is the instabilities under 1 and 2 above which are most likely to be significant in detonating a major future crisis or in changing more gradually the nature of the Soviet regime; although those in 3 and 4 are likely to play an important part in the working out of a crisis should a split among the instruments of power develop and generate into open struggle. The present portion of the analysis considers separately the nature of each of these potentially unstable elements. Their relation to each other in the context of alternative possible patterns of evolution of Soviet society is left to Part Three of the analysis.

Before examining in more detail the nature of these instabilities and tensions, it may be useful to give them a quantitative setting by indicating the breakdown of the Russian social structure, by rough groupings, for the years 1914 and 1939–40. The rise in the proportion of the working force in industry and the bureaucracy, as opposed to agriculture, roughly measures the consequence for the social structure of Russia's economic and administrative transition under Soviet rule. The Soviet Union remains, however, a country still approximately half peasant.

CLASS COMPOSITION OF RUSSIA, 1914, 1939, 1940

1914*	Per cent	1939†	Per cent	1940*	Per cent
Nobility and army officers	3	Bureaucracy Top administrators 1.3 Intermediate, including army and probably secret police 4.0 Intermediate, without power of command, mainly technical and intellectual 3.5 Lower, including teachers, clerical, and deputies of local soviets 8.7	17.5	Top officials and intellectuals	.02–.03
Middle class	4			State employees and intellectuals	12–14
Intellectual and clerical	2				
Workers	13	Workers	32.2	Workers (of whom forced labor 8–11 per cent)	28–33
Peasants	74	Individual peasants, craft workers, etc. Collectivized peasantry	5.7 44.6	Peasants, collectivized and individual	53
Balance (armed forces, pensioners, etc.)	4			Balance (armed forces, pensioners, etc.)	7–0
	100		100		100–100

* D. Dallin, *The Real Soviet Russia.*
† B. Moore, *Soviet Politics.* Moore's figures include an estimate of families for each category, rather than merely a proportionate breakdown of the working force.

Chapter Eleven

THE INSTABILITY OF EXECUTIVE POWER

CHAPTER 15 considers the actual sequence of events in the period from the Party Congress of October 1952 through the early months of Malenkov's regime. The present chapter and the three chapters that follow have the limited purpose of posing the problem created by Stalin's death in the framework of Soviet society as a whole. They aim to establish the broad perspective within which more recent events are examined in Chapter 15.

1. INTRODUCTION

The greatest potential instability in the structure of Soviet society lies in what was, from about 1929 to Stalin's death, its main source of strength, namely, the extreme centralization of executive power achieved by Stalin. The long-run instability of Stalin's dictatorship derives from its chief characteristics, which may be summarized as follows:

1. Stalin's position was achieved as the consequence of a protracted historical process; it was not simply a post in a table of organization that can be mechanically filled.

2. Its consolidation appeared to require not only Stalin's personal domination of the Party and Politburo but also the replacement with his own appointees of the high-level bureaucracy, and his subsequent direct control of major appointments.

3. Its subsequent efficient and responsive operation appeared to require detailed surveillance and intervention not merely by the Politburo but, on key issues, by Stalin himself; this, in turn, demanded that Stalin maintain independent intelligence and police services directly in his own hands.

4. Its subsequent operation tended also to diminish considerably

the relative role in policy-execution as well as policy-making of the Party apparatus, as opposed to the state administration, the secret police, and the armed forces.

5. When Stalin died there was no single individual in a position to succeed easily to the role which Stalin created over the period of some thirty years during which he had sought, achieved, and exercised supreme power; and this situation resulted directly from the conditions required for the success of Stalin's rule—above all, from his careful, fluctuating rationing of secondary authority to lesser figures.

Stalin's previous success in acquiring and maintaining intimate and effective control over all the instruments of force in the Soviet state thus constitutes the greatest current source of potential instability in Soviet society, because the continuity of such unified exercise of power is not and cannot be assured. The authority exercised in Russia by the Communist Party arose through a raw struggle for power. Similarly, Stalin's authority was consolidated by a raw exercise of power. No rules exist for the exercise of this power or for its smooth passage to other hands. The problem of successful succession to absolute rulers has bedeviled Russia in the past, and we are now witnessing the regime's effort to solve this problem without uprooting Soviet domination over Russian life.

The nature of the searching set of issues confronted by Stalin's successors can best be seen, perhaps, by examining separately three related elements undoubtedly now at play within the higher reaches of Soviet life, all set in motion by the end of Stalin's reign: (1) the structural alternatives for handling executive authority; (2) the interplay of personal ambitions; and (3) alternative views on the substance of Soviet policy.

2. THE STRUCTURAL ALTERNATIVES

Four major alternatives, which, over time, may not be mutually exclusive, were open to Stalin's successors and remain open to them: (1) A collective leadership by a small group (say three to five); (2) A "constitutional" dictator; (3) A full successor; (4) An overt indecisive struggle leading to civil war.

The notion of Stalin's power passing to a small group emerged naturally (as it did before Lenin's death), as his important subordinates, each of whom apparently bore primary responsibility for administering one or another of the key instruments of power under

Stalin's intimate direction, rose in the hierarchy. Moreover, it was undoubtedly suggested by the triumvirate of Stalin, Zinoviev, and Kamenev, who assumed headship of the party at the time of Lenin's demise—although the fate of their effort was not calculated to encourage hopes of its stability, or to commend this solution to men with a strong sense of their own collective history.

Formulated simply as a group succession this solution can, on the whole, be ruled out for any substantial time period. It is the essence of the problem of exercising executive power in an anarchic situation of this type, where no external rules are accepted, that decisions must be reached clearly within the self-appointed ruling group. Three or four men, even when they are fully agreed on broad policy, are unlikely to agree in detail on day-to-day decisions. Further, the policy problems which confront the Politburo-Presidium [1] do not break down in such manner that they can be allocated to one or another instrument of the Soviet state for decision. The domestic and foreign policy problems requiring decision in the Presidium have their implications for all aspects of the state and its machinery. An allocation of issues of different types to different men for ultimate decision would not appear a possible or likely solution. Like the President's Cabinet in the United States, or any other executive body, the Presidium would appear to require a recognized decisive voice in order to function, and this a group executive would not supply.

It is, of course, possible to envisage a small group (or even the Presidium as a whole) operating on a majority vote basis. It will be recalled that such a procedure was followed formally within Lenin's and Stalin's Politburo, in its early days. It was officially abandoned in 1929 when Stalin announced that Politburo decisions were unanimous; but it had been undermined earlier by Stalin who gradually acquired enough organizational power to remove his opponents from the Politburo and replace them with his own appointees. A serious use of voting in the Politburo would require voting also for new appointees which, in turn, would involve collective control over the whole process of appointment and promotion in the structure of the Communist Party and, probably, also in the other chief agencies of state power. The trend of Stalin's regime from its beginnings was away from reliance on diffuse power in the operation of the Party and the state. Taken seriously, rather than as a short-run

---

[1] Hereafter, post-October 1952 references to the old Politburo will be made simply as "Presidium."

tactical device, decision by voting in the Presidium would constitute nothing less than a full reversal of modern Soviet history and a type of constitutional revolution. It would involve, in fact, the legitimizing of an opposition position.

A second possibility, given the apparently indecisive distribution of authority among Stalin's old lieutenants, and their tremendous common incentive to avoid an overt struggle for power, is an agreement to accept one man as arbiter among the Presidium members or an inner grouping of them. It may be that some such function is now (May 15, 1953) envisaged for Malenkov, the Premier stripped of direct control over any bureaucratic agency of power. It should be noted that the role of arbiter within the Presidium would be profoundly different from that which Stalin created and exercised down to the last years (about 1947) for which direct evidence exists on his mode of operation.[2] Stalin did not deal at arm's length with the institutions which administer power. They were his personal instruments. He determined the appointments to key posts and was prepared to intervene intimately in their activities. A successor whose action was limited to negotiating or arbitrating agreement within the Politburo would be fulfilling one of Stalin's functions, but not operating as his successor. In particular, such an arm's-length relation between the head of state and the intimate day-to-day workings of the principal instruments of state power would give increased scope for the existing bureaucratic structures to develop along independent lines, as will be discussed in Chapter 12.

The Soviet system has been not merely a dictatorship in the formal sense, but a system of concentrated executive rule in which direct interference was possible at all levels and in which the unity of force at the top was sufficient to permit the operation of the bureaucratic arms at low levels on a purposely conflicting basis. A weakening in the unity of executive power such as that represented by a group succession, with Malenkov as arbiter, would make difficult the continuation of the present strong executive system. Soviet administration would run the risk of generating either major conflicts among the various arms of power or of "clarifying" the areas of responsibility of each in order to avoid such conflicts. In the latter case, areas of executive authority would increasingly accumulate within the bureaucratic chains of command. The fear which

[2] The manner in which the Party Congress of October 1952 was conducted would appear to indicate that Stalin was in full command as late as that time, at least.

may well have played a part in Stalin's decision to conduct the purges of the 1930's might then become a reality.

The problem of a single successor to Stalin arises from two aspects of the position created by his rule:

1. None of his principal lieutenants is apparently now so placed that he can, from his present position, easily achieve the dominance that Stalin could from his base in the Party in 1924.

2. On present evidence, no single person has yet emerged who has earned a position of leadership acceptable to all those within the Presidium; and, indeed, by the nature of the case it is hard to see such an emergence arising from common consent, since true leadership would require the appointment of the leader's own men to positions of secondary command, and peaceful retirement of public figures has not yet developed as a Soviet tradition.

It was the essence of Stalin's rise to dominance that it was earned in a struggle for power. Those who opposed his assumption of control were ousted from the Party or eliminated from positions of power and later liquidated. Stalin made the Soviet structure of command and control his own, from top to bottom. Malenkov, who before Stalin's death appeared to control the Party, did not enjoy the monopoly of power and patronage that Stalin did from the Party base of the 1920's. Beria [3] almost certainly, and perhaps Bulganin and others have had their own limited areas of power and patronage or the possibilities of creating them now. But Stalin consistently so handled his subordinates as to avoid a disproportionate accretion of power to any one of them. If Stalin is to have a single full successor, that man would appear to be confronted by the need to create his new position, in a living struggle for power, under circumstances where he starts with important limitations and where serious opposition is likely.

It cannot be emphasized too strongly that the surviving members of the Presidium are under the strongest compulsions to avoid an open conflict in the transference or distribution of Stalin's power. They are fully aware that only complete unity of the instruments of power has permitted the internal maintenance of the Soviet regime, and that the Western nations would be tempted to exploit fully any inner conflict which became manifest.

As the formal alternatives cited above indicate, however, Stalin's

[3] This chapter was written, of course, before Beria's arrest. A footnote comment on this event appears on p. 241.

lieutenants confront a real dilemma. The succession of one individual to power would place the present members of the Politburo at the mercy of one of their colleagues, while a diffusion of power, in one form or another, might well undermine the strength and unity of the Soviet system.

It is, of course, impossible to predict which course will be followed or whether an effort by one man to seize the full measure of Stalin's authority would quickly succeed or fail. It would be wholly unjustified on present evidence to rule out the possibility that one man might move from the present indecisive position, overcome the difficulties, and fully succeed to Stalin; the difficulties, however, appear real.

If the effort to seize full power should not meet with prompt success, forces might be set in motion which would be difficult to contain, short of full-scale civil conflict. As self-appointed rulers of the state, subject to no rules other than those they have created, the members of the Presidium have no authority or accepted procedures to appeal to if they fall out, unless the Central Committee is to exercise an authority it has not enjoyed for thirty years, if at all. Despite the formidable bureaucratic structure of Soviet institutions, beneath the Presidium there exists political anarchy: as presently organized, the bureaucracy is simply the Presidium's instrument. Under conditions of protracted struggle for power one might, say, see the force of the army brought into action against the Party and, especially, the secret police over which Beria appeared briefly to have re-established full personal command. Further, one might see one group or another vying for power, making an appeal for popular support to Soviet citizens, and bringing at last into effective political play the dissatisfactions and frustrations of various popular groups within the Russian Empire.

Present evidence does not justify a prediction of this outcome. This case is cited to dramatize the dilemma of the succession problem. In the past the death of powerful Russian rulers has occasionally led to the indecisive diffusion of power, followed by open struggle. In earlier times, while such struggles weakened the power of the Russian state, they could be confined within tolerable limits. By and large the country could proceed with its relatively stable life of feudal agriculture. However, Russian life in the mid-twentieth century is intimately tied to the state by instruments of control which reach down from Moscow, in complex chains of command, into the life of the factories, villages, and lesser military units. A struggle which separated these instruments would be reflected promptly throughout the land and would be extremely difficult to control. A modern "Time of Troubles" would involve full-scale civil war, not merely a series of palace squabbles or localized coups.

3. THE MEN

The evolution of executive power in the Soviet regime is not merely an abstract question of providing for executive decision and control over the bureaucracy. Its future will be determined largely by the group of men who are now members of the Presidium, although the rapid emergence of some new figure of importance cannot be ignored, especially if open conflict over the succession breaks out. For the Presidium members the succession issue involves the extent of their own authority relative to that of their colleagues. The question of succession thus raises profound issues of power among a group who are thorough professionals in its manipulation and whose personal careers, as well as the history of the regime they serve, have been centered on power as the central goal for action.

The form or sequence of forms in which the succession process unfolds will certainly be determined in part by the relative power motivations and abilities of various key individuals and by the instruments they have at hand for enlarging their power from the positions they now hold. The personal power motivations of these men will be restrained, as emphasized above, by a most persuasive inducement to curb personal ambition and to maintain unity as a group. The possibility of a raw struggle for power cannot, however, be ruled out; and maneuvering for authority, short of an overt struggle, will almost certainly play an important part in the evolution of the Soviet regime.

There are now ten figures who appear to share Soviet power, at its highest levels. The following are brief observations on their history and significance:

MALENKOV

Now in his fifty-first year, Malenkov is probably the ablest and most widely experienced politician of the generation brought up under Stalin's rule. He was drawn to Moscow at the age of twenty-four, after working as a Political Commissar with the Red Army in Central Asia under Kaganovich, and he has remained close to the center of power ever since. From 1925 on he was close to Stalin personally. His experience over the intervening years included not only work in and, later, direction of the Party apparatus and its personnel, in the post-Purge period, but also high responsibilities within the economy during World War II. Although overshadowed by the rise of Zhdanov in the period 1946–48, he successfully bided his time and triumphed as leader of the Party, under Stalin, in the years 1948–53.

Throughout his career he has exhibited, and even symbolized, the criteria for the New Soviet Man: hard, competent, practical, enterprising, faithful to orders, openly scornful of ideology as a motivation for the regime and the peoples it controls. Further, he exhibited marked talent for building up within the structure of the bureaucracy his own group of henchmen. His relatively few public statements before Stalin's death were marked by boldness and confidence, although always within the orbit of policy laid down by Stalin.

Malenkov has never taken part openly in negotiations with non-Communist diplomats although, undoubtedly, he has observed intimately the course of these negotiations in Moscow and has had a hand in the foreign policy decisions of the Politburo.

Malenkov is a tough, ambitious man at the height of his powers, evidently capable of a high degree of self-control and patience. He has been contained by his colleagues; but may well try to break out and assume a full succession to Stalin.

BERIA [4]

Although Beria's career has been associated since 1921 with the Soviet secret police, he has evidently (since 1939 at least) accumulated a wide experience of both domestic and foreign policy problems. The economic functions of the secret police, which probably include the production of fissionable materials, give Beria power beyond that which would in any case accompany his authority over Soviet intelligence and punitive institutions.

Like Malenkov, he has shown a talent for building up his own chain of command within the Soviet bureaucracy, and he is undoubtedly a formidable in-fighter at the higher reaches of Soviet politics. Somewhat older than Malenkov (fifty-four), he has been active politically ever since the November Revolution.

Because he is a Georgian and a police chief, it is generally agreed among Russian experts that Beria could not successfully assume the role of Soviet chief of state. Although Stalin was a Georgian,

[4] See footnote, p. 241.

it is believed that the rise of Great Russian nationalism in the past two decades would exclude a second ruler from the southern province at this time.

Like Malenkov, he has appeared to have little serious concern with ideology; his whole mature life has been built on the manipulation of the basic domestic source of power of the Soviet regime—the secret police. His vigorous reassertion after Stalin's death of his authority, over both the secret police and other elements of political power, appears to indicate that he is not likely to permit himself to be disposed of as easily as his two predecessors, Yagoda and Yezhov.

If, in fact, Beria has successfully gathered the control over the police fully into his hands, and if it is true that he cannot aspire to full dictatorship, he represents the most substantial stumbling block to the re-establishment of Stalin's full powers by another figure.

MOLOTOV

Even in Lenin's day Molotov's reputation was that of the impeccable, unimaginative Bolshevik bureaucrat. Now sixty-three, he has been an active professional Communist since 1905. From 1925 at least, but probably earlier, he was associated with Stalin's personal entourage, and was his most reliable administrative agent. Unlike Malenkov, who was given responsibility in the field for a number of trouble-shooting jobs, both political and economic, Molotov in recent times has been a headquarters bureaucrat at the highest level.

Of Stalin's successors, Molotov has had, of course, the widest experience of the non-Communist world, including primary administrative responsibility for foreign relations since 1939.

Unlike Malenkov and Beria, Molotov has never developed a substantial group of men under him tied by personal loyalty. In part, this stems from his long connection with the specialist field of foreign affairs, but he may have shown a lesser aptitude for bureaucratic politics than some of his colleagues.

Although vastly experienced in the techniques, and knowledgeable in the dangers of higher Soviet politics, Molotov appears one of the more vulnerable figures in the present "collective leadership." It is unlikely that he can aspire to Stalin's succession, and, from a distance, he gives the impression of an aging man, somewhat lost without his boss and protector, still useful to the regime but with distinctly ambiguous future prospects.

VOROSHILOV

Recently elevated to the hitherto purely symbolic post of Chairman of the Presidium of the Supreme Soviet, Voroshilov is a somewhat more considerable figure than his predecessor, Shvernik. He is, perhaps, more active in the present "collective leadership" than is generally credited. A vigorous man of seventy-two, Voroshilov was one of Stalin's closest personal associates. Although he showed no great aptitude in modern military operations during World War II, Voroshilov nevertheless survived as a figure high in the Soviet regime. He conducted his post as Chairman of the Allied Control Commission in Hungary after the war with some poise and skill, as well as ruthlessness.

A tough old soldier from the original Red Army, with enormous knowledge of the workings of Soviet higher politics and an innocence of ideological matters, Voroshilov is not likely to be eliminated easily from his present comfortable position and is unlikely to be found in a Soviet court making an elaborate confession of guilt to some alleged conspiratorial crime. Of the galaxy of men at or close to the top of the Soviet regime in the past quarter-century, Voroshilov alone appears to have some personal popularity among Soviet citizens, if Zhukov is excepted.

KHRUSHCHEV

Under Stalin, Khrushchev was distinctly a figure of the third echelon in Soviet power, and it is altogether likely that in his present post of Secretary of the Communist Party he is not a leader of independent force. Now fifty-eight years old, he has spent a long official life in the Soviet regime, almost all of it as a member of the Party apparatus. Khrushchev is of an age and a history which distinguish him from the group of Malenkov's younger protégés; nevertheless he worked under Malenkov in recent years when the latter was at the head of the Party organization.

Several passages in Malenkov's speech at the October Party Congress can be interpreted as critical of Khrushchev's administrative ability and his views on agricultural policy. It is by no means evident that he holds his present high post as General Secretary of the Party simply as Malenkov's man. He may well have acquired this position, not because of Malenkov's support but because Malenkov's fellow-successors to high power wished to see Malenkov's authority over Party affairs diluted.

Like Molotov at a higher level, Khrushchev appears to be a figure being used by the major forces at work at high levels of the Soviet regime, rather than an independent manipulator or conniver for the highest policy-making power.

KAGANOVICH

On his record there is no more able, formidable, or experienced figure at the second level of Soviet power than Kaganovich. Although his name has been associated for many years with trouble-shooting jobs in the development of Soviet economy, and his responsibilities remain primarily economic, Kaganovich is a tough and experienced Soviet politician.

It is doubtful that Kaganovich has built up a group of personal followers, along the lines of Malenkov and Beria. He may well, however, have the confidence of many men in the economic chains of command, and his long record of success on difficult missions gives him a special prestige. Since his influence in power was wholly derived from the confidence that Stalin placed in him over several decades, and since, in a showdown struggle for power, the economic ministries would be relatively weak, Kaganovich is likely to be important in the future of the Soviet regime as a secondary figure, throwing his considerable personal weight and influence in one direction or another.

The fact that he is Jewish removes him from consideration as a possible sole successor to Stalin's authority. Like Voroshilov, however, Kaganovich is not a man who can be easily or lightly disposed of by the primary contenders for Stalin's authority.

BULGANIN

Like Khrushchev, Bulganin rose to the high levels of Soviet power relatively late in life. He is now fifty-seven years old. During World War II he moved from his previous position as a major industrial administrator to the State Defense Committee, where he replaced Voroshilov. It was only after the war that he became Minister of Defense, that is, the chief administrative director, under Stalin, of the operations of the armed forces.

There is no reason to believe that this bureaucrat, who proved his worth to Stalin, is likely to maneuver for a larger share of power than he now holds. Nor is there any reason to believe that he personally enjoys the confidence of the major military figures within the armed forces, for example, Zhukov or Sokolovsky. He belongs, rather, with Molotov, Khrushchev, and Kaganovich, as an able man developed by Stalin over whom Malenkov has developed no personal or moral authority. Like others in his category, Bulganin has undoubtedly thrown his weight toward some form of "collective leadership" to succeed Stalin's rule, the only form of executive operation which would permit his continuance at a comfortable, high, secondary level.

MIKOYAN

Like Kaganovich, Mikoyan has been for a generation or more associated with the economic policy and operations of the Soviet Union—in his case, foreign and domestic trade. Even less than Kaganovich has Mikoyan ventured outside the area of his special competence and assigned authority. Nevertheless, he has seen a great deal of higher Soviet politics from the inside, and, like the others who survived this long under Stalin, is unlikely to leave himself open to being maneuvered cheaply from his present high position. Further, his believed positive interest in Soviet trade with the outside world may, under present circumstances, give him some influence over the actual course of Soviet external policy.

SABUROV AND PERVUKHIN

The Presidium now includes two men of the younger generation associated with economic affairs: M. Saburov and M. G. Pervukhin. Little is known of their histories, except that they rose to prominence through two key, rapidly expanding sectors of the Soviet economy: the engineering and electrical industries, respectively. Saburov is believed to be a general industrial planner.

4. THE ISSUES

The succession process involves not only a question of the form of executive power and of the relative distribution of authority among a group of power-conscious men, but it is likely also to interweave with differences of judgment on questions of policy. It will be recalled that the struggle of the 1920's between Stalin and his rivals was shot through with real or apparent disagreements on the orientation of Soviet external and internal policy. There were opposition movements to Stalin's left and to his right.

In one sense the problem of avoiding struggle would appear to be easier after Stalin's death than after Lenin's. There is no evidence that substantive and ideological issues of the order of magnitude that appeared to divide Stalin from Trotsky, Bukharin, Rykov, and Tomsky now exist or are likely to arise among the residual Presidium members. The issues of collectivization and industrialization appear to be settled firmly so far as broad policy is concerned. The Russian peasant still presents problems to the regime, and Russia's industrialization is not complete. Nevertheless, the broad lines of development have been set, and, more important, institutions are now regularly operating to keep Russia moving, year by year, along its present paths. No member of the Presidium is likely to favor reallocation of substantial independent powers to the trades unions, for example, or to reopen the question of democratic centralism. There have evidently been tactical disagreements on agricultural policy in recent years, and there have almost certainly been differences of judgment on specific lines of Soviet postwar foreign policy, within the Presidium; but these are unlikely to have been profound or fundamental, by external objective standards.

It does not follow from this picture of broad agreement on goals and even methods that policy issues will be unimportant in the evolution of Soviet high power. In the first instance, it is evident that men may disagree violently in politics over issues of tactics as well as broad strategy. This is especially likely to be the case when tactical decisions are bound up with the power position of individual men and the bureaucratic organizations with which they are associated.

An extremely important range of such apparently tactical issues confronts the Presidium in relation to its external policy. The present lines of policy have stimulated heavy Western rearmament. In turn, this has been judged to require increased allocations of resources to military end products at the expense of other objectives of Soviet power. As in any government, differences in judgment come to rest on the allocation of resources in different directions. Those charged with internal capital development, foreign trade, light industry, or the control of the satellites may well feel, and resent, the pinch of increased armament outlays. If these increased outlays for armaments are accompanied by a successful frustration of Soviet ambitions vis-à-vis the external world, serious differences on an appropriate foreign policy could arise within the Presidium. Among the converging elements which have probably determined current Soviet diplomatic peace gestures, motivations of this kind almost certainly figure. The potentialities of disagreement on appropriate policy toward the external world are believed to be enhanced if they are viewed in the light of relations between the Presidium and the higher levels of the Soviet bureaucracy.

Chapter Twelve

THE HIGHER BUREAUCRACY AND EXECUTIVE POWER

1. INTRODUCTION

THE EVOLUTION of Soviet executive power is likely to affect and be influenced by the evolving position within the higher levels of the Soviet bureaucracy. A political system of the kind that has evolved within Russia over the past three decades has within it an important internal contradiction. Its unity, flexibility, and effectiveness, from the point of view of the dictatorial group, depend on the maintenance of a clear line between the making of policy and its execution by the bureaucracy; but this line is difficult, if not impossible, to maintain sharply in practice, especially over considerable time periods. The regime has sought to install a system which separates authority from administrative responsibility. This separation violates the natural two-way workings of an administrative structure in a complex society.

In the army, the Party, the state administration, and the secret police, the Soviet system requires a considerable number of men who must take the responsibility for important day-to-day decisions, within the framework of executive policies sometimes only generally formulated. These higher bureaucrats in fact control, for practical day-to-day purposes, very wide areas of Soviet society. They not only carry out policy in the usual sense; they also hold that special form of policy-making power which consists in the right to hire and fire men, to promote and demote. Inevitably, despite the purposeful procedures of surveillance and overlap instituted from the top, they create areas of patronage and limited power. Above all, as a group if not as individuals, they are needed by those who exercise high power.

The actions the Presidium may wish to take at any moment of

time are thus conditioned by the capabilities of the administrative arms they themselves have created, and the methods by which they operate. From its beginnings, the Soviet state was troubled about the problem of bureaucratic administration. In part this uneasiness stemmed from the role of the bureaucracy under the tsar, and from its place in Marxist ideology as an instrument of repressive class rule. As the Soviet regime acquired responsibility, the Marxist view was rapidly superseded by a realization that bureaucratic organization was necessary in order to run a modern society. Power must be, in a real sense, shared between those who make high policy decisions and those who execute them. An endless problem thus exists for the centralized executive authority which desires to keep policy effectively in its hands. It must find ways of preventing the bureaucracy either from achieving a partial *de facto* usurpation of its powers, or from retreating from responsibility into mechanical administrative formulae.

This problem has obsessed the Soviet rulers from the first. It was manifest in the early relations of the Soviet rulers to the army; and in the postrevolutionary years, when the need for a state bureaucracy was increasingly accepted, the regime steadily faced, on a wider front, the problems of maintaining conformity in detail to high-level policy decisions and of preventing the growth of that lethargy and inflexibility which appears endemic to bureaucratic structures. It appears reasonably certain that the Great Purge of the late 1930's represented, in one of its aspects, a violent and even pathological response to this dilemma of the executive. In a clean sweep Stalin drove from the positions of higher bureaucratic command those who, having held bureaucratic power for some time, were evidently judged by him to have drawn to themselves elements of power which constituted an actual or potential challenge to his policy-making powers. These men were superseded by a new generation of bureaucrats who have held their position more or less steadily for some fifteen years.

2. THE DILEMMA OF OVERLAPPING CONTROLS

It does not follow, of course, that this second generation of bureaucrats has been permitted to work quietly within one or another of the chains of command which run down from the Kremlin. The Soviet regime under Stalin evolved a system of internal espionage, checks, and balances, which was evidently designed to prevent the bureaucrat from either settling into security and lethargy or straying from the policy line promulgated from the top downward. This result was achieved through concurrent control, at every bureaucratic level, by the Party and the secret police as well as by the relevant operational chain of command. The higher bureaucrat must do his job and live his life in a framework of continuing insecurity.

The bureaucrat under Stalin lived in a world of three criteria, institutionally personified, sometimes converging but often in conflict. First, there was the classic bureaucratic criterion of strictly disciplined loyalty to the letter of administrative procedures, as formally laid down. Second, there was ideological conformity to the current version of the Party line. Third, there was a brute, continuing pressure to achieve the specific substantive result required in the centrally determined plan.

Of these, efficiency in performance has emerged as the most powerful (but not overriding) criterion for success or failure in the higher echelons of the Soviet system. Put another way, it appears that a considerable degree of casualness toward ideology, and a considerable range of extra-legal operations, are tolerated if the substantive result desired by the Kremlin is achieved. The net consequence of these priorities has been the emergence of men at the top of the bureaucratic hierarchies who, above all, are effective operators. They approach their tasks in a practical way. The word "concrete" marks their vocabulary and symbolizes the empirical standards which dominate their action. They are determined to get results and prepared to take the risks which this demands in the complex structure of Soviet society.

Although every device of education, incentive, and threat is maintained to avoid a centering of loyalty by the higher bureaucrat in his job and the organization to which it relates, rather than in the top level of the regime, it appears inevitable that the continuance of bureaucratic administration of this kind generates a frame of mind which may clash with the continued exercise of high policy in an arbitrary and flexible manner.

Thus, the nature of the bureaucratic techniques which have been built up to meet the mixed criteria of efficiency, ideological conformity, and order limits and, in fact, partially determines the policies which may be pursued by the Presidium at any moment of time. It is altogether likely, for example, that the nature of the relations which the Soviet Union could maintain with its wartime allies in postwar Europe was partially determined by the fact that it felt it could handle its authority safely in areas abroad only by the means generated out of Soviet experience at home. The Control Council in Berlin, which required the day-to-day making of compromise decisions if it was to work, ran counter to the normal bureaucratic practices within the Soviet Union, where orders flowed down from the top and were executed within a direct chain of command hedged about with surveillance and controls, also centered at the top. Similarly, in the satellites, whether or not it was planned from the beginning, the Soviet method of control has moved step-by-step toward a reproduction of its bureaucratic method for exercising power within the Soviet Union. At almost every stage where it confronted a choice, the Soviet Union has chosen to play for absolute direct exercise of power, at the expense of perhaps wider areas of more limited power, where the authority of the Kremlin would be diluted and its techniques of bureaucratic operation would be inapplicable. Many factors, obviously, entered into the decision which led to the present disposition of Soviet influence in postwar Europe and the manner of its exercise. The rigidity of its bureaucratic instruments for executing power may, however, have helped determine the kinds of policies which, in the end, the Soviet Union had to adopt. The joint, distributed administration of power which flows so naturally from Western political ideas and methods, and which is now incorporated in a multitude of operating international organizations, is incompatible with the peculiar techniques of administration which the Soviet regime has developed in consequence of its power priority. This encroachment of means on ends may, over the long period, increasingly embarrass the Soviet Union and limit its capabilities for flexible adjustment to and exploitation of the possibilities opened to it by the course of history.

The maintenance in authority for considerable periods of time of higher bureaucrats has, perhaps, an even more direct bearing on policy-making. By the nature of their jobs, such men must have access to much information on the whole context of Soviet policy. In their own terrain, moreover, they are forced to make evaluations and to take responsibility for "correct" courses of action. This experience of real, if lesser, responsibility may well lead to the view in one or another higher echelon of the bureaucracy that the policy coming down from above is not the policy most in the interests of the Soviet Union. It is extremely difficult, given the fine gradations of policy-making which must exist in a bureaucratic chain of command, to maintain a frame of mind in which men close to the top deny themselves the right to formulate, at least privately, the sort of high-level policy which they regard as appropriate. There is a steady danger, then, that a view of appropriate Soviet policy different from that of the Presidium may emerge privately in the minds of men in the higher levels of the bureaucracy. So long as the present control system remains unified and in full force, these private judgments are unlikely to be exchanged or crystallized in group opposition. But at a time, such as the present, when unity of command has been weakened, or at a time of crisis in Soviet affairs, they may assume importance.

3. THE BUREAUCRACY AND THE NATIONAL INTEREST

The possibility of private reservations regarding dictated policy is likely to be strengthened by the nature of the regime's relation to Russia and the Russian interest. The regime has sought increasingly since the mid-1930's, by every device of education and propaganda, to identify its own policies and motivations with the Russian national interest. It has made important ideological and other concessions in order to make this identity persuasive. In fact, however, the Presidium aims primarily to maintain its own political power. It is altogether possible that the higher bureaucrats in various fields may have come to feel that there is a lack of identity between the policy being pursued and the Russian national interest as they come to see it. Those concerned, for example, with the internal industrialization of the country may very well come to resent a foreign policy which is judged unnecessarily aggressive and therefore involves important unnecessary diversion of resources from the areas of their own responsibility and power to military end products. Military men and high diplomats who have experienced direct negotiations with the West may have come to feel that an accommodation in the Russian national interest might be possible, if the regime were prepared to pursue a somewhat different course. In short, there is every reason to believe, from an examination of Soviet society and from an examination of the history of other bureaucracies in autocratic states, that the absolute supremacy of the executive is not easily or automatically maintained over a long period of time. The higher bureaucracy may play, in particular, an important and even a decisive role when the unity of the executive authority is violated or if the executive power is exercised with diminished energy or competence.

Given the extreme suspicion and distrust with which the higher bureaucrat is evidently regarded by the executive, which is incorporated institutionally in the operations of the secret police and to some extent the Party, it is inevitable that certain of the higher officials develop resentment toward and dislike for the executive authority. The fact that the regime has needed men of vigor and enterprise to execute its tasks has increased the likelihood that resentment and dissidence might develop and has thus increased the necessity for substantial efforts at surveillance and discipline by fear.

4. THE TECHNOCRATIC OUTLOOK

The bulk of the bureaucracy is now professionally trained in one or another field of specialization where criteria for efficient performance are rationally evolved, e.g., engineering. The outlook of the good technician, with his built-in standards of order and efficiency, is bound to conflict with the workings of a system where the arbitrary and apparently irrational exercise of power erratically intrudes on the normal business of life. Whether openly articulated or not, the conception of a more orderly and (from the technician's perspective) rational organization of society is altogether likely to develop; and it might become politically meaningful should the instruments of high power split or operate less strongly on the bureaucratic chain of command. The technician's conception of an optimum political organization may well not be democratic, by Western standards, but it is also likely to diverge from Stalin's practice.

5. THE POLITICAL POTENTIAL OF THE ARMED FORCES

Of all the higher bureaucratic elements, the armed forces might play the most decisive role in the event of an open and protracted violation of the unity of the executive. The importance of the armed forces lies in the fact that, even more than other forms of bureaucracy, they have access to decisive instruments of raw force; and the regime is dependent upon them and their capabilities in a fundamental way, notably at a time of international tension. The manner in which the regime has sought, since the 1930's, to maintain a sense of dignity and responsibility in the armed forces has already been described.

Aware of the danger, particularly prominent in Russian history, that the armed forces might play an important political role, the Soviet regime has done everything in its power, by stick and carrot, to guarantee political loyalty in the army and to avoid the crystallization of an independent political line. Recruitment policies, material incentives, public acclaim—all have been directed to making the army loyal to the regime in a very direct way. The daily presence of agents of the Party and the police emphasizes the dangers and costs of violation of this loyalty. Nevertheless, there is an accumulating body of evidence that the army, perhaps more than any of the other bureaucracies, has resented the incessant intrusion of the police; and it may have generated a considerable body of potentially dissident political opinion on both domestic and foreign policy, which might be turned against the regime should a real opportunity emerge.

The importance of the armed forces at a time when the executive power has been weakened by inner conflict or dissension appears, then, to be considerable. Beneath the very top level of a dictatorship there is, almost by definition, anarchy. The Presidium maintains its short-run unity and coherence only by the acceptance of a single binding line of policy; and, in the long run, its unity hinges on the co-option of new members. There are no objective rules for the making of decisions on which it can fall back should its own unity be violated. The bureaucrats themselves are intentionally forced to operate at cross purposes, in the particular sense that differences cannot, ultimately, be resolved below the level of the Presidium. Should the unity of this system be violated, the armed forces, representing raw power, would take on disproportionate importance, as they have systematically in other Russian succession crises. The extent of their political effectiveness would depend, in particular, on the extent to which disagreement at the top had degenerated into open conflict: if disagreement is contained, as it were, within the Presidium family the army might never be brought into play, or its stirrings might be effectively checked by the MVD and the Party. If conflict continues and becomes increasingly overt, the role of the army in its solution is likely to expand.

Chapter Thirteen

GENERAL POPULAR DISSATISFACTIONS

As DISCUSSED above, the Soviet regime from its beginnings has counted on the existence of considerable popular dissatisfaction in the society it dominates. It was, perhaps, believed in the early days that, after a reasonable period of control and Marxist education, the people would accept the "dictatorship of the proletariat" and some form of government by consent would be possible. But dissatisfactions continued. The pattern of policy and control developed over the years is designed to contain these persistent dissatisfactions and to prevent them from interfering with the attainment of the specific goals set by the regime in terms of its own complex of motivations.

It is extremely difficult to identify with confidence the impact of this system on the lives of individual men or specific groups. The conception of dissatisfaction itself is not without ambiguity, implying the conscious desire for an alternative situation even if that alternative is not clearly articulated. The combination of incentives and restraints which are projected by the regime out onto Soviet society is designed to minimize the possibility that individuals might formulate in their minds an alternative to Soviet society as it is, acknowledge their aspiration for an alternative to themselves, and exchange such fundamental views with others.

The most general description of the mood of the Soviet citizenry is, almost certainly, political apathy, a negative acceptance of its lot and a channeling of interest into areas where positive human satisfactions are to be derived—a mood well characterized by George Fischer as "inertness and passive disaffection" in his study of the Vlasov movement. The demands of work (including enforced group activity), and the problems of acquiring food, shelter, and clothing, and of maintaining a personal life, absorb so high a

democratic society tl
able degree of respor
This assumption of
societies. In the deca
and political life wa
all, about three-qua
made up of peasants
shared the ideas and
trend." The trend w
social organization,
of its autocratic pov
reversion, which has
secret police, as col
on the whole, produ
maintained or stimi
the past have also
Russia. The extent t
of responsibility—in
their less responsible
personality. What ai
Soviet society accer
viduals.

An awareness of
Russians with the s
available, remove th
source of popular di
of which Soviet citiz

Despite a lack of
side Russia, the Sov
provement in his sta
these expectations ha
in the revolutionary
form or another, w
stimulated by incre
standards in Eastern
the West.

The prevailing lo
stems both from the
ment in the Soviet

proportion of the energies of most Soviet citizens that little positive attention is directed to the political workings of the society. Lacking a realistic alternative within the borders of the Soviet Union, the Soviet citizen by and large simply accepts the regime as a fact outside his powers to alter.

Nevertheless, it appears to be the case that important conflicts exist between the aspirations and expectations which are generated by life in Soviet Russia and the realities which are confronted. The following discussion is to be regarded as a partial interim sketch of such conflicts. As the knowledge accumulated from defectors and other sources is analyzed, we should be able to draw up a more accurate human balance sheet than is now possible.

We would now identify two major groups of popular dissatisfactions, some virtually universal throughout Soviet society, others having their impact on certain particular groups. Before examining briefly each of these aspects of dissidence, two general observations are to be made:

1. Since these dissatisfactions take their shape from the interplay of individual men and an environment created by the policy of the regime, they are to be understood only in the light of the unfolding course of the regime's policy, i.e., they are the product of a past experience and are not static phenomena.

2. The identification and evaluation of these dissatisfactions is made in the light of what we know or what we can deduce of attitudes within the Soviet Union, at a time when the regime is in reasonably full control. Should the regime undergo an internal crisis, or should some other circumstance offer Soviet citizens the possibility of an alternative organization of their society, it does not follow that their aspirations would simply constitute a positive projection of current dissatisfactions. The attitude of Soviet citizens is partially determined by the alternatives they have open to them. Their response to a change or widening in those alternatives cannot be automatically predicted from their believed current state of mind.

1. THE SECRET POLICE

The evolution of the role of the secret police in Soviet society is examined briefly in Chapter 3. Although there has been no recurrence of the Great Purge in Russia since 1939, the memory of that passage in Soviet history is probably still fresh, touching as it did

the lives of r
tive operatic
a feature of t
feature.

The impa
various level
The greatest
positions of g
constant sur
tion and hos
The power o
and other g
unreliable. N
fices, factori
forced recrui
home the ex
when the av
his life with
bureaucracies
ner, but they
environment
symbol of th

Although
in such evide
the existence
more normal
be in the W
of Russian c
life, and fron
by an arbitra
sible that the
Soviet educa
and then gra
sponsibility,
human perso
police in Sov
viduals of thi
haps, embede
tainly reinfor
assumed, not

Put anothe

tensive capital accumulation at the expense of consumers' income. Military outlays and war damage have added to the burden carried by the Soviet economy, again at the expense of living standard as well as the rate of capital development. The long, apparently endless experience of privation has been a source of frustration and active dissatisfaction. In particular, the disappointment of hopes for a rapid improvement in living standards after 1945 apparently intensified this discontent. Such disaffection has certainly been accentuated by direct and indirect knowledge of European living standards acquired by the armed forces when abroad.

Real wages have never regained the peak level of 1928, although there was some improvement after the inflation which accompanied the First Five-Year Plan. A rough index of Soviet industrial real wages follows: [1]

1928	703	1938	404
1932	710*	1940	348
1936	344	1948	251
1937	364		

* 1932 figure grossly distorted upward by rationing.

The war imposed extreme hardship, but there has been gradual improvement since; by about 1950 real wages appear to have reached the 1938 level. The currency reform, price reductions, and derationing of December 1947 resulted in a substantial improvement in the position of the workers at the expense of the peasants and those who managed in one way or another (including the black market) to prosper during the war. The impact of accelerated Soviet rearmament in the past year or so cannot yet be accurately assessed.

Consumer goods industries continue to lag behind heavy industry and the quality of their product is still a serious problem, openly discussed. Retail distribution and personal services, on the other hand, are reasonably effective. Population increase, the rapid urbanization of the thirties, and the extremely heavy damage caused by the war have made housing definitely the worst aspect of the Soviet urban standard of living. With an average space allotment of one room or less per family, the housing condition undoubtedly has a serious and probably cumulative detrimental effect on popular morale and efficiency.

[1] H. Schwartz, *Russia's Soviet Economy* (New York, 1950), p. 461.

3. RELIGION

As discussed above, the Soviet regime's position with respect to religion is ambivalent. On the one hand, anti-religious propaganda, notably among the youth, persists, but since 1936 a substantial *de facto* toleration, notably of the Orthodox Church, has obtained. The increased toleration during the war has been somewhat diminished in the postwar years. Given the ideological foundations of the regime, however, a surprisingly high proportion of the Soviet population (about 50 per cent) remain believers and find means for expressing their belief.

It does not follow from this limited toleration that dissatisfaction concerning the religious position is unimportant. The fact that religious feeling is permitted some expression may, in fact, increase rather than decrease dissatisfaction with its second-class status in Soviet society. Further, the relative toleration of the Orthodox Church does not extend to other faiths. There has been a growing anti-Semitism in the Soviet Union; the Roman Catholic Church is severely restricted; and the Moslem and other faiths associated with particular nationality areas have been consistently harassed.

The status of religion may thus be rated an important cause of popular dissatisfaction of varying acuteness in different groups and areas.

4. IDEOLOGY AND PROPAGANDA

As described in Chapter 3, a fundamental weakness in the Soviet political system is its necessity for maintaining and enforcing an ideology which, despite important modifications, remains largely at variance with the facts of Soviet life. In terms of its best citizens, this situation confronts the regime with a dilemma: the idealistic Communist who makes its most impassioned supporter may be, in the end, the least reliable. A young Komsomol, fired with the revolutionary tradition, eager for adventure and the implementation of his ideals, makes a poor bureaucrat. In contrast to the careerist whose ideological principles are derived from his personal identification with the regime as an institution, the idealist's loyalty to the regime is derived from principles he has accepted, and is prepared to apply as criteria for the worth of actions or situations more or less independently. Thus, whenever he may become sufficiently aware of the discrepancy between the regime's ideology which he accepts and the *de facto* performance of the regime, his loyalty may turn into hostility.

Such idealist disaffection, generated by progressive development of the regime away from its still articulated ideals, may have accounted in part for the severe impact of the Great Purge on the Party, particularly on its middle-level leadership who had previously been firm supporters of Stalin. On the other hand, the purge was probably in many cases the critical event which translated ideological misgivings into a more profound repudiation of the regime.

Although since the mid-1930's Soviet education and propaganda have sought to minimize the possibility of men distinguishing the regime from its initial ideology, it is unlikely that this effort is wholly successful. It is evident to virtually all Soviet citizens that many men join the Communist Party and play their part in the regime for familiar human motives of personal aggrandizement and satisfaction. Over time, this quality of the bureaucratized state undoubtedly has some corrosive effect. The attempt to marry an ideological heritage to the efficient pursuit of power has had significant costs, notably in the frustration and even disillusion of idealists.

With respect to the Soviet citizen in general, by and large propaganda appears notable for its lack of positive success. This is due first of all to the discrepancy between what the regime evidently is and the substantive welfare goals embedded in its ideology. Facts of material deficiency or failure cannot be concealed; and although popular criticism of the bureaucracy is used both as a device to channel off such dissatisfactions and to help keep the bureaucracy efficient, the deeper roots of the gap between promise and performance are not wholly concealed. The effort to excite political enthusiasm may thus backfire when a political consciousness is generated which then turns against the regime for its failure to fulfill the expectations it has generated, e.g., with respect to the standard of living and the ideal of social equality.

Finally, and perhaps most important, men are bored by the dull repetitions of Soviet propaganda. In spite of constant pressure on the Party organization to improve propaganda work, the level of results seems to remain uniformly low. Apathy and indifference to politics are characteristic of the Soviet population, although the mushrooming of political organizations among recent Russian émigrés indicates that this is merely a reaction to a repressive situation. In this reaction, however, lies the accomplishment of the negative function of Soviet propaganda, i.e., prevention of independent thought and formulation of a realistic alternative to the Soviet regime in men's minds.

The position of patriotism in the Soviet Union appears to constitute an important exception to these observations. As part of its general reversion to traditionalism, carried out between 1934 and World War II, the Soviet regime sought to effect a thoroughgoing identification of itself and its Marxian rationalizations with Russian nationalism and the traditions of the Russian past. Patriotism is the main area in which the regime appears to have evoked a positive emotional response from the people. The war showed Great Russian nationalism to be a powerful force in support of the regime, in the context of its then-defensive posture, and in the face of Hitler's implacable anti-Slav policy.

The postwar ideological retightening has not involved any formal conflict between Marxism (as currently interpreted) and nationalism. Soviet ideology, now centered on the glorification of the state and the great men who lead it, has become itself a vehicle for rabid nationalism and xenophobia. The current phrase "Socialist Patriotism" reflects the crystallization of this policy. The combination of ideological form and nationalist substance finds its most intense expression in the postwar campaigns of anti-Westernism, and anti-Americanism in particular.

Contact with the West by Soviet citizens during and immediately after the war caused widespread disillusion with Soviet propaganda and with the conditions of Soviet life. Soviet officials and the rank-and-file who learned something of the West appear to have been drawn both by its conditions of freedom and its standard of living. Against this background of disturbance, the Soviet government has suppressed all save minimum official contact between Soviet citizens and Westerners, and it has elevated in its propaganda to a new high point the sense of the external enemy. This state of mind is evidently judged important for Soviet political stability, as the optimum device for mobilizing behind the regime important sentiments of patriotism and unity in a common cause.

The relative success of Soviet propaganda in identifying the regime with the most primitive national fears and aspirations cannot be accurately gauged. The long experience of Soviet propaganda on the part of its own citizens has yielded a general skepticism and indifference. Some, no doubt, regard the gigantic effort at identification as false. There is evidence of views of the United States and the West less hostile than those Soviet propaganda would wish to project. On the other hand, the long national experience of Russia, reinforced by Hitler's invasion, gives the regime advantages and presents the West with a formidable challenge in the formulation and effective projection of its aims vis-à-vis the Soviet Union.

5. LACK OF POPULAR PARTICIPATION IN GOVERNMENT

Before 1917, as was noted earlier, Russian politics were slowly moving along a path toward recognizably Western forms of democracy. A profound popular desire to participate in government helped give strength to the Revolutions of 1917 and even to the Bolsheviks in the early days of their power. Despite the conversion of their power into a totalitarian state, the Soviet rulers have recognized in the Constitution, in the maintenance of forms of an election procedure, and in residual aspects of their ideology the force of this aspiration. It is, therefore, germane to attempt an assessment of the extent to which dissatisfaction appears to be felt with the denial of the substance of democratic procedures within the Soviet Union.

In general it would appear that the dissatisfaction of the Soviet citizen is not channelled strongly in this direction. A multi-party political system, operating within a firm constitutional framework and based on periodic appeal on the substance of policy to the individual citizen does not now appear to have strong roots in Soviet society. Dissatisfactions with the regime are substantial, but they do not, on present evidence, appear to come to rest on the nature of the political process in this abstract and general sense.

This aspect of the popular outlook may stem from the shallowness of the pre-1917 democratic tradition in Russia combined with a lack of direct knowledge or experience as to the means by which a system of diffused power operates. The present generation of Russians certainly lacks a firm democratic tradition. Against this background of noncomprehension, Soviet propaganda may have had some success in identifying political democracy with private industrial capitalism, which, again, does not now appear an attractive alternative to the Soviet citizen.

It should also be noted that a degree of limited and carefully directed popular political action is permitted in Soviet society. The Soviet regime, in its effort to combat bureaucratic corruption, inefficiency, and complacence, has not relied only on cross-checks among various bureaucratic institutions. It has also used (in a limited way) one democratic element in the revolutionary ideology, i.e., mass participation in the administrative process. The encouragement of popular pressure on the middle and lower levels of administration provides the regime with an additional counterweight to the bureaucracy. The forms of popular participation in administration—through the local Soviets, the trade unions, and "self-criticism"—give the people some sense of sharing in the government. They can blow off steam—in approved directions—and can sometimes secure redress of grievances against the lower officialdom, who are made scapegoats in order to deflect hostility away from the regime per se.

The lack of political freedom—of any opportunity for basic criticism of the regime or for a positive voice in the nation's policies—does not in itself appear to be regarded as particularly onerous. Specific grievances and tensions, which to the Western mind are symptoms of the political process, seem to take precedence in the mind of the Soviet citizen. General political ideas are conspicuous by their absence within the Soviet Union, although, once outside, the Soviet citizen appears to take to politics with vigor. In this as in the other instances noted here, the apparent reaction of the Soviet citizen to his present environment can not be used directly as a means of prediction of his response should that environment radically alter.

Chapter Fourteen

GROUP DISSATISFACTIONS

In ADDITION to these general clashes between men's expectations and the realities of Soviet life, the system has a particular impact on groups within the social structure. The apparent position and outlook of certain more important groups is discussed below.

1. THE PEASANT

There appears little doubt that the most substantial area of conscious dissatisfaction within Soviet society exists among the peasantry, who still constitute something like half the population of the Soviet Union. Their dissatisfaction has its roots in the simple fact that they have maintained to an important extent their aspiration for private ownership and cultivation of the land. It has been accentuated by memories of the brutality of collectivization which followed a decade of relative economic freedom under NEP, and, latterly, by the relaxation (toward use of private plots of land) which took place in the course of World War II. It may be that the ideological foundations of the regime, which involved the giving of the land to the peasantry, and the continued external propaganda concern of the regime with the plight of the small and medium farmer, may somewhat enhance dissatisfaction with collective farming as it is, in fact, organized and administered within the Soviet Union.

When, in 1935, the stabilization of collectivized agriculture was marked by the *kolkhoz* (collective farm) statute, a definite compromise with the individualist inclinations of the peasantry was made. The *artel* system was generally adopted, whereby the peasants were allowed to keep and work individual plots in addition to doing their collective work on *kolkhoz* land. This compromise, though it provided the minimum reconciliation of the interests of the state and the peasantry, has been unstable. The basic picture of Soviet agriculture since 1935 has been one of chronic friction between the individual interests of the peasants and the interests of the state in the collective system. Certain major specific frictions can be noted:

1. The peasant prefers to work on his own plot, and seeks to enlarge it whenever possible. During the relative freedom of the war period, individual work and marketing expanded greatly, and actually produced a substantial portion of the urban food supply. In 1946 the regime undertook a major effort to restore land to the *kolkhozy*. To induce quantitatively and qualitatively adequate collective work, constant efforts have been necessary: minimum work standards, monetary incentives, tax discrimination against income derived from individual work, and disciplinary measures.

2. There have been difficulties in organizing the units for collective work, i.e., the controversy of link vs. brigade. The small group, the link, prevailed until after the war, but has been in the process of replacement by the larger brigade to improve work discipline and check the individualist or familial tendencies allegedly encouraged by the link.

3. There has been a chronic and fundamental weakness in creating a collective spirit, attested by the constant problem of theft of collective property both by the peasants and by the *kolkhoz* administrators.

4. Hostility has continued steadily between the peasants and the *kolkhoz* administrators who are frequently regarded as outsiders endeavoring to enrich themselves. Periodic efforts have been made by the government to increase the degree of responsibility of the *kolkhoz* administrators to the peasants, and thus to check the power and abuses of the regime's local plenipotentiaries.

5. Frictions are evident between the *kolkhozy* and the state, primarily because of the large obligatory crop deliveries (at a very low price) imposed by the state. Adjustments to price changes or local difficulties are inadequate. In general, the peasants are left to bear the burden of crop fluctuations. Otherwise, state administrative controls are usually loose, leaving the peasantry at the mercy of local officials.

6. Income differentiation within the *kolkhoz* has caused evident dissatisfaction, especially between administrators and field workers; but income differentiation between *kolkhozy* has also raised difficulties.

7. Machine tractor stations and the *kolkhoz* have generated

chronic friction due to believed unsatisfactory MTS services. Dependence of the peasants on bureaucratic MTS functions, which are judged unreliable, has been resented.

After the initial violence of the collectivization process, village life was again more or less stabilized. Mass voluntary migration to the cities after the middle thirties fell off greatly—to the point where the state had to resort to the State Labor Reserve draft in 1940. The peasants, on balance, evidently prefer agricultural life despite the hardships which it imposes. Although their average standard of living is low, there is a fair opportunity for individual peasants or their children to advance socially. They may earn differential wages, enter the *kolkhoz* administration, move into urban employment, or even acquire a higher education.

The peasant's grievance appears to be not that he must remain a peasant, but that he cannot till the soil in the individual fashion which he prefers. The full range of powers of the Soviet state in altering the setting of his life and in determining the education and information available to him has not destroyed this aspiration.

From the point of view of the state, the system of control over agriculture appears to be judged inadequate. The problem of the regime is not to balance considerations of central control and local execution, but to attain what is believed to be a necessary minimum of political and administrative leverage over agricultural life. To further these objectives, the policy of amalgamating collective farms has been undertaken in the postwar years.

The general trend of Soviet policy toward the peasantry since 1929 has been in the direction of proletarianization, i.e., toward the creation of an agricultural working force divorced in fact and in aspiration from land ownership. This policy, like collectivization itself, was probably the result of converging economic and political interests. Economically the regime desired to acquire the nation's food supply at lowered real cost and with a diminished allocation of income to agriculture. This appeared to justify large-scale farms, accelerated mechanization, and controlled prices for the bulk of agricultural output. This system also commended itself as a means of drawing labor from the land into the cities and factories. Politically, the system commended itself, in a rare throw-back to deterministic Marxism, as a way of altering the individualistic social outlook which is associated with small independent landowners.

Whether agricultural output per man and capital formation in general have been accelerated by Soviet policy toward the peasantry since 1929 is debatable. What is clear is that the social and political problem of the peasants' outlook has not yet been resolved. The problem, however, is not acute, since the direct administrative machinery of the *kolkhozy*, in combination with the Party and secret police, keep the peasants' dissidence under adequate control. Separated and without organization, the Soviet peasantry is not an independent active political force. Its very existence, however, appears to constitute a nagging problem to the regime, as well as an important potential factor in the ultimate resolution of an internal crisis, should it develop.

2. THE NATIONAL MINORITIES

There is no more complex or elusive task in the field of Russian studies than the evaluation of the strength of nationality sentiment within the Soviet Union. The problem is difficult both because nationality feelings must be distinguished from other, more universal sources of dissatisfaction, and because the position in the different nationality areas is believed to vary widely. The appraisal here given is made in general terms and excludes regions brought within the Soviet Empire after World War II, notably the Baltic states.

From its very beginning the Bolshevik regime inherited the ancient Russian problem of handling the diverse hostile and separatist national minorities. Under the tsarist regime national differences had been encouraged in some areas only as a tactical means of inciting one minority group against another and thus increasing the power of the central authority. Tsarist policy in general is reflected in its slogans: "One Tsar, one religion, one language"; "Russia one and indivisible." Contrary to the desired effect, it left a heritage of bitterness and resulted in an increase of national political consciousness as well as the growth of a national intelligentsia who, in one way or another, have remained a key element in the nationality problem down to the present.

The view of the early Russian Marxists on the nationality question deprecated national sentiment as a serious political force and looked to its adaptation to the class criteria of socialism, a view which led to a concept of ultimate unification and amalgamation of the ethnic groups under socialism. Lenin and his followers, however, in considering the nationality question before the Revolution, took an early stand in favor of self-determination insofar as it did not lead to the breakdown of ethnic groups into self-governing bodies. Fearing the development of the national-cultural autonomy concept, Lenin sent Stalin to Vienna in 1913 to study the minority question and to prepare an article. The resulting work, entitled "Marxism and the National Question," was directed primarily against the doctrine of national-cultural autonomy as proposed by the Austrian Social Democrats. Before the Revolution, then, the Bolsheviks were somewhat ambivalent on this issue, recognizing the force of nationality sentiment and, at the same time, struggling for a formula which would take account of its reality without interfering with the workings of a centralized socialist state.

Nevertheless, despite this measure of realism about nationality sentiment, the strength of the centrifugal forces unleashed among the nationalities following the Revolution was a surprise to the Bolsheviks, who had believed that the nationalities would rally with greater unity around the banners of the socialist revolution. Lenin and his followers quickly relaxed their earlier opposition to federalism and advanced a new policy with a triple objective:

1. To assure the Russians that their national geographic heritage would be preserved.

2. To convince the non-Russians that they would not be discriminated against.

3. To assure the non-Russians that the tsarist program of forcible Russification had been abandoned.

Politically, the policy adopted was to grant varying forms of apparent political self-expression which were effectively nullified by the fact that they could operate only through the Communist Party which was, of course, centrally controlled and operated. The grant of linguistic autonomy was considered to be a responsive answer to the cultural demands of the minority peoples.

The new Bolshevik policy quite effectively reduced initial friction engendered between the Bolshevik regime and the minorities. The Soviet leaders were hopeful that, through the extension of cultural freedom, political loyalty would be assured. They sharply criticized those who would proclaim the supremacy of Russian culture, and continued to assert that "national cultures must be permitted to develop and expand."

This policy of fostering a national culture, including the use of native languages, was hailed as a forward step by the non-Russian intelligentsia and particularly by its younger representatives. In the

Soviet Ukraine however, many Russians and Russified Ukrainians opposed Ukrainization as they had the policy of the ill-fated Ukrainian Republic of 1918. They felt that their position, bound as it was to Russia rather than to the Ukraine, was threatened. Despite opposition, the policy of fostering minority cultures was well on the way to implementation by 1924. The institution of this minority policy was accompanied by and, in fact, was part of the same phase of concessions to popular feeling as the New Economic Policy. In general, the cultural and economic policies of these years created a feeling of relative satisfaction among the peasantry, workers, and intelligentsia; and, taken as a whole, they fostered the rise of a feeling of national political and cultural consciousness within the Ukrainian Republic and, to a lesser degree, in the Caucasus.

Gradually, however, from about 1927, as Stalin assured his personal grip on the Soviet state, the regime executed a definite shift of policy regarding cultural autonomy and the relations between Great Russians and non-Russians, a change of attitude which had a major effect on many sections of the population. The greatest impact was on literature and the arts—perhaps the most important immediate factors in sustaining a sense of national identity. National leaders and writers were subject to purges beginning in the late twenties and continuing until 1938.

The change in nationality policy coincided approximately with the end of NEP and the shift in economic policy to a concentration on large-scale development of industry and the collectivization of agriculture. The opposition to collectivization was particularly bitter in the Ukraine. In the Georgian and Armenian Republics opposition took the form of peasant uprisings and, in part, was translated into antagonism toward the Great Russians. As the Ukrainian urban working class was largely Russified, there were no apparent major tensions in the Ukrainian factories. In the Caucasus, where the industrial working class was small, minor tensions resulted from the mixing of nationalities in the new industrial enterprises. For the Armenians and Georgians, industrialization signified a new source of wealth of which the native elements were proud; but the lowering of living standards under the Soviet convinced many of the older and middle generations that this newly developed industrial wealth was being exploited by Moscow.

Stalin clarified this change in policy by declaring in 1934 that "local chauvinism has grown into a danger to the state." His policy included a throwback to tsarist Russification, with emphasis on

Russian as the second language of all nationalities. Russian officials, particularly in the late thirties, were sent into the non-Russian areas as "more reliable elements" to assume responsible positions. The program for cultural uniformity was given new impetus with the emergence of the concept of "Soviet patriotism." This doctrine, giving priority to the Soviet state over the regional attachments of the non-Russian peoples, made it possible to emphasize the cultural leveling and assimilating aspects of Soviet life, and to deflate the spirit of autonomous culture which earlier Soviet policy had encouraged.

The nationality policy of the thirties was, in effect, a thorough reversal of previous policy and resulted in a rise of resentment and bitterness, particularly among the intelligentsia. The Soviet regime made efforts to temper this reaction by continuing to stress the importance of the nationalities in Soviet politics and by popularization among the peasants and workers of their cultures, although in a greatly censored form. In these efforts the regime was not entirely successful. National consciousness was still alive and in evidence in some areas, although its extent was difficult to gauge. The underlying tenor of prewar Soviet policy was well reflected in the Great Purge, when the nationality groups (including Communist Party leaders) were hit with particular force and thoroughness.

In economic terms, the regime had succeeded by 1941 in bringing the economies of the nationality areas fully within the orbit of the central planning and administrative machinery of the Soviet Union as a whole.

It is evident that, in general, the regime was not sufficiently successful in gaining the loyalty of Soviet citizens to avoid major defections when war and invasion made that possibility realistic. The rapid advance of the German army created a condition under which pent-up dissatisfactions could be translated into action. Antagonism toward the Soviet regime expressed itself in wholesale desertions and surrender of army units to the Germans, and in the initial welcome extended by the villagers to their believed liberators.

The Soviet Ukrainians, Russians, Belorussians, and other nationals deserted and surrendered to and welcomed the Germans—not as such, but as the enemy of the regime. The conditions created in the initial rout of the Soviet armies were seized upon as a promise of liberation from oppression rather than as an opportunity to establish independent national minority states. The fact that the Ukrainians predominated among the defectors was principally a geographical accident of war. The same pattern of behavior on the part of the Soviet population was repeated—if more hesitantly—in other than predominantly Ukrainian areas.

Although defection was not primarily a function of nationalist impulses, mass desertions and attempts to co-operate with the Germans on a community basis were the more easily organized and effected where a given community or a given military unit was unified ethnically and linguistically. In that sense the concentration and the density of nationally and culturally similar people did play an important role. It was this experience which has probably determined the postwar Soviet policy of breaking up and diluting the population of the nationality areas by cross-migration and other means. Similarly the postwar reorganization of the Soviet army has seen the elimination of distinct nationality units.

More broadly, postwar Soviet policy has sharply increased the trend toward Russification, including the growing numbers of Russian officials in nationality areas, the expanding use of the Russian language, the rewriting of non-Russian histories, emphasis on the special status of the Great Russians in Soviet propaganda, and continued resettlement of peoples. Reaction to this policy has been reflected in the recurrent minor purges since the war and the more recent drastic housecleaning in the Ukrainian and Georgian Republics. Apparently segments of the non-Russian intelligentsia are having a difficult time keeping within the formula "national in form—socialist in content," which suggests that a nationalist spirit is by no means defunct, and that it has, perhaps, been increased as a result of current Russification policy. Having been encouraged to develop in the past a degree of at least cultural identification with their nationality region, some non-Russians may now acutely resent an accentuated shift in policy in the other direction.

On the other hand, the greatly intensified Russification program has probably achieved some success. The application of the Great Russian symbols to the non-Russians cannot be judged wholly ineffective. The Russian language and many aspects of Russian culture may increasingly influence, either consciously or unconsciously, the minds of the youth of Soviet minorities, since their educational opportunities have increased under the Soviet system. Soviet officials, engineers, and others among the non-Russians probably derive some satisfaction from participation in the economic and political life of a large and strong country. Perhaps the greatest strength of the Soviet nationality policy is that it tends to draw the individual non-Russian into the Soviet pattern and to diminish his sense of identity with his ethnic group. "Voluntary" migration and resettlement of peoples may also contribute to the success of the Russification policy. Something akin to the American "melting pot" does appear to operate, to a degree, in the Soviet Union, notably at the level of the bureaucratic middle class.

This does not mean, of course, that non-Russian Soviet citizens are satisfied with their lot. The peoples of the Soviet Union are dissatisfied with their economic position; they resent the rigid police and party controls which penetrate even their personal lives; and they are subject to other frustrations. These general dissatisfactions are fully shared by the non-Russians, and in some areas are undoubtedly accentuated by the clash between a sense of cultural identity and the policies of the Muscovite regime. It appears that the attitudes toward the regime of the non-Russians are stronger versions of those of Soviet citizens in other social categories and areas, and that the most important grievances of the non-Russians are similar to those of the Great Russians. It does not follow that the animus or frustration of the non-Russians is firmly attached to the aspiration for national independence, nor that the nationality dimension of popular dissatisfaction is of uniform strength in all the non-Russian areas.

The political power of national sentiment at the present time is, as in the other cases of popular dissatisfaction, relatively slight: first, because, lacking opportunities for effective expression, the bulk of the citizens of these areas are probably apathetic with respect to the usefulness of independent political thought and action; second, because the regime, so long as it maintains its unity, has ample resources to contain manifestations of discontent.

Effective political action motivated by nationality sentiment is likely to flare up only when opportunity for it exists. The form it may take, and, in particular, whether it is likely to be directed against the regime or against identification with Great Russia, cannot be predicted on present evidence, which shows a clear persistence of regional and cultural self-consciousness but little or no aspiration for political independence. The outcome for the future may well be determined by the form in which the opportunity, if any, arises. A protracted internal crisis in Russia, in which the power of Moscow disintegrated, or a war in which a nationality area is held by one of Russia's enemies, might see this sentiment channelled into a move for independence. An alteration in the central regime which offered greater tolerance for the individual citizen in general and some of the substance of federalism for the nationality areas (while the regime sustained its ultimate authority throughout the Russian Empire) might well see this feeling effectively placated.

Our broad conclusions then, are as follows:

1. The discontents within the nationality areas are, essentially, similar to those which characterize Soviet citizens in other regions, including the Great Russians.

2. In addition, with varying force, these general discontents are heightened by a sense of cultural identity which is increasingly violated by current Soviet policy.

3. There is no evidence to indicate that the discontents of these peoples, whatever their source, are now positively associated to any substantial degree with an aspiration for national political independence.

3. THE INTELLECTUAL

As described in Chapter 6, Soviet intellectuals and creative artists have had a peculiarly stormy history. The successive transitions from relative freedom in the 1920's to the brief *partiinost* phase, with its domination by literal propaganda, to the continuing regime of "Socialist realism" since the early 1930's, have altered the setting in which they have worked and the goals they have been permitted to pursue. The postwar tightening of the regime's controls has been particularly painful, since a substantial degree of individual creative liberty was granted in the years of World War II, including enlarged contact with men and work going forward in the outside world. Like many other elements in Soviet society, the intellectual apparently felt and hoped that the successful and loyal defense of the Soviet Union over the period 1941–45 would result in a sea-change, which would ease the degree and character of controls and recognize the capabilities of the Soviet peoples for responsible national citizenship.

The intellectual and artistic professions carry with them a long heritage of individual expression—almost of egoism—which, from about 1929, the Soviet regime has systematically sought either to harness to its own ends or to constrain. As if aware that a policy of harnessing the intellectual could, by the nature of the case, not wholly succeed, it has engaged over recent years in chronic harassing tactics. While these appear to result in reprimand, demotion, or temporary public eclipse rather than liquidation, they undoubtedly give to intellectual and creative life a distinctly uneasy quality.

The criteria on which the regime bestows its praise or criticism can no longer be deduced from external first principles; nor can appeal be made in terms of alternative interpretations of such principles. There are at least two fundamental ambiguities at work here:

1. The profound modifications in deterministic Marxism which have been made over the years by the regime are not fully acknowledged or codified; thus, even with a will to conform, the intellectual must await the arbitrary application of the regime's current view of his output's usefulness before knowing his status.

2. The bias of the regime over the past two decades toward, broadly, traditional intellectual and artistic forms makes precarious any original creative effort.

Intellectual controls under these circumstances can only be applied negatively. The will of the regime can only be learned by trial and error.

The situation is further complicated by the bureaucratic organization of intellectual and creative life, which introduces into each field powerful bosses whose tastes and empire-building undoubtedly tinge the judgments passed on individual men and works. Fadeev has held such a position of postwar command in literature; Lysenko in biology.

Like other men of talent, the intellectual and the artist in Soviet life find themselves tempted by the substantial rewards offered: high real income, public acclaim, and widespread publication, display, or performance. These rewards can be attained, however, only at heavy costs—including personal risk and compromise with both professional standards and personal insight. These latter criteria evidently remain alive among the criteria for performance. Many take the risk and make the compromises, but few can be wholly satisfied. Many intellectuals find a retreat into areas where the exposure to the regime's interest is believed to be minimum, e.g., ancient history. Novelists pour their creative human insights into villains and secondary characters, larding over their works with vindications of the current Party line and the vacuous prototype hero. Performers and audiences exploit to the full the potentialities offered by the regime's tolerance of selected pre-1917 Russian drama and the ballet.

What is central here, as in the case of religion, is that the mixed position of intellectual and cultural life—partially but not wholly regimented in terms of the regime's ambiguous criteria—sustains, though they are muted, individualistic and humanistic conceptions and expectations not in harmony with the major realities of a totalitarian state. After all, one part of Soviet policy would place current writers in the tradition of Tolstoy, Turgenev, Gogol, and others whose works are published on a large scale and are extremely popular. Artistic integrity and independence as well as a compassionate concern for the individual in society are not unknown conceptions in Soviet Russia. The awkward and evidently unsatisfactory position of the intellectual and creative artist in Soviet life may prove of great importance should the control system weaken or break down. The artist-intellectual, perhaps uniquely among Soviet social groups, because of the partially accidental history of the regime and because of the nature of his profession, has kept alive the conception of a realistic alternative.

4. THE MIDDLE AND LOWER BUREAUCRAT

The Soviet regime, in a step-by-step process, gradually came to acknowledge its requirement for an efficient, loyal, and enterprising bureaucracy. The norms of the educational and social system shifted steadily away from the revolutionary conception of reliance on the industrial worker toward the development and rewarding of the bureaucrat. This progressive transition was symbolized at various stages by the permission of wide differentiations in real income heavily favorable to the bureaucracy, the ending of social and political discrimination in favor of "proletarians" within the Party (1939), and by Malenkov's enunciation of the criteria of education and ability for promotion within the bureaucracy (1941). There is no doubt that the base of the regime has been shifted from the bottom to the top of the social (and real income) pyramid.

This transition, with its powerful incentives, has been accompanied by the imposition of a complex system of surveillance and overlapping controls designed at once to keep the bureaucracy efficient and to maintain it as the servant, not the master, of the regime. As discussed in Chapter 12, it is believed that the nature of the regime raises special problems with respect to limitations of power of the upper reaches of the bureaucracy. With respect to the lower levels of bureaucracy, further removed from the area where major decisions are made, a similar but less acute set of problems appears to exist.

Under Stalin's rule the bureaucracy was not a ruling class so much as a group of important and, therefore, privileged servants of the state, analogous in its position to the upper class under Ivan IV or Peter the Great, or in the ancient empires when a strong king prevailed. The Soviet administrator commonly shoulders important responsibility. He is given broad authority within the directives handed down, and the principle of individual management generally holds. But the bureaucrat is subjected to rigorous standards of political conformity, plan-fulfillment, and so on. The ultimate sanction for error or failure is powerful—liquidation or the labor camp. The extreme penalty was applied on an extensive scale only during the Great Purge of 1936-38, but minor purges as well as the memory of 1936-38 have kept alive an awareness of the risks of even modest elevation in the Soviet structure.

The efforts of the regime to secure both the control advantages of intense centralization and the performance advantages of subordinate and local autonomy and initiative in all of its various administrative systems have typically placed the Soviet administrator in a position of extreme tension. On the one hand, he can aspire to high material rewards, great authority and prestige, and opportunities for satisfaction by achievement. On the other hand, his responsibility is heavy; he is subjected to the scrutiny of several control hierarchies; his efforts can be hamstrung by regulations or the arbitrary action of higher authority; and he works under risks barely short of mortal. High tension—the higher, the more responsible the position—is a basic feature of the life of the Soviet bureaucrat.

Probably crucial for the morale of the administrators is the balance between the sense of achievement and the sense of futility which they experience in their work. The workings of a control system of this kind are not likely to be highly efficient or fully rational, from the perspective of the orderly bureaucrat. He must try to do his job and, at the same time, contend with a system which contains irrational elements of arbitrarily exercised power and mechanical political conformity.

This type of administrator selected out by Soviet conditions as the most successful is extremely ambitious, willing to take risks to satisfy his desire for achievement, tough and aggressive, but highly adaptable in making his ambitions conform to the demands of the system. He is prepared to violate the law to further the effective performance of his function and, when he can get away with it, is inclined to use his official power for personal advantage. Local bureaucratic cliques are formed to protect the interests of the administrators and allay the tensions to which the central authority endeavors to subject them. The over-all picture seems to be one of an uneasy balance of power between the central authority and its agents.

Common results of the tension experienced by the administrator are the avoidance of responsibility and initiative, and a retreat into bureaucratic routine and relative safety. These force the top authority, in turn, to intensify the pressures impinging on the administrator in order to maintain the necessary minimum of initiative. There are elements here of a potential vicious circle, i.e., a failure of efficiency leading to a greater control and pressure leading, in turn, to a further reduction in enterprise and efficiency. An awareness of this danger may partially account for the sporadic nature of the purge process in different sectors of the bureaucracy, notable since the Great Purge.

On the other hand, it is not clear that the Soviet regime has formed a technique of stable equilibrium between centralization of executive power and efficient administrative operations. The long-term trend was, under Stalin, toward increased use of police power. This trend, combined with an apparent reluctance to undertake another Great Purge, undoubtedly led to a diminution of vigor in the bureaucracy similar to the withdrawal to be noted among intellectuals and creative artists. On the other hand, the various potential instabilities within the executive authority and between that authority and the higher bureaucracy may lead to an assumption of greater authority by the bureaucracy in the making of policy. The attempt to separate power from responsibility, in the extreme manner which Stalin attempted, is not likely to prove stable over long periods.

The dissatisfactions felt by the bureaucrat are evident enough from the nature of the structure in which he operates. The returns for success are sufficiently real and attractive to draw recruits; but the risks are great, the pressure is intense, and built-in conflicts exist between the fulfillment of objectives the bureaucrat has not determined, procedural rules laid down from above, and the changing requirements of political conformity externally enunciated. In this setting some careerists accept the system as it is and seek to move forward in terms of its peculiar complex of demands. Others may seek the compromise of accepting its rewards at a modest level while avoiding its risks, thus in effect reducing the extent to which they accept responsibility. Others—probably few—may actively resent its workings and, at least privately, look to its change. The attachment of the bureaucrat to the regime is evidently, where it exists, an attachment to a system in which he has done well, rather than an attachment to a set of abstract ideals. Although the average medium- and low-level Soviet administrator is not likely to play a major role in detonating or expanding a crisis in the system, he is also not likely to resist its change especially actively, if the change is in the direction of a reduced exercise of the multi-armed executive authority on the bureaucratic chain of command.

5. THE INDUSTRIAL WORKER

The Soviet proletariat is a new class, composed largely of peasants recruited into industry within the last generation, without long tradition or collective memory. The working class of 1917, in whose name the Bolshevik Revolution was carried out, was substantially dissipated with the collapse of industry during the civil war and with recruitment into the ranks of the Party organization and administrative groups. Social mobility for old workers was high through the 1930's.

Although many individual workers have risen in the power structure, the proletariat as a class has progressively lost touch with power. Workers' control in industry was eliminated during 1918–21; with the NEP, state-owned industry was organized on bureaucratic lines, as it has since remained. The real influence of the industrial worker in the Party was reduced to a negligible quantity by 1921, with the dominance of the Party apparatus and the suppression of the Workers' Opposition. In 1928–29 the trade unions lost what autonomy they still held. Since the inception of the First Five-Year Plan, the "productionist" view has prevailed, i.e., disciplinary and incentive measures are combined, in the familiar stick-and-carrot combination, to insure maximum productivity.

With the intensive industrialization of the First Five-Year Plan, vast numbers of peasant recruits, released from or forced out of the farms by collectivization, were taken into industry. New problems of education and incentives to overcome the peasants' backwardness and easy-going psychology were then posed. The combination of propaganda and premiums represented by the Stakhanov movement was the upshot. Similar problems of education and incentives were faced in securing managerial material from among the workers. These problems of industry figured prominently in the repudiation of equalitarianism and of a deterministic psychology. They also contributed to the extreme anxiety about industrial errors or failures, treated as "wrecking" or "sabotage."

The standard of living of the average worker fell, as inflation more than offset wage increases. However, it is probable that many, if not most, individual workers maintained or improved their condition through upgrading, while the average was depressed by the influx of new workers at real wages lower than earlier rates but possibly higher than their income on the farm.

With the stabilization of agriculture by 1935 and the concession of private plots, the influx of peasants to the cities fell off. This was followed by drastic changes in labor policy to counteract the increased bargaining power of labor, and to prevent a rise in real wages at the expense of investment resources. Collective agreements between unions and enterprises were terminated in 1935–36. Labor turnover—the effect of seeking the best possible conditions—was attacked by the institution of labor books for each worker in 1938, and by a comprehensive job freeze in 1940.

These measures have been continued since the war but enforcement is difficult, since employers, eager to get men, connive in their violation and tend to bid up wages over the planned levels. With the growing shortage of labor, discharge as the principal disciplinary sanction had to be replaced, as it was in 1940, with pay cuts, forced labor, and penal sanctions. Also in 1940 the State Labor Reserve draft was instituted; but this technique now appears to be on the decline. Harsh discipline and arbitrary managerial authority remain in the postwar picture, but they are tempered by management's plan-fulfillment interest in attracting good workers and keeping their morale high.

Along with the subjection of the new industrial working class to quasi-military discipline has come a sharp loss in political privileges and social status. Party ideology has ceased to emphasize proletarian superiority. By 1939 the preference accorded industrial workers in getting education, appointments, and Party membership was terminated. Ability, rather than social background, has become the prime criterion for advancement, and the new technicians and intelligentsia—composed in a significant degree, to be sure, of former workers—is now the real upper class. Workers play a diminished role in the Party, a noteworthy symptom being the tendency for managerial personnel to assume the function of Party agitation in the factory. The social distance between the workers and the people who run the institutions of power has increased. Social mobility is diminishing. The recruitment of the managerial elite, save for the replacement of war losses, is substantially complete; and the continuing flow of replacements to that class may now come, in increasing proportion, from the families of bureaucrats. The labor draft and educational fees instituted in 1940 suggest the felt need to stabilize the acquired status of the social classes which have emerged.

The aspirations of the Soviet worker—still close to peasant origins—are probably of limited range and material in emphasis. An improvement in living standards is probably his main aspiration, and the extent of his labors and inadequate improvement in welfare the main source of his dissatisfaction.

To the extent that workers absorb the ideal of the classless society and the conception of broad opportunity for advancement, and can contrast the ideal with the increasing exclusion of themselves from upper-level activities of the society, there is material for further disaffection. The ideology on which the regime partially depends to keep the masses satisfied makes future satisfaction increasingly difficult. The possibility can not be excluded of the future emergence, possibly through the trade unions, of a working-class movement directed against the regime, although at the present time the evidence would suggest only a low level of political interest or even awareness in the Soviet industrial working class.

6. PRISON AND FORCED LABOR

The process whereby the secret police was set up as an arm of the Revolution, and prison camps were established for "unreliable" political groups as well as conventional prisoners, has already been described in Chapter 3. From 1923 forward, at least four motives have converged to sustain the institutions of prison and forced labor:

1. The fear and docility they help create within the population in general.

2. The recurrent desire of the regime to neutralize one group or another judged politically unreliable: those believed domestic enemies during and after the Revolution; those purged in the late 1930's; nationality groups not trusted during World War II; believed Baltic dissidents after the war; groups from the European satellites; retained prisoners of war, etc.

3. The desire to mobilize quickly large pools of cheap labor for special tasks of capital construction.

4. The vested interest of the MVD bureaucracy in the continuance of the prison camps.

Estimates of the population directly affected vary widely. As a minimum estimate, about three and a half million Soviet citizens are held in prison camps, including, presumably, those who have been transported (with their families) to live under supervised and limited conditions in remote areas. Both groups are under MVD control. At a minimum something like 2 per cent of the total Soviet population is thus directly caught up in the system of prison and forced labor, a figure to be compared with the U.S. (federal and state) prison population of one-tenth of 1 per cent (150,000). Other responsible estimates in this difficult field run twice or three times as large. On present evidence, 8,000,000 is a quite reasonable estimate. An estimate for 1941 would suggest that 14 per cent of gross capital investment in the Soviet Union was executed under MVD supervision. Although total planned investment in that year may have been somewhat reduced because of heavy military outlays, it is, nevertheless, evident that prison and forced labor is a massive social and economic fact.

Since the population of the prison camps is so large and, almost by definition, dissident, it is important to establish the character of its outlook on the Soviet system. In a manner made familiar by our knowledge of Hitler's concentration camps, a rather complex human re-orientation takes place within the prison camps which affects heavily the political attitudes of inmates and, in a wider sense, their political significance for the long-run stability of the society. Groups and cliques, tensions and solidarities emerge. At the top of the hierarchy is the MVD personnel: the MVD commandant in charge of the camp and his associates. The camp director has at his command ordinary troops of the MVD army. The main division of the prison population is between criminals and political prisoners. This division is real and acute, and the criminals appear to have higher status and more privileges.

The better treatment of the criminals does not consist primarily of superior rations, since officially every prisoner gets rations in accordance with his individual performance in relation to the work norm assigned to him. The privileged position of the criminal consists rather in the kind of job to which he is usually assigned. Jobs are performed in units called brigades, which consist of from twenty to forty people. The man in charge of the brigade, a prisoner himself, is called the brigadier, and he is reported to be almost invariably a criminal prisoner. He submits at the end of every working day a detailed report showing the individual performance of each member of his brigade. It is according to work performance that food and other necessities of life are given. While the total output of the whole brigade is checked by men who are over the brigadiers and whose specific function is to verify the production figures, no one checks the subdivision of those figures between the individual members of the brigade. The brigadier has the power to write down as little or as much for each prisoner as he wishes. Thus he wields an ultimate power over each member of his brigade.

Another privileged clique which may consist of both political and criminal prisoners, but weighted toward the criminal faction, is the veterans. These are men who survived the initial hardships, who succeeded in adjusting themselves successfully to the rigors of the camp regime, who know the situation well, including the legal, semilegal, and illegal means of procedure, and who hold the administrative jobs of the camps which give them the opportunity to manipulate the lives of their fellow prisoners. *Blat,* or pull, plays generally an important part in Soviet life, but nowhere more so than in the prison camps.

A somewhat different relation between prisoners and camp guards appears to emerge than was normal under the Nazi experience. In the Nazi camps the prisoners in authority, the block leaders and others, tended to identify themselves socially and psychologically with the Gestapo men. In the Soviet camp the social and psychological division is apparently more complex and subtle. Thus a regular rank-and-file MVD soldier whose duty is to watch over a given working unit, often in bitter cold, tends to identify himself, through common hardship, with the working group. This conclusion is, of course, based wholly on the personal observations and feelings of escaped prisoners rather than on direct evidence. The guard would never jeopardize his position by open sympathy with his charges. Further, he is better clad and fed than his charges. It is, nevertheless, the general conclusion of prisoners who have escaped that the guard generally felt that he was a victim of the system in much the same manner as the prisoner.

The upper elements of the MVD bureaucracy in charge of the camp administration seem to have considerable rapport with the upper groups in the hierarchy of the camp population. Technicians and engineers as well as office workers, in order to perform their specific duties, are given special passes to go about the camp without guard. These jobs are usually held by veterans who have been in the camp for many years, and who live better than ordinary MVD guards.

The attitude of the typical political prisoner appears to develop into an admixture of cynicism and resignation. Before being sent to camp his spirit may be broken in prison during the days and nights of continuous interrogation. Bowing to the pressure of physical and psychological torture, he is likely to confess, although neither he nor his interrogators believe in the truth of the confessions. In the camp, he is quite bewildered and still does not know quite why he is there. He tends usually to blame his fate on some sort of mistake—on the jealousy of local competitors who wanted, perhaps, his job, or his apartment, or his social position, or his wife. It is hard for him, especially if he was a Party member and held high positions in the Party, to blame the Communist hierarchy for his fate. He is often convinced that he is still a good Communist, and the leaders of the Party could not possibly know of his fate since, if they knew of it, they would make good the evident error. In a modern version of the old Russian peasant's attitude toward the Tsar, good will is attributed to the leaders of the regime —or was, at least, to Stalin. But time goes on and the prisoner remains where he is. He works hard, becomes ill; his friends may die; and his letters to various organs of the Ministry of Justice which are supposed to review his pleas and check the irregularities of the secret police, and his letters and petitions to the other organs of Soviet power, remain unanswered. Thus he becomes increasingly bitter and resigned to his fate. Since he is only too well aware of the impossibility of any organized activity that could bring a change in his condition, he resigns himself to it and devotes his energies to making the best adjustment he can. Under Soviet control, with its intricate systems of check and cross-check, under the eyes of informers and spies, his opportunity for organization or common political activity is almost nonexistent. When one is continuously supervised, when one is continuously searched, when one's correspondence is scrutinized, hope for subversive political activity soon dies. The political outlook of the typical camp prisoner thus constitutes an extreme version of the political apathy which characterizes Soviet society as a whole; and, in general, the massive phenomenon of forced and prison labor in the Soviet Union is better understood as a shading off of normal life under totalitarianism, toward higher degrees of control and surveillance, than as a highly distinct phenomenon, like prison life in Western societies.

The position of removed populations living and working under MVD supervision is, of course, somewhat less acute; but they are almost certainly weighted down equally by the burdens of labor and the unbreakable power of the setting within which the regime has placed them. Unless a disintegrating internal crisis or war fractures the control system, they are almost certainly incapable of independent political activity.

Among those outside prison and forced labor camps, the existence of these institutions is an oppressive fact. Although these camps may be taken for granted in a way unfamiliar to the traditions of the West, they remain perhaps the most powerful single reminder of the unsatisfactory character of the regime. Men who know nothing of democratic life and who do not feel the lack of the relatively free political procedures of democracy, nevertheless understand that the arbitrary seizure of men, their secret trial, and their indefinite incarceration are inherently unjust. They may well give little conscious thought and no open expression to their view; but the scale on which the Soviet prison and forced labor systems operate makes their existence known, feared, and disliked.

Part Three

CONCLUSIONS

Chapter Fifteen

POST-STALIN

1. INTRODUCTION

THE PURPOSE of this final chapter is to take stock of the position within the Soviet Union as of the interim date May 15, 1953,[1] and, in particular, to assess the forces now at work shaping the Soviet future. By the time this book appears more will certainly be known of the meaning of recent changes in the structure of Soviet power and of recent moves in both foreign and domestic policy. It would be foolhardy at this stage and under these circumstances to pretend to omniscience concerning the recent past or to predict how, in fact, the succession process now under way will proceed in the coming months and years.

What may be useful is to consider the known facts in the light of the views developed in Parts One and Two of this essay, and to examine the alternatives. The succession process is proceeding not in a flexible revolutionary setting but in a system that is now some thirty-six years old, almost two generations beyond its revolution and about a generation beyond Stalin's totalitarian settlement of the 1930's. It is, therefore, worth looking at the current scene against the background of its past. Situations in life are always too complex to permit exact prediction on the basis of history; but, since the past helps determine the realistic alternatives available at any moment of time, there may be some use in examining more recent events in the setting from which they have arisen.

This chapter will, therefore, follow the categories developed in the earlier portions of the analysis, notably in Chapters 11–14. Starting back with the October 1952 Congress of the Communist Party, changes in the structure of Soviet rule, the relative position of the principle political figures, and real or apparent changes in

[1] See footnote 4a, page 241. This chapter has not been revised to fit developments since it was written.

the substance of policy at home and abroad will be examined.
Finally, certain concluding observations will be made on the operative motivations of current Soviet rulers and the prospects for
further change in Soviet society, as they may now be discerned.

<h2>2. CHANGES IN THE STRUCTURE OF POWER</h2>

The Nineteenth Party Congress was held October 5–14, 1952, the
first such gathering in almost fourteen years.[1a] In the course of the
Congress certain structural changes at the highest levels of the regime were announced. There may well have been some important
redisposition of authority among the figures secondary to Stalin imbedded in these changes, but their exact meaning remains obscure
as was, certainly, Stalin's intent. The most dramatic change was
the abolition of the Politburo and its replacement by a Presidium.
The Politburo usually had nine members and two alternates, while
the short-lived Presidium created at the Nineteenth Congress had
twenty-five members and eleven alternates. This apparent enlargement in the number of those making policy at the highest level
may well have been illusory. The Politburo is known to have operated by a committee system where major decisions were arrived
at by less than full membership. It is unlikely that the Presidium
represented, in fact, a substantial diffusion of decision-making; for
Stalin was evidently still in full command at the time of the conference, and only nine of the tried-and-true old Politburo members,
aside from Stalin, had their portraits featured prominently in the
ritual of celebration of the November Revolution.

It is, nevertheless, possible that the widened membership in the
Presidium was designed as a kind of counterweight to the second
major structural change formally accomplished by the Congress.
The Secretariat of the Central Committee, aside from Stalin and
Khrushchev, appeared to concentrate considerable authority in the
hands of Malenkov and some of the younger Soviet leaders believed
to be associated with him in recent years. The members of the
Secretariat were: Stalin, Aristov, Brezhnev, Ignatov, Malenkov,
Mikhailov, Peyov, Ponomarenko, Suslov, and Khrushchev. The
composition of the Secretariat, combined with Malenkov's public
presentation as the principal elaborator of Stalin's views, may have
indicated that Stalin regarded the structural arrangements of the
Conference as an interim device to permit Malenkov to develop

[1a] The interested reader should consult the authoritative discussion of the
Congress by Philip E. Moseley in the January 1953 issue of *Foreign Affairs*.

his position as heir apparent, while in no way gaining full control over the levers of power. All the indications at this time were that, while Stalin was prepared to push Malenkov forward, within the orbit of his own unquestioned authority, he did not regard his death as imminent and he was unprepared to take the steps necessary to smooth Malenkov's path to a full succession.

Beyond these ambiguous and, in a sense, contradictory shifts in the Soviet structure, the Conference saw formal and symbolic confirmation of certain changes which had taken place, in fact, some time before. Not only was the Politburo changed to the Presidium, but the functions of the Orgburo were formally assigned to the Secretariat, where they had already been. Of greater symbolic interest, perhaps, is the fact that the name of the Party itself was altered from the All-Union Communist Party, Bolsheviks, to the Communist Party of the Soviet Union; and with this change the title of the magazine in which Stalin had laid down the policy lines for the meeting (in his article, "On Economic Problems of Socialism in the U.S.S.R.") was changed from *Bolshevik* to *Communist*. The names Politburo, Orgburo, and Bolshevik, with their historical overtones derived from the era of Russian Revolution, have evidently been judged inappropriate to the bureaucratized machinery of state which has developed in the Soviet Union.

Like other changes in the Soviet past, these merely brought form in line with an older substance. Broadly, they appeared to confirm the reshaping of Soviet institutions around the outlook and experience of the generation of state bureaucrats now rising to dominance as opposed to the older generation of men who had at least some part in the November Revolution and the formative period in which the Party, as a living institution, was, in fact, the center of power.

In the five months between the Party Congress and Stalin's death there were no major known changes in the structure of Soviet power. However, there may well have been alterations of importance behind the scenes, notably between the announcement of the doctors' plot on January 13, 1953, and Stalin's death early in March; but those are for future historians to establish.

In the days after Stalin's death was announced, on March 6, 1953, the structure of Soviet power was rapidly reformed once again. The somewhat obscure and possibly transitional arrangements laid down by Stalin at the Party Congress were set aside; a new structure was announced on March 15, 1953, which, superficially, followed the executive methods used by the regime during World War II. In his speech of March 16 before the Supreme Soviet, Malenkov stated that these changes had been maturing for a long time, with Stalin's assistance.

In general, the new structure appears to concentrate power in the hands of a few familiar, experienced figures, grouping beneath them the many particular ministries which make up the vast Soviet bureaucracy. In the Council of Ministers, which now consists of five members only, are the following: Malenkov (Premier), Beria (Security), Molotov (Foreign Affairs), Bulganin (Armed Forces), and Kaganovich (the economy?). The Presidium of the Central Committee of the Party (the old Politburo) includes, in addition to the five key figures named above, Khrushchev (the Party), Voroshilov (President), Mikoyan (Foreign and Domestic Trade), Saburov (economic planner), and Pervukhin (industrial expert). In an act evidently charged with meaning, and perhaps achieved only after some inner struggle, the role of General Secretary of the Party was surrendered by Malenkov and turned over to Khrushchev on March 15, as the result of a Central Committee meeting the previous day. Each of the major Soviet figures, with the exception of Malenkov, the Premier, and Voroshilov, who succeeded Shvernik as President of the Supreme Soviet, is apparently charged with major administrative responsibilities, although Kaganovich is not officially designated as a responsible administrator.

In the first four days after Stalin's death, the Moscow press appeared to be in the process of elevating Malenkov rapidly to a position as Stalin's full and lone successor, in a publicity campaign which included the famous fake photograph of Stalin, Mao, and Malenkov, published in *Pravda* on March 10. But from, roughly, March 11 forward it became increasingly apparent that this is a power structure thoroughly different from that achieved and operated by Stalin.[2] All the principal secondary figures Stalin developed are close to high policy decisions, and bear, almost certainly, direct administrative responsibility for a major bureaucratic chain of command, except Malenkov himself. It has been explained in high pronouncements and repeated in the Soviet press that decisions are now collectively arrived at; and, by implication, the virtues of one-man rule as conducted and proclaimed by Stalin have

[2] For an excellent account and analysis of these formative days see S. Schwartz, "V Sovetskom Soyuze posle smerti Stalina" ("Soviet Union After the Death of Stalin"), *Novoye Russkoye Slovo* (New York), April 30–May 1, 1953.

been all but overtly denied. Whether in fact decisions are collective, in the sense that votes are taken and followed, or whether Malenkov or some other figure in the inner circle of power (perhaps, even, Voroshilov) is the arbiter, is not now known. It is clear, however, that for the time being at least, the major secondary figures under Stalin, excepting Malenkov, have seized or clung to the administrative instruments from which their authority derives and have produced a version of what is described in Chapter 11 as the "Constitutional" case.

On April 16, 1953, the rationale for this method of rule was officially put forward in *Pravda*. Leaders were attacked who "began to conduct themselves as if they alone knew everything, as if only they can say anything sensible and intelligible, and it only remains to the lot of the others to support their opinion. . . . Leaders cannot take a critical statement aimed at them as a personal offense. They must know how to meet criticism courageously. The manifest way is to subordinate their will to the will of the collective." This editorial refers, significantly, to the Central Committee of the Party as the highest expression of the collective principle, echoing a theme Beria notably stressed in his speech after Stalin's death, which contains five key references to the Central Committee. From the time that Malenkov was relieved of his duties as Secretary of the Party on March 14—if not a few days earlier—his name has been referred to much less often than Beria's, Molotov's, Mikoyan's, or even Voroshilov's, in the Moscow press. All the evidence points, then, to a purposeful and thus far successful effort to avoid the passing of the totality of Stalin's power into Malenkov's hands.

This dilution of power must have had important effects on the operation of the bureaucratic chains of command, for the reasons considered at length in Chapters 11 and 12. It was the degree of concentration of Stalin's power which permitted them to operate, below the level of the top, in an uneasy overlapping relationship. It is evident that, immediately upon Stalin's death, pressures arose for the chains of command to be given a greater degree of autonomy vis-à-vis each other and especially vis-à-vis the secret police. The evidence—or, better, symptoms—which justify this tentative view are the following:

1. As part of the amnesty decree of March 27 a revision of the criminal code was ordered by the Presidium of the Supreme Soviet (headed by Voroshilov) which would remove a considerable range

of bureaucratic crimes (offenses committed in an official capacity) from among those handled by the secret police. These are to be dealt with by administrative rather than police measures. If implemented this revision would significantly dilute the powers of the secret police over the arms of the bureaucracy.

2. An editorial of April 26, 1953, in *Pravda* declared that Soviet ministries had received substantially widened individual authority as a result of the government reorganization in March. It was noted, particularly, that the principle of unified command within individual ministries had been strengthened and that plenipotentiary powers had been granted to ministers, including the right of allocating material and money resources within their total ministry allotments as well as the right of decision on all basic questions of activity and enterprise within the institutions subordinate to them.

3. Perhaps the most important of the bureaucratic changes concern the armed forces. It is notable that Zhukov, potentially the most substantial political figure in the armed forces, was formally made Vice Minister of Defense on March 15, and may have assumed important status in Moscow at an earlier date; while, in a move whose exact significance is not now established, Marshal Sokolovsky (previously a member of the Central Committee) was made Chief-of-Staff of the Soviet Armed Forces as early as February 20, 1953. These two men had closer political and personal relations with the West, and especially with high American officers, than any others, in the immediate postwar period in Berlin.

The dilution of executive authority and the assertion of a degree of autonomy on the part of the bureaucratic chains of command have been accompanied by a startling public emphasis on the importance of legality in Soviet rule. A major occasion for this display of concern for legality was, of course, the reversal of the judgment on the guilt of the doctors who had been alleged, in January 1953, to have murdered several key figures in the Soviet state. On April 6 it was announced that the whole charge had been fabricated, and that S. D. Ignatiev had been taken in by his deputy, the unfortunate Ryumin, who ended his career characterized by *Pravda* as a "despicable adventurer." Both the original charge and its reversal were obviously tied to maneuvers for power at the highest level of the regime. The reversal was accompanied, however, by the publication of a remarkable editorial in *Pravda*, on April 6, which discussed in some detail the previous fabrication of evidence and the violation of the "inviolable rights of Soviet citizens, which are inscribed in our Constitution." The rights of citizens under Article 127 of the Constitution, ensuring inviolability of person, were referred to with a fervor that carried more conviction than most *Pravda* editorials.

It is, of course, impossible now to judge the meaning of this new public emphasis on legality—the first such wave of public reference since the end of the Great Purge late in 1938. The implied limitation on the arbitrary powers of the secret police would undoubtedly be immensely popular with the peoples of the Soviet Union. The amnesty of March 27, if its broad provisions should in fact be carried out, would mean the liberation of hundreds of thousands, perhaps millions, of people now confined in forced labor camps of various types. But if there is substance in this new line— and this is still to be demonstrated—it is much more likely to derive from the battle of the bureaucracies (and the uneasy men who now head them) against any reconcentration of Stalin's power than from a serious direct concern with popular aspiration for civil liberties. It is to be noted, for example, that the amnesty's references to the release of prisoners held for minor military offenses is more precise than for any other category; this characteristic, shared with the 1945 amnesty, may indicate a special deference to the armed forces and an intent to implement the decree in this category at least. There is absolutely no evidence that the basic role of the secret police in the Soviet structure has been altered or, even, that the amnesty provisions have been applied. We are talking now of gestures and symptoms, not of accomplished facts.

The evident rise of Beria as the major champion of collective leadership makes this apparent deflation of the secret police particularly anomalous. He came to prominence in 1938–39 as the man who established order after the anarchy of the Great Purge. Under him the powers and scope of the police have undoubtedly expanded. He has been the bureaucrat of terror. In his speech on Stalin's death Beria referred respectfully to the people's rights "recorded in the Stalin Constitution." It is not impossible that he is now prepared to consolidate his personal position as a political figure, within the collective leadership, at the expense—perhaps temporary—of some reduction—perhaps minor—in the arbitrariness of the powers wielded by the secret police against the armed forces and the other bureaucratic chains of command. It would not follow, however, that there is any question of Beria's liquidating the empire of police, intelligence, and forced-labor institutions over which he presides.

3. THE MEN

Whereas the structural shape of the Soviet Union and its overt domestic and external policies are difficult to conceal for any period of time, the exact position within the power structure of various individual figures and especially their relations to one another are notably obscure. The evolution of their respective positions since the October Conference has been the subject of wide and contradictory speculation. This speculation has centered on the meaning of the rise and fall of Ignatiev and, therefore, around the relative power and the relationship between Beria and Malenkov. The major facts are these:

1. After a career which (as Nicolaevsky has demonstrated) [3] was not notably associated with Malenkov's entourage down to 1948, Ignatiev emerged as a new member of the enlarged Presidium after the October 1952 Congress.

2. In February 1953, when the doctors' plot was in full vogue, it was publicly indicated for the first time that Ignatiev was Minister of State Security, when his nomination to the Moscow Municipal Soviet was announced.

3. Even after Stalin's death Ignatiev was named a member of the Secretariat of the Central Committee, although he was dropped from the Presidium at the time its membership was reduced. He held his Secretariat post until March 21, at least.

4. On April 4 Beria announced that the doctors' plot had been fabrication; and, on April 6, it was announced that Ignatiev, duped by his deputy Ryumin, had been removed from the Secretariat and from his post as Minister of Security.

5. In May,[4] a Tiflis newspaper announced that Ryumin had been implicated in a fabricated plot which had resulted in the removal to jail of key Communist leaders. Some time before the announcement the leaders had been returned to their posts in a move evidently instigated by Beria. The reversal of the doctors' plot was thus openly linked to political maneuvers within the Soviet apparatus.

[3] Boris I. Nicolaevsky, "How Did Stalin Die," in *The New Leader*, April 20, 1953.
[4] Reported from Moscow, *New York Times*, May 14, 1953, p. 14.

The most conventional line of speculation on these events is as follows: The announcement of the doctors' plot in January, with its implication that the secret police had been poorly administered under Beria, is taken to have been a maneuver by Malenkov to get within his own hands, through his alleged agent Ignatiev, control of the key security services. This authority would have given him, for the first time, the powers required fully to succeed to Stalin's role (the Party being now an inadequate power base). The reversal of the doctors' plot, and the removal of Ignatiev, on this view, are judged major moves in sealing off Malenkov's direct control over the instruments of power, as well as part of a program of consolidation by Beria designed to ensure his own administrative base in the struggle for power.

Although there are many unanswered questions concerning the meaning of the doctors' plot and its April reversal, some such hypothesis remains, as of the present, the most likely. It is supported by the purposeful overt efforts of Beria to consolidate his political position after Stalin's death and to pose as the advocate of the collective-leadership principle.

Behind Beria's recent initiatives lies a more fundamental fact. The secondary figures developed in the course of Stalin's rule know all there is to be known about the complex and dangerous game of higher Soviet politics. They know that peaceful retirement from power is not yet a Soviet convention. A succession to Stalin, at its core, requires that one man seize the instruments of power and replace the secondary figures created by Stalin with men of his own choosing. Whatever their abstract, ideological views might be concerning the optimum manner of conducting the Soviet state, the succession problem is, for Stalin's old henchmen, also a simple matter of life or death. More than that, Malenkov, whatever his abilities, is, to men like Molotov, Kaganovich, Voroshilov, and the others, a junior figure elevated by Stalin long after their comradeship with him had been consolidated. In this human context it is almost unthinkable that they assume a position of absolute deference to Malenkov in the making of policy, similar to that they were prepared to accept in relation to Stalin. It is, therefore, natural for them to worry along with some form of collective-leadership method, even if it violates the accumulated experience of Communist success from Lenin's prerevolutionary days down to Stalin's death.

They know that the basic rule of the Communist Party, since its modern beginnings, has been the laying down of the line by one powerful leader. The alternatives open to them, however, are not easy: either an open struggle for power, which would risk the continuity of the Soviet regime and all of their lives; or the acceptance of rule by (say) Malenkov, in the manner of Stalin, which would almost certainly involve their personal elimination from power, or worse.

Where, then, does Malenkov stand in the new structure of power, and what are likely to be his intentions? At the present time this question cannot, of course, be answered with confidence. It is clear, however, from Malenkov's whole past performance, that he is an able, experienced, and strong figure. He did not persist among the secondary figures and rise to the position of Premier without gaining a vast experience of Soviet higher politics and developing considerable powers of survival in the unstable secondary level beneath Stalin. Moreover, he has exhibited an ability to bide his time when suffering setbacks, as he did in the period from 1946, when Zhdanov took over the Party under Stalin, to 1948, when Zhdanov died or was killed. Malenkov now appears to have had his powers as head of the Soviet state limited, how severely it is impossible to say. On the other hand, it is most unlikely, in the longer run, that he will accept a dilution of his power to the point of becoming a figurehead, without at some stage attempting to assert his authority. If those with a stake in collective leadership (as opposed to effective rule by Malenkov) have rallied around Beria and the secret police as their principal agency of basic strength, Malenkov may well look to the Soviet armed forces as a counterweight. In fact, it is not at all unlikely that he has had a hand in bringing Zhukov and Sokolovsky to the elevated positions they now hold in the Soviet hierarchy. The only effective counterweight to the secret police in a fundamental struggle for power would be the Soviet armed forces.

As Malenkov and his colleagues well know, however, the political use of the Soviet armed forces would be exceedingly dangerous to the continuity of Soviet rule. It would, in fact, almost certainly involve civil war unless, in the meantime, by a slow process of erosion, the powers of the secret police, and notably their powers over the armed forces, had been drastically reduced. It has been a major continuing function of the secret police to watch closely over the army and especially to prevent any consolidation of a political view or grouping within the armed forces. More than that, the secret police itself contains major fully armed units which would have to be dealt with unless the unity of command over the secret police were fractured in a single drastic blow. Nevertheless, so long as Malenkov does not have full and direct authority over the secret police he cannot exercise effective unilateral command over the Soviet power structure.

If this general view of the present circumstances of the Soviet regime is correct, what we observe is the strong figure of Malenkov surrounded not by the younger men of his entourage in a new Soviet administration, but Malenkov as an individual dealing at arm's length with a group of his peers who are united in their intent to deny him—or any other single person—the totality of Stalin's command, as a means of assuring their own power prerogatives and their lives. Malenkov's chief personal subordinates undoubtedly retain important lesser positions, probably in the Secretariat of the Central Committee and elsewhere in the policy-making structure. On the other hand, certainly, Beria, and probably others, are seeking to consolidate their positions within their respective administrative chains of command by elevating men whom they personally trust. And above all, the armed forces, with major figures holding high posts in Moscow, add an important element of ambiguity to the unsettled circumstances which have evolved since Stalin's death.[4a]

4. THE ISSUES

Against the background of unsettled position in the higher reaches of Soviet power, the new regime struck out in both domestic and foreign policy with important gestures whose substance is yet to be established. At home, an amnesty from the prisons and forced labor camps was announced; a price reduction was decreed; and the intent to pursue peace as a major goal of Soviet policy was promulgated with special emphasis. Abroad, a brisk series of peace gestures covering virtually the whole range of Soviet relations with the external world, converted the rather shopworn propaganda peace offensive of recent years to what might be called a diplomatic peace

---

[4a] As these proofs are put to bed, Beria, arrested on or about June 26, awaits public trial. No dogmatic conclusion is justified on the basis of the author's knowledge concerning the meaning of this event. The most plausible hypothesis is that Beria's exceedingly active exploitation of his administrative base—the secret police—after Stalin's death permitted Malenkov to organize the same sort of coalition against Beria as that which limited Malenkov's powers in March 1953. With Beria removed, Malenkov's authority has undoubtedly risen. As of this date (August 17, 1953), however, there is no evidence that Malenkov has assembled the powers required for a true succession to Stalin.

offensive. But the only act of substance, as of the present date, has been the exchange of sick and wounded prisoners in Korea, which makes it not impossible that a truce might emerge there.

In a sense, recent events in the Soviet Union conform to an old Soviet pattern. At least twice before in Soviet history gestures of popular appeasement and conciliatory moves toward the external world have accompanied moments of internal crisis at the higher reaches of Soviet power. The first such occasion was, of course, when, at the time of the Kronstadt Revolt and serious internal Party difficulties, Lenin launched the NEP and a concerted effort to establish normal diplomatic relations with the external world. The second major occasion was during the mid-1930's when the Great Purge was accompanied by the promulgation of the Constitution and other moves of domestic conciliation and by a Popular Front program for Communists abroad.[5] It seems evident that, once again, the Soviet rulers do not regard the time as propitious for a tightening of controls over the Soviet peoples or for dangerous schemes of external expansion—a mood whose duration, however, cannot easily be predicted.

Within this broad pattern of behavior, consistent with the Soviet past, there may well be additional and more proximate motivations at play within the Soviet leadership. Stalin's prestige, and in a sense his legitimacy as a ruler, was created, in the end, by his success in the development of Soviet basic industries, in the course of the Five-Year Plans, and by his successful leadership of the Soviet Union at war against Germany. A continuance of the pattern of the Five-Year Plans is not calculated to add to the prestige of the new regime. Mounting figures of total production, concentrated on investment goods and military equipment, with only slight concessions to welfare, are an old and painful story. It will be noted that the latest Five-Year Plan, put forward officially at the time of the October Congress (but announced and applied earlier) involved surprisingly high goals for consumers' goods (notably food) as compared with the previous plans. The latest lowering of consumers' goods prices was undoubtedly, in part, a move to indicate to the Soviet peoples

[5] On two previous occasions broad amnesties were announced: the first in November 1927, on the tenth anniversary of the Revolution; the second on July 7, 1945, in commemoration of the victory over Hitler. In neither case, of course, did the amnesty alter the nature of the forced labor system or even halt its trend to expansion.

that the new regime seriously sought to make good the implications of the new Plan for welfare.

As for major military ventures, the regime must appreciate, in the face of the new weapons which would be applied in a major war, that the Soviet rulers would not only risk military defeat but, much worse, would endanger the continuity of the Soviet regime.

Thus, gestures toward peace, welfare, and civil liberty—the three greatest aspirations of the Russian peoples—may well appear to be the best means for acquiring a minimum popular acceptance for the new regime.

The amnesty, along with the new emphasis on the inviolability of persons, is a development of some interest, even as a mere propaganda gesture, when considered in connection with recent Soviet attitudes toward the external world. After the Party Congress in October, the general mood of Soviet propaganda, in conformity with Stalin's theoretical pronouncements in *Bolshevik*, was one of quiet confidence at home and efforts to push the propaganda peace offensive abroad, with the enunciated purpose of splitting off the U.S. from its allies in Western Europe and Asia. With the announcement of the doctors' plot in January, however, the mood of Soviet propaganda sharply changed. From January 13 down to Stalin's death, an internal campaign of vigilance was pushed with a feverish ugly quality reminiscent of that which preceded the Great Purge of the 1930's. The danger of externally fomented sabotage and wrecking was day by day presented in the Soviet press and over the domestic radio; and a heightened vigilance against such internal and external enemies was called for. The external world was presented as distinctly more hostile and threatening than had been the case between October and January.

Virtually from its beginning the new regime appeared to reverse these themes. The preamble to the amnesty decree, suddenly switching from the alarming tone of the vigilance campaign, asserted blandly that "the law and socialist order have been strengthened and crime has considerably declined. . . ." Malenkov, in particular, emphasized his intent to pursue peace in his speech of March 16 before the Supreme Soviet. And, starting at the end of March, a whole series of conciliatory gestures was made, including the Chinese acceptance of the UN offer to exchange sick and wounded prisoners, immediately backed by Molotov; Soviet willingness to launch discussions with Britain on air safety along the approaches to Berlin;

agreement to the appointment of a new Swedish Secretary-General for the UN; the acceptance of a visit by American newspaper editors; the businesslike Soviet performance at the Geneva meeting on East-West trade; and a massive demonstration of professional good-fellowship by Soviet diplomats at a variety of points where they were in contact with the external world.

Had it not been for the reversal of atmosphere between January and March 1953, all of this might be regarded merely as the fruition of the line developed at the time of the Congress in October. Although there were contradictory strands in Stalin's article in *Bolshevik*, on the whole it forecast an intensification of diplomatic and other efforts to split the Western coalition by nonmilitary devices. Stalin himself reinforced this likelihood at Christmas 1952 with his answers to the questions put to him by Mr. Reston of the *New York Times*. And, indeed, the whole Soviet diplomatic performance of April 1953 bears the marks of a psychological and diplomatic operation, long prepared.

Two things, however, distinguish the current effort from previous Soviet peace operations. First, the main reliance is not placed, as on earlier occasions, on peace conferences organized by the Communists and frequented by fellow-travellers, and on other such forms of propaganda. The latest Soviet effort has brought diplomacy to the center of its psychological warfare. Second, there is a notable increase in the degree of sophistication in the Soviet diplomatic moves and in the flexibility of language and method employed. The texture of the Soviet reply to President Eisenhower's speech of April 16, published in the Moscow newspapers of April 25, appears to indicate the presence in Soviet councils of younger, less rigid minds, well attuned tactically to the outlook and sensibilities of the outside world. This document, and other aspects of the Soviet diplomatic peace offensive, give the impression that there are those in Moscow who have for long felt that Stalin's handling of the diplomatic weapons available to the Soviet Union had been clumsy, and had unnecessarily united the outside world. One senses a search for a lighter touch, phrasing more comprehensible to the outside world, and gestures of somewhat more apparent substance.

Is there, in fact, more to the Soviet peace offensive than this? Are we to see, merely, at most, a truce in Korea, an avoidance of major war, and a more urbane effort to split the coalition arrayed against Soviet aggressive purposes? Leaving aside the questions of

Korea and Indo-China, the touchstones for any serious effort to end the Cold War are two:

1. A willingness to see Germany reunified by free elections, with all that would imply for the ability of the Soviet Union to hold together its satellite empire in Eastern Europe.

2. An effective system of atomic energy control, as the basis for a general control of the level of world armaments.

As of this writing, there is no evidence whatsoever that those effectively governing Soviet policy are prepared to move seriously on these issues. There is, however, sufficient ambiguity concerning the intent of the Soviet diplomatic peace offensive to justify current Western efforts to establish its meaning.

5. THE OPERATIVE MOTIVATIONS OF THE SOVIET RULERS

This skepticism concerning the seriousness of the Soviet diplomatic peace offensive stems from a view of the long history from which its present leaders have emerged; and it may be well to recall that history in the midst of the day-to-day speculations of the present.

It is the burden of this essay that there has been a remarkable continuity in the priorities, or effective scale of values, in terms of which dominant Soviet leaders have decided the issues with which they have been confronted. Malenkov, Beria, Molotov, and the others now at the apex of Soviet power have lived their mature lives wholly within the Soviet tradition whose continuity can be traced over a half century, from the publication in 1902 of Lenin's "What Is To Be Done" down to the present. The priority of power takes form first in Lenin's conception of the disciplined party as the chosen instrument for implementing the Marxist historical progression; it marks the series of complex *ad hoc* decisions taken by Lenin in the course of the revolutionary and postrevolutionary period which add up to the seizure and maintenance of power by force in defiance of the instruments for registering consent; it governs Stalin's maneuvering to unique authority; and it gradually transforms the whole range of policy of the Soviet state, to become institutionalized in bureaucratic habits of day-to-day totalitarian performance.

It is the essence of that developing scheme of priority that the success of the Bolshevik Party and the Soviet regime became identified with the goals of Marxist ideology. That identification having been made, and reinforced with a further personal identification of certain men with the success of the Party and regime, decisions could be taken by them in the light of the consequences for the power and efficiency of the organizations they dominated and of their own places within those organizations. By this dual identification the transition from an ideologically defined revolution to the pursuit of power as a virtually independent goal was accomplished.

This transition was essentially completed early in the history of the Soviet regime. Its course is clearly marked by the decisions regarding Brest-Litovsk, the Kronstadt rebellion, and NEP. In these early days, however, decisions were reached only after an examination of the alternatives within the minds of the Soviet leaders, and often after an overt struggle within the Communist Party. As time went on, however, and notably in the decade following the full consolidation of Stalin's rule (say, 1929–39), the norms for decision were fully institutionalized in methods of education, thought, and administration which confirmed for Soviet society as a whole the pattern of one-man leadership and organizational discipline which had previously been generated in the Communist Party.

Just as Stalin worked out to a logical conclusion the potentialities of his early dominance over the Secretariat and over the other elements of the control machinery of the Communist Party, from about 1929 he worked out the implications of maintaining and enlarging his over-all domestic power and the international power of the Soviet state from his position of dominance within the Politburo. The keystone of this system was, of course, the unification within Stalin's own hands of all the instruments of power. More than that, his authority permitted him to intervene intimately and directly at any level in the chain of command of the bureaucratized instruments for the handling of power, and to avoid a disproportionate accretion of power to any single bureaucratic organization or subordinate. This effective and intimate control over an enormous machine Stalin accomplished by the following basic administrative devices:

1. A large independent intelligence system and secretariat, which permitted him to select the issues on which he chose to intervene in detail—interventions which generated a pervasive insecurity, as they were designed to do, by their arbitrary, unpredictable character.

2. The power of appointment, which kept the strings of patron-

age and the lines of political loyalty from becoming too diffuse.

3. The overlapping allocation of function, which prevented any single chain of command from making major decisions without confronting other arms of the state's bureaucracy and thus bringing the issues into the open at a high level.

The first and primary purpose of this system of power has been its own preservation. From Brest-Litovsk and NEP, down through the period of the German-Russian pact of 1939, to the elaborate conflict between Russia and the non-Communist world in the years since 1945, there seems little doubt that the maintenance of the internal power machine has had a clear priority over any other goal of Soviet policy.

Just as the maintenance of absolute internal power became institutionalized in attitudes and organizations, a similar fixing of the Soviet position toward the external world took place. The habit of hostility took hold early in Soviet history. It was founded in Marxist ideology and confirmed in the experience of the external world from 1917 to 1921, which, in turn, conformed to older Russian experience of aggression from the outside. Fundamental hostility to the outside world was made a continuing part of Soviet internal life and became embedded in the automatic habits of thought and action of Soviet institutions. External aggression, however, has thus far in Soviet history enjoyed a lower priority than the maintenance of the regime's internal dominance.

The relation between Soviet internal and external power is not simply that of a first and second priority in Soviet thought and policy. The two goals are more intimately connected. First, the posture of hostility toward the outside world was soon appreciated to be a major asset to the Soviet regime in handling its internal power position. The postulation of the external enemy, with its roots both in the Communist ideology and in the Russian national experience, was early recognized as useful if not essential for the workings of the internal system of absolute control which the Soviet regime, in any case, required. The external enemy was needed as a rationale for the role of the secret police, for a system of resource allocations which gave low priority to economic welfare, and, later, for a policy of cultural isolation from the rest of the world. There were, indeed, periods in Soviet history, notably after 1922, when a persuasive external enemy did not exist, when the civil war and foreign intervention had ended and the rest of the world was more concerned with difficult domestic problems of the 1920's than with the arena of world power. Under these circumstances the French General Staff was, for a time, the chief villain of Soviet propaganda in the continuing "foreign conspiracy" against Russia. And, as Kennan has noted, in international as in human relations, the postulating of hostility is an assured means for creating it.

A second relation of the internal control system to external power constitutes, in fact, a fundamental limitation on the ultimate power of the Soviet Empire to expand. On the basis of its post-1945 performance the Soviet regime appears to have evolved three methods for conducting its relations with other countries: formal diplomatic negotiation including overt propaganda; subversive influence on internal affairs, exerted through the local Communist parties and other agents under direct Moscow control; virtually complete domination, on the pattern of the Soviet system of internal control. The first two techniques of power appear to be regarded as tactical devices to permit movement toward the third. Soviet relations to Communist China have, of course, posed a special case whose resolution is still to be determined.

In its policy toward the European satellites, for example, the Soviet government appears to have planned or been driven by events step by step to install a system of control virtually as absolute as that exercised within the borders of the Soviet Union. It was evidently on this issue of the extent and character of Soviet control that Yugoslavia broke with the Soviet Union. The habits and institutions of internal administration appear now to be deeply ingrained and inflexible. Where the Soviet Union has the capability of exerting full control it appears driven to demand that all instruments of power of the captive state be directly and immediately subservient to Moscow. The potentialities of holding effective power by less clear-cut means and of exploiting what would be judged, from a Western point of view, to be authentic political assets have not appealed to the Soviet regime at its present mature bureaucratic stage. It is evidently prepared to play politics, in the Western sense, when its power is not assured; witness, for example, the current Soviet maneuvers vis-à-vis Germany and Western Europe. But power having been achieved, there appears to exist a compulsion to exercise it by the same absolute techniques which have been developed at home. Ideological enthusiasm and popular good will have an exceedingly small place in those techniques.

On the whole this external projection of the Soviet domestic control system is likely to constitute a limit on the potentialities for Soviet expansion. The desire to maintain virtually total detailed control at the center of the Soviet regime appears, in particular, to have the following effects:

1. It increases the number of decisions which must be taken at the Presidium level, and limits the flexibility of action within the Soviet Empire.

2. It makes it impossible for the Soviet system to engage the support of and to use independent strong men in the satellite areas, and increasingly requires direct Soviet responsibility for operating decisions, if not full administration.

3. It denies the Soviet Union important possibilities of popular support (including ideological support) and increases the scale of allocations required for internal security purposes within the Soviet Empire.

4. It limits the appeal of Communism outside the Soviet Empire and reduces the potentialities of extending Soviet power by non-military means.

Although it is certainly too soon to make a firm historical judgment, evidence would suggest that the cumulative long-run effect of the Soviet bias toward the exercise of absolute centralized power is likely to limit the total power and influence it can effectively generate. The great successful empires of the past have not been built and sustained on a policy of all or nothing. The extremely firm grip which the Soviet regime exerts within the area it controls is thus achieved at a long-run cost still to be fully reckoned.

It does not follow from these conclusions on past performance, concerning the priority of internal over external power, that the Soviet Union, under any future circumstances, will not undertake aggressive major war. What can be said is that the scheme of priorities of the Soviet regime, crystallized and institutionalized under Stalin, has systematically placed a premium on the security of the domestic base of the regime as against the extension of its external power; and, since major war involves important risk to the domestic base, the regime, as presently organized by Stalin's heirs, appears likely to try to avoid major war.

Nevertheless, the initiation of major war by the Soviet regime is not to be ruled out. Given its persistent objectives, the regime would almost certainly initiate a major war if it felt with a substantial margin of assurance that war could be decisively won without endangering its hold on Soviet society. In turn, such a decision would imply that the external world was judged sufficiently weak and lacking in political unity and purpose to rally from an initial blow sufficiently to mount a military effort which might damage or destroy the regime's domestic position.

The regime might also undertake major war in a variety of conditions under which it became convinced that major war was the only realistic alternative to loss of control over Soviet society. In other terms, the regime is likely to choose to go down fighting rather than surrender its domestic base without a fight. For example, on the knowledge available to us it seems likely that an overt ultimatum to the regime, whose acceptance would be judged to involve both loss of essential positions and open capitulation to an external threat, would be rejected. On the other hand, the Soviet regime has, in its history, exhibited a marked ability to retreat and to take its losses without detonating major war when it felt such losses were not incompatible with the continued maintenance of power over its domestic base. The significance the regime attached to any given loss in its external position might thus turn, in part, on the manner in which it was induced and, especially, on the believed consequences of the loss for its internal position.

If this view is correct it implies that the avoidance of major war with the Soviet Union under present tense circumstances, when a limited conflict of interest might flare into general mutual defiance, may hinge in part on the diplomatic techniques by which such conflict is handled on both sides. It seems altogether possible that war might begin not because the substantive interest at stake in a given conflict were judged to be decisive, but because the Soviet regime felt that overt defeat on the limited issue might have general decisive consequences at home. It is to be noted that in its postwar aggressions against Greece, Berlin, and South Korea the Soviet regime has taken pains to avoid taking positions such that limited defeat would be tantamount to general defeat. However, as the competitive armaments race proceeds—with increasingly powerful weapons—the danger is likely to recur in an acute form if it is believed that the side which strikes first will gain, thereby, a major military advantage.

There is a third and more remote category of danger that the Soviet Union initiate major war. We have thus far considered the Soviet regime as it is and has been, a state committed deeply to external expansion, but with a long time scale in mind, a willing-

ness to wait, and a substantial vested interest in avoiding external
action which would endanger its internal security position. There
is no guarantee, however, that its internal position will remain secure
indefinitely. The present precarious balance of power within the
Soviet regime might slide into an open struggle for power, despite
the powerful common interest of the present collective leadership
in its avoidance. Such a struggle would, of course, weaken the
external power of the Soviet Union in the first instance; and, to this
extent, it would make the undertaking of major war on the grounds
of a rational calculus less likely rather than more likely. It might also,
however, make one group or another contending for power more
desperate and, in a sense, less responsible than the Soviet regime
has hitherto been. If real or imagined action by the external world
could be successfully presented to the Russian peoples as a recurrence of foreign interference or aggression, war might be undertaken
as a last desperate means of reuniting the nation and establishing
the internal control of a group which sought power.

We need not count, then, on Soviet initiation of a major war in
terms of a fixed plan for world conquest; and it is proper to underline
the apparent inhibitions on the regime's use of war. But we cannot
rule out the possibility of such action, notably under conditions of
weakness and disunity in the external world, under actual or believed
conditions of an external ultimatum or imminent attack, or even
under conditions of grave internal instability.

It might be thought that both Marxism and the experience of
Communism in two World Wars would make the regime look to
major war with hope as well as fear. The wars of this century have,
in perspective, resulted in weakening of the non-Communist world
and in great advance for Communism. But the Soviet regime, from
its early days, has shown an ability to distinguish sharply between
the spread of Communism and the stability and extension of Soviet
power. The ideological argument for war is thus, in itself, probably
not judged persuasive, especially under conditions where Soviet
internal rule is judged stable by the regime. A spread of Communism
at the cost of weakening or endangering domestic Soviet power is
not now likely to be judged appealing within the Presidium.

It is also a conclusion of this analysis, however, that the same basic
operational motivations which inhibit Soviet military aggression
inhibit the establishment of a true peace, as this is understood in
the West. The leaders of the Soviet Union could not, up to the
present, accept a basic settlement with the external world because

the nature of that settlement would threaten the bases upon which their domestic rule is founded. To admit to the Soviet peoples that their security is guaranteed by collective security arrangements (such as effective atomic energy control), would remove from the secret police a basic historic justification, i.e., to combat the domestic agents of a militarily hostile external world. It would also remove the rationale for the sense of continued tension in Soviet life and for the chronic postponement of the day when Russian resources might be devoted substantially to improvements in welfare. To accept the dismantling, by bourgeois free elections, of a satellite structure (such as Germany) modeled on Soviet life itself, would raise problems of the greatest difficulty with the other Eastern satellites. And it would pose forcefully this question: Why, indeed, if free elections are the appropriate technique for Eastern Germany, are they not also appropriate for the Soviet Union?

It is, thus, our judgment that the ultimate obstacles to a diplomatic agreement on the decisive issues of the Cold War stem not from problems of Russian national security, but from the overriding priority of Soviet policy, namely, the maintenance of that regime's power over its Russian base. It follows, therefore, that a true liquidation of the Cold War—as opposed to a mitigation convenient, perhaps, for both sides—hinges on the possibility of change in the nature of the Soviet regime, which would make its foreign policy a reflex of Russian national interest rather than the interest of a regime in perpetuating its own domestic power.

6. ALTERNATIVE EVOLUTIONS FOR THE SOVIET SYSTEM

If this view is correct—that the decisive questions of peace hinge on an internal change of the Soviet structure—how are we to rate the possibilities of such change over the foreseeable future? There are, roughly, two major possibilities for change favorable to peace:

1. The present regime, caught in a set of cross-purposes it cannot resolve, may make internal changes by a sequence of *ad hoc* decisions, leading, step by step, to a situation which permits an end to the Cold War.

2. There may be a major, violent internal crisis leading to the formation of a new Russian government prepared to make a fresh accommodation to the external world, in terms of the Russian national interest in the narrow sense.

The first possibility, that is, a major internal change in the structure of Soviet society and an accommodation to the external world brought about by the present regime in the fairly near future, appears doubtful indeed. Nevertheless, certain implications of the regime's current dilemma should be noted.

It appears to be the case that no single successor to Stalin has felt himself strong enough to seize full power, or has been willing to risk the destructive possibilities of the attempt. The Presidium appears to have organized itself on the basis of an agreed ruler with limited authority. Thus far it would appear that Malenkov, having been separated from intimate control of the bureaucratic agents of power, has, at most, the right of executive decision or arbitration as among equals. In turn, this separation, which in effect has distributed the elements of Stalin's authority, has appeared to require more sharp and firm definition of the limits and competence of the various bureaucratic instruments than has previously existed. And, indeed, failure to achieve an agreed delimitation of powers might well lead to dangerous conflicts of authority among the instruments of power and among the men controlling them, which without the presence of Stalin could disrupt the minimum unity necessary for the survival of the regime. If these tendencies to bureaucratic "constitutionality" are maintained, and extend themselves downward to the lower levels, they might well have further profound consequences. The inherent long-run tendency of the bureaucracies to develop independent policy positions would be accentuated; for, in affect, decisions would be reached in the Presidium more nearly by an open negotiation, with the head of the state as an arbitrator, than by a dictator's fiat.

Over time, a system of this kind, if in fact it can work on the Soviet scene, might well have its consequences for the individual Soviet citizen. The diminished unity of power, and the need to organize its structure on more explicit rules for the handling of authority, might serve to diminish the arbitrariness with which the individual Soviet citizen has been controlled. It is an old story in history that the rights of the citizen are, in the end, protected by the division of power. Many of the rules of law which now protect the citizen's civil rights in the West arose from the struggle of the nobility against royal absolutism, centuries ago. The mechanism for this protection arises from the fact that the manipulation of distributed power requires the existence of accepted rules which define the procedures and limits by which authority is exercised. It is the lack of such known procedures and limits which defines, in one of its central aspects, a totalitarian state. Habeas corpus is the ultimate foundation for the quality of democratic organization in a society. A continued distribution of authority among Stalin's heirs along these lines would necessarily require, for example, a more sharp definition of the powers of the secret police than was necessary when the secret police was firmly and directly under the control of a single dictator; and so also with the Party, the army, and the arms of state administration in industry and agriculture. In such a situation the citizen might have increased potentialities for finding protection and even, perhaps, for making his political interests felt.

It is by no means evident that the group of men trained under Stalin are capable of operating in a stable manner, for a substantial period, in a situation of this kind. Moreover, as noted earlier, it is not reassuring that the apparent leader of the move toward collective leadership and constitutionality is also the chief of the secret police. What can be said is that some such evolution is implicit in any successful effort to separate the multiple powers generated, unified, and operated by Stalin; and that, as of the present, certain possible symptoms of this evolution can be discerned in the Soviet system.

The touchstone of this evolution is, of course, the erosion of the powers of the secret police which, in the end, is not only the principal symbol but the principal pillar of Soviet power as it has in fact emerged. The amnesty gesture and the public reassertion of constitutional legality are undoubtedly measures popular not only among Soviet citizens generally but also in the high bureaucracy and the armed forces. But it is only when we have evidence that the prisons and forced labor camps are being substantially reduced and that the ability of the police to interfere arbitrarily with the lives of Soviet citizens has been effectively curbed that we can regard this process as seriously under way. Such evidence is not now in hand.

Historians, however, may well look back to two events in the months after Stalin's death as having had considerable long-run importance: the *Pravda* editorial of April 7, with its open acknowledgment of the fabrication of evidence by the secret police; and the publication in Moscow on April 25 of the full text of President Eisenhower's speech of April 16. There are, indeed, precedents for both actions in Stalin's practice in the past. Such accusations against the police, for example, accompanied the removal of Beria's predecessor Yezhov; and textual statements of other Western leaders have occasionally been presented in the Soviet press. Nevertheless, to have permitted, and even encouraged, public discussion of the performance characteristics of the secret police (which every Soviet citizen already knows), and to have permitted President Eisenhower's text, with the evident sincerity of its peaceful purposes, to circulate, are notable acts. They are particularly striking at a time when the position of Soviet high power is unsettled. And they may make a deeper and longer impression on the Soviet peoples than envisaged by those who may have permitted these moves for tactical purposes. They may help to crystallize within the Soviet Union views which lie, in any case, just below the surface of consciousness and beyond the range of normal discussion. Men may be encouraged to consider more explicitly whether Russian society might well be run without the benefit of a secret police and with serious and sustained constitutional protection for its citizens, and whether the purposes of the external world are not such that a decent accommodation might be achieved for Russian interests on a collective security foundation. In a fundamental sense these two acts of publicity may not prove to be wholly reversible.

In short, by failing to agree on a single total successor to Stalin his heirs may be driven, essentially against their will, into a form of Soviet organization which would bring into play the interests and outlook of the higher bureaucracy and even, to some extent, the Soviet citizenry in general. This outlook is judged to be more nationalist in spirit, more concerned with peace, welfare, and civil liberty than that of the top political figures. There is, thus, some small possibility of an internal transformation of the Soviet Union out of the dynamics of the succession process.

The second major possibility of internal change enhancing the possibilities of peace is, of course, that the successors to Stalin prove incapable of achieving either a fully unified succession or a stable distribution of Stalin's authority, and, in consequence, that they permit a degeneration into an overt struggle for power. Although the lessons of history and the position in which Stalin left his regime make this a thoroughly possible case, the legatees of Stalin have an almost overriding interest in maintaining their unity in some form, or, at least, in preventing any struggle for power from spreading outside the Kremlin. If such a struggle proceeds for any time, however, it is likely to engage the main instruments of bureaucratic power, i.e., the main contestants for dominance are likely to bring into play the potentialities of the secret police, the Party, the army, and the state administration. If the Soviet armed forces remain outside (or are kept outside) the contest, it is likely that the secret police, as presently organized, could master the situation. Although the Communist tradition and experience would emphasize the dangers of invoking the armed forces, or even the secret police, as quasi-independent participants in a political struggle, that tradition and experience would also underline the importance of instruments of raw power in such a situation. It is altogether typical of the modern Soviet mentality that, in its political contest with Tito's government, the Soviet regime devoted a major effort to subverting the Yugoslav army. It is thus wholly possible that one contestant for power or another, under the assumed circumstances, would look to the armed forces as a counterweight against his rivals.

It is not useful to peer too far into such a wholly imaginary situation. Three characteristics of such a contest for power are, however, to be emphasized:

1. In modern Russia (as opposed to Russia of previous centuries) an overt struggle for the succession would be difficult to confine; once the bureaucratic instruments of force became engaged the struggle might well fan out over the whole Soviet Empire.

2. If such a struggle were to proceed for any considerable period of time, the contestants might well reach back into the society for popular support and thus bring politically into play the dissatisfactions and positive aspirations of various groups. In any case, a split among the instruments of power is likely to give popular political feelings (for virtually the first time since 1917) a realistic opportunity to have their impact on public policy.

3. The evolution of such a full political crisis, and its outcome, may well be affected by the actions taken with respect to it by the non-Communist world, and notably by the extent and manner of foreign intervention; in this context there is a possibility that real or feared intervention might cause a surge of nationalist feeling in Russia which would override the divisive forces at work in the crisis.

The Soviet domestic situation can, of course, move for the worse as well as for the better, in terms of the possibilities of peace. The succession process now under way might well lead at some stage, by some form of transition, to the emergence of a true successor to Stalin. Given the relatively mature, inflexible nature of Russian society in the 1950's—as opposed to the 1930's and 1920's—the transition might well be painful. A repetition of the Great Purge of 1936–38 would be no simple matter, but some such grand-scale replacement of key bureaucrats may be a necessary condition for a true succession. Nevertheless, such a maneuver for the totality of Soviet power may be attempted; and it could succeed, and thus postpone the day when history destroys or dissolves Soviet inhibitions on a stable collective security resolution of present conflicts with the external world.

Whether the danger arises in the course of the succession process or otherwise it is a judgment of this essay that the possibility of Soviet-initiated major war may be intimately tied to the degree of insecurity felt by the regime concerning control over its domestic base. And, as noted earlier, this relationship, if correctly identified, may pose subtle problems for Western diplomacy at moments of domestic Soviet crisis.

In general, then, it may be said that the resolution to the problem of Stalin's succession may move in any one of several directions. We may see a successful effort by (say) Malenkov, to recapture the secret police and to recreate something like the unity of power enjoyed by Stalin. We may see the presently indecisive balance of power break into open conflict and even into civil war, in which two underlying instruments of raw force (the secret police and the army) are pitted against one another. We may see Stalin's heirs learn painfully to live within the dilemma which confronts them, permitting widening areas of autonomy for the arms of bureaucracy, the development of common-law rules for the negotiation of policy positions among themselves, and the emergence of a method for bureaucratizing the one element which Lenin and Stalin had kept free—the ultimate policy-making powers of the state.

While no dogmatic prediction on the solution of the succession problem is justified on present evidence, we can be reasonably firm concerning the principal forces likely to cause change in the nature of Soviet society over the years and decades to come. On the whole, by the values of most societies, they are to be judged hopeful.

The problem of adjusting, by one means or another, to Stalin's death certainly belongs at the head of the list of dynamic elements in Soviet society. Aside from this factor, the following appear to be the most important elements making for change:

1. The existence of a generation of well-trained higher bureaucrats, now moving toward self-perpetuation as a Soviet elite, whose

experience and motivating forces differ appreciably from those which have largely determined the performance of present Soviet rulers.

2. The progressive weakening of ideological motivation throughout Soviet society and the substitution for it of standards of patriotism and efficiency as well as incentives for individual reward and recognition.

3. The gradual but well-attested development of indifference and disbelief in the main lines of the regime's propaganda among Soviet citizens generally; and the *de facto* abandonment by the regime of any serious notion that it will prove possible to educate its citizens to positive support of the "dictatorship of the proletariat" or to operate the society without centralized systems of force and restraint, including the secret police.

4. The growth of popular literacy, the enlargement of popular knowledge of Russian and Western culture, the growth of popular knowledge of the outside world (much accelerated by the Second World War and not completely halted by postwar Soviet policy). and the progressive enlargement of that group capable of forming a critical judgment of public affairs.

5. The widespread desire of the Russian peoples for peace and, especially, for a let-up in the unremitting pressure of work and poverty they have experienced over the past three decades, especially since 1929.

Without change or conflict at the top of the Soviet structure we can expect no dramatic overt reflection of these forces, all of which have arisen from the dynamics of Soviet evolution but lie outside the capabilities of the regime wholly to control. The stability of Soviet policy since the mid-1930's is artificial. It represents a complete short-term tactical success in maintaining the pattern of Soviet rule; but this success has been achieved by holding in check or frustrating forces and attitudes which are not diminishing but are probably gaining in strength as a secondary consequence of that pattern of rule.

It would be dangerous to underestimate the capabilities of the Soviet regime to maintain domestic order so long as it maintains a minimum unity at the top, and, in particular, so long as the secret police continues in existence as an effective agent of the regime. Nothing in this analysis justifies an easy optimism concerning the timing of a change in the Soviet system or concerning the process of transition. Nor will such change necessarily and automatically work in the interests of the United States and common humanity everywhere.

On the other hand, it is important to recognize the existence of these deeper forces and to take those actions which would maximize the chance that their ultimate coming into play contribute to the development of a more peaceful and stable world, and thus accord with our own interests.

A SELECT BIBLIOGRAPHY

Suggestions for Further Reading

The following list makes no pretension to completeness. It is meant simply as a guide to some of the works in English pertinent to the present study. In many cases it was impossible to give anything like adequate coverage with bibliographical suggestions. Without wishing to deny our own limitations in this vast field, it must be noted that, in some areas (that of the nationalities, for instance), adequate works in English are as yet nonexistent.

I. THE PRE-1917 FOUNDATIONS FOR SOVIET RULE

Berdyaev, Nicholas. *The Origin of Russian Communism*. London, 1948. A minor classic on the evolution of Leninism as a Russian phenomenon.

Berlin, Isaiah. *Karl Marx, His Life and Environment*. New York, 1948. A well-written penetrating study.

Hare, Richard. *Pioneers of Russian Social Thought*. New York, 1951. Essays on Herzen, Chernyshevsky, and others.

Hunt, R. N. Carew. *The Theory and Practice of Communism*. New York, 1950. The most recent of several competent studies of the subject.

Kucharzewski, Jan. *The Origins of Modern Russia*. New York, 1948. Militantly anti-Russian, but full of insights on the intellectual history of the revolutionary movement.

Laski, H. J. *Communism*. London, 1927. A brief, vivid account by a famous British socialist.

Maynard, John. *Russia in Flux*. S. Haden Guest, ed., New York, 1948. The first part of this work is one of the best treatments of modern Russian thought, revolutionary and otherwise.

Shub, David. *Lenin, a Biography*. New York, 1948. A highly personalized account.

Wilson, E. *To the Finland Station*. New York, 1940. A famous and still valuable work by the distinguished literary critic.

Wolfe, Bertram D. *Three Who Made a Revolution*. New York, 1948. Without doubt the best book on the early history of the Bolsheviks.

II. THE HIGHER POLITICS OF SOVIET RULE

Basseches, N. *Stalin.* E. W. Dickes, trans., New York, 1952. Interesting but somewhat over-optimistic in its interpretation and predictions of Soviet policy.

Carr, E. H. *The Bolshevik Revolution, 1917–1923.* 2 vols. New York, 1950–52. The first two volumes of a projected three-volume history. These volumes cover party, state, nationality, and economic policy. The next volume will treat foreign policy. These three volumes were conceived as the beginning of a still larger history of the USSR. The treatment is analytical rather than chronological. The performance is of a high order, but the author's deterministic view of history should be noted and discounted.

Chamberlin, William H. *The Russian Revolution, 1917–1921.* New York, 1935. A classic.

Deutscher, Isaac. *Stalin, a Political Biography.* New York, 1949. An excellent biography and, more, a good one-volume history of the USSR.

Florinsky, M. T. *The End of the Russian Empire.* New Haven, 1931. One of the "Russian series" in the *Economic and Social History of the World War.* There are other scholarly studies of Russia in the series.

Pares, Bernard. *The Fall of the Russian Monarchy.* New York, 1939. An outstanding work by one of the great modern scholars of Russian history.

Radkey, Oliver H. *The Election of the Russian Constituent Assembly of 1917.* Cambridge, Mass., 1950. A scholarly analysis of Russia's only fully democratic election, too often forgotten.

Schuman, F. L. *Soviet Politics, at Home and Abroad.* New York, 1946. A favorable account. While strained in its interpretation of events after 1929, this remains the only serious academic attempt at a sympathetic evaluation of Soviet history down to the end of World War II.

Trotsky, Leon. *The History of the Russian Revolution.* 3 vols. New York, 1936. An indispensable source.

III. THE BUREAUCRATIZATION OF THE INSTRUMENTS OF POWER

Beck, F., and Godin, W. *Russian Purge and the Extraction of Confessions.* New York, 1951. A remarkable account of the Great Purge, embracing the direct knowledge of the two authors, information derived from fellow-prisoners, and a survey of theories of the Purge.

Dallin, D., and Nicolaevsky, B. *Forced Labor in Soviet Russia.* New Haven, 1947. The fullest account now available.

Deutscher, Isaac. *Soviet Trade Unions.* London, 1950. A standard work.

Fainsod, Merle. "Komsomols; a Study of Youth under Dictatorship,"

American Political Science Review, March 1951, pp. 18–40. A splendid analysis of an important Communist group.

Herling, Gustav. *A World Apart*. Joseph Marek, trans., London, 1951. Memoirs of a former political prisoner.

History of the Communist Party of the Soviet Union (Bolsheviks). New York, 1939. The chief author is J. Stalin.

Meisel, J. H., and Kozera, E. S. *Materials for the Study of the Soviet Union: State and Party Constitutions, Laws, Decrees, Decisions and Official Statements of the Leaders in Translation*. Ann Arbor, 1950. A handy collection.

Moore, Barrington, Jr. *Soviet Politics—the Dilemma of Power*. Cambridge, Mass., 1950. A first-rate essay, unique in its effort to unite and relate modern tools of sociological and political analysis.

Schueller, George K. *The Politburo*. Stanford, 1951. Summarizes such inadequate information as is available on the individual members of the Politburo.

Schwarz, Solomon M. *Labor in the Soviet Union*. New York, 1952. A scrupulous, scholarly analysis.

Stypulkowski, Z. *Invitation to Moscow*. London, 1951. The story of a brave man.

Towster, Julian. *Political Power in the U.S.S.R., 1917–1947. The Theory and Structure of Government in the Soviet State*. New York, 1948. Though rather hard reading and somewhat too exclusively descriptive, this book is based entirely on source materials. Indispensable.

Vyshinsky, A. Y. *The Law of the Soviet State*. Hugh W. Babb, trans., New York, 1948. An official Soviet text.

White, D. F. *The Growth of the Red Army*. Princeton, 1944. The only full treatment of the history of political controls in the Soviet armed forces.

IV. SOVIET POWER AND THE ECONOMY

Baykov, Alexander. *The Development of the Soviet Economic System*. New York, 1947. A full and technical description.

Bergson, A. (ed.) *Soviet Economic Growth*. Evanston, White Plains, 1953. A valuable symposium reflecting the results of recent research and especially refinements in estimates of national income and capital formation.

Bienstock, G., Schwarz, S., Yugow, M. *Management in Russian Industry and Agriculture*. New York, 1944. Particularly valuable for its analysis of relationships between political and economic objectives.

Dobb, Maurice. *Soviet Economic Development Since 1917*. London, 1948. The story from the point of view of a competent British Marxist.

Gerschenkron, Alexander. "The Rate of Industrial Growth in Russia since 1885," *The Tasks of Economic History*. Supplement VII, 1947, to *The Journal of Economic History*. An analysis of first importance in placing the Soviet economic performance in proper historical perspective.

Jasny, Naum. *The Socialized Agriculture of the U.S.S.R.* Stanford, 1949. The big book on the subject.

Jasny, Naum. *The Soviet Economy during the Plan Era*. Stanford, 1951. A scholarly survey, basic in the field.

Nicolaevsky, Boris I. "The New Soviet Campaign Against the Peasants," *Russian Review*, April 1951, pp. 81–98. On the new "supercollectives."

Schwartz, Harry. *Russia's Soviet Economy*. New York, 1950. A sound textbook.

Shimkin, D. B. *Minerals, a Key to Soviet Power*. Cambridge, Mass., 1953. An important monograph on an area that may determine the future rate and character of Soviet economic development.

V. IDEOLOGY, SOCIAL AND CULTURAL LIFE

Bauer, Raymond A. *The New Man in Soviet Psychology*. Cambridge, Mass., 1952. One of the best books on the ideological transformation, focused on the field of psychology but drawing general implications from that area.

Berman, H. J. *Justice in Russia: an Interpretation of Soviet Law*. Cambridge, Mass., 1950. An account and interpretation of the transformation of Soviet law.

Carr, E. H. *Studies in Revolution*. London, 1950. Contains two chapters on Stalinism.

Counts, G. S., and Lodge, N. P. *The Country of the Blind: the Soviet System of Mind Control*. New York, 1949. A study of the significant tightening up of ideological controls after World War II.

Denicke, G. "Links with the Past in Soviet Society," Series 3, No. 84, External Research Staff, Office of Intelligence Research, Department of State, Washington, D.C., March 12, 1952. A valuable estimate of the role of the Russian nineteenth-century classics in contemporary Soviet life.

Ellis, J., and Davies, R. W. "The Crisis in Soviet Linguistics," *Soviet Studies*, Jan. 1951, pp. 209–64. A good survey of the Marr affair.

Gurian, Waldemar. *Bolshevism, an Introduction to Soviet Communism*. Notre Dame, 1952. Though rather loosely organized, this book contains many valuable insights.

Harper, S. N. *Civic Training in Soviet Russia*. Chicago, 1929. A classic on the early years of the Soviet regime.

Historicus. "Stalin on Revolution," *Foreign Affairs*, Jan. 1949. A scholarly essay on Stalinist theory.

Hoover, Calvin B. "The Soviet State Fails to Wither," *Foreign Affairs,* Oct. 1952. An excellent analysis of the Soviet rationale for the successive postponement of the euthanasia of the state.

Inkeles, A., "Family and Church in the Postwar U.S.S.R.," *Annals of the American Academy of Political and Social Science.* May 1949, pp. 33–44. A useful article by one of the major figures among the younger generation of American scholars of the Soviet Union.

Inkeles, A. "Social Stratification and Mobility in the Soviet Union, 1940–1950," *American Sociological Review,* August 1950, pp. 465–79. A basic analysis of first importance.

Inkeles, A. *Public Opinion in Soviet Russia.* Cambridge, Mass., 1950. A thoroughly competent book on the mechanisms of Soviet communication and the content of Soviet information policy.

London, Kurt. *The Seven Soviet Arts.* London, 1938. The transformation of the mid-1930's.

Schlesinger, R. "Recent Soviet Historiography," *Soviet Studies,* Jan. 1951, pp. 265–88. Surveys the post-Pokrovsky era.

Schlesinger, R. "Stalinism," *Soviet Studies,* Jan. 1950, pp. 240–58. A short paper on Stalin's social and cultural policy.

Schlesinger, R. (ed.) *Changing Attitudes in Soviet Russia.* Vol. I, *The Family.* London, 1949. A source collection.

Stalin, J. *Problems of Leninism.* Moscow, 1940. A basic source on ideology.

Struve, Gleb. *Soviet Russian Literature, 1917–1950.* Norman, Okla., 1951. A standard survey, somewhat polemical in tone.

Timasheff, N. S. *The Great Retreat, the Growth and Decline of Communism in Russia.* New York, 1946. A great work dealing with the transformation under Soviet rule of many aspects of social and cultural life.

Timasheff, N. S. *Religion in Soviet Russia, 1917–1942.* New York, 1942. The standard work on the subject. For developments in the 1940's, see also Timasheff's article in W. Gurian, ed., *The Soviet Union: Background, Ideology, Reality.* Notre Dame, 1951.

Trotsky, L. *The Revolution Betrayed.* New York, 1937. Interesting and, for our day, unusual criticisms of Soviet social and cultural policy of the 1930's by the exiled old revolutionary in his latter days.

Zirkle, Conway (ed.) *Death of a Science in Russia; the Fate of Genetics as Described in* Pravda *and Elsewhere.* Philadelphia, 1949. A fascinating collection of sources on Lysenko and company.

VI. THE ROLE OF RUSSIA IN THE EVOLUTION OF THE SOVIET STATE

Dicks, Henry V., "Observations on Contemporary Russian Behaviour," *Human Relations,* Vol. V, No. 20, 1952, pp. 111–75. A first-rate psychiatrist's insights.

Goldman, I., "Psychiatric Interpretation of Russian History," *American*

Slavic and East European Review, Oct. 1950, pp. 151–61. A criticism of psychiatric approaches to the interpretation of Russian history.

Gorer, G., and Rickman, J. *People of Great Russia; a Psychological Study.* London, 1949. The insights of a cultural anthropologist. Subject of much controversy, even among anthropologists.

Kennan, G. F., "America and the Russian Future," *Foreign Affairs,* April 1951, pp. 351–70. An interesting speculation on Russian potentialities for democracy.

Kornilov, A. *Modern Russian History.* New York, 1943. The best history of nineteenth-century Russia (though weak on foreign affairs).

Kurganov, Ivan, "The Problem of Nationality in Soviet Russia," *Russian Review,* Oct. 1951, pp. 253–67. First appeared in Russian in the *Novyi Zhurnal,* a Russian-language periodical published in New York. A sound essay.

Maynard, J. *The Russian Peasant and Other Studies.* London, 1942. Contains two good essays on the nationalities (as well as some excellent material on Soviet politics and economics).

Mead, Margaret. *Soviet Attitudes Toward Authority.* New York, 1951. A diffuse and uneven collection of essays, but the best work thus far of this experimental genre.

Pipes, Richard E., "The First Experiment in Soviet National Policy: The Bashkir Republic (1917–1920)," *Russian Review,* Oct. 1950, pp. 303–19. A scholarly case study.

Sumner, B. H. *A Short History of Russia.* New York, 1949. Probably the best one-volume history of Russia. Organized analytically in terms of continuing strands of Russian history, rather than chronologically.

Tyrkova-Williams, A., "Russian Liberalism," *Russian Review,* Jan. 1951, pp. 3–14. A good summary by the author of a lengthy work in Russian on the subject.

VII. SOVIET FOREIGN RELATIONS

Barghoorn, Frederick C. *The Soviet Image of the United States.* New York, 1950. An unusually good and imaginative treatment of a difficult subject.

Beloff, M. *The Foreign Policy of Soviet Russia.* 2 vols. New York, 1947–49. Covers 1929 to 1941. A basic survey.

Borkeman, F. *The Communist International.* London, 1938. An important study by an anti-Stalinist Marxist.

Dallin, D. *Soviet Russia's Foreign Policy, 1939–1942.* New Haven, 1942. An outstanding book on a crucial period.

Fischer, Louis. *The Soviets in World Affairs.* 2 vols. New York, 1930. Covers 1917–1929. Though now somewhat outdated, this book is still valuable.

X, "The Sources of Soviet Conduct," *Foreign Affairs,* July 1947, pp.

566–82. A famous basic statement of American policy toward Russia by George Kennan.

Nazi-Soviet Relations 1939–1941: Documents from the Archives of the German Foreign Office. Published by U.S. Dept. of State, 1948.

Rosenberg, Arthur. *A History of Bolshevism.* Ian F. Morrow, trans., London, 1939. By a former German Communist. Excellent on the Comintern.

Sherwood, Robert E. *Roosevelt and Hopkins, an Intimate History.* New York, 1948. Full of information on Russo-American relations during World War II.

Smith, W. B. *My Three Years in Moscow.* Philadelphia, 1950. The early years of the Cold War, as seen by the American ambassador.

Taracouzio, T. A. *War and Peace in Soviet Diplomacy.* New York, 1940. Legalistic and solid.

VIII. THE EUROPEAN SATELLITES

Armstrong, H. F. *Tito and Goliath.* New York, 1951. A vivid account of Tito's break with the Kremlin. Includes chapters on other Eastern European countries.

Gluckstein, Ygael. *Stalin's Satellites in Europe.* Boston, 1952. A full and competent survey.

Roucek, J. S. (ed.) "Moscow's European Satellites," *The Annals of the American Academy of Political and Social Science,* September 1950. Articles by various experts.

Ulam, Adam B. *Titoism and the Cominform.* Cambridge, Mass., 1952. A scholarly analysis of the roots of the Yugoslav schism.

IX. COHESIVE FORCES, INSTABILITIES, AND TENSIONS IN CONTEMPORARY SOVIET SOCIETY

Note: This is a field in which comparatively little work has been done to date. We therefore mention only two readings below. A number of studies connected with these problems are in progress at the Harvard Russian Research Center. Barrington Moore, Jr., is preparing a book on the subject. Raymond A. Bauer's forthcoming *Gallery of Soviet Prototypes* should also prove important in this regard.

Fainsod, M., "Controls and Tensions in the Soviet System," *American Political Science Review,* June 1950, pp. 266–82. One of the first attempts to examine this problem.

Fischer, George. *Soviet Opposition to Stalin.* Cambridge, Mass., 1952. On General Vlasov, his program, and his relations with Hitler.

INDEX

Index